EPISTLES
OF
JOHN

NOTES
ON
1, 2, 3 JOHN

by
Roy H. Lanier Jr.

IBSN: 0-89137-136-2

Preface

Many thanks are due to numerous ones who have made the writing of this book of notes possible. Without the invitation of Bennie Whitehead to do this work, I would not have begun it. The encouragement and support of my home congregation, the Broadway Church of Christ in Garland, Texas, made it possible for me to arrange my time to do this work. Thanks to these fine elders: Alan Dodson, Tom Savage, and Bill Sisk.

Other churches who help in my support encouraged me to spend the time in this writing also. I mention the Hoffman Heights Church in Aurora, Colorado; the Granbury St. Church in Cleburne, Texas; churches in Earth, Texas; Sayre, Oklahoma; Vealmoor, Texas; and Hardin, Kentucky; and the Southside Church in Waco, Texas. In addition to these congregations, there are several individuals who also help in my work.

Special help came in the person of my sister, Dr. Joy Henshall, who proofed, rewrote, corrected and stimulated my efforts. Any plaudits for correct spelling, grammar, and readability should go to her.

And to my wife Patricia goes the largest possible thanks for her unfailing support, encouragement, and patience.

May this study be of value to those dedicated to God's Word.

Roy H. Lanier Jr.
August 31, 1989

i

TABLE OF CONTENTS

1 JOHN

EPISTLES OF JOHN

NOTES ON 1 JOHN

by
Roy H. Lanier Jr.

Introduction

Three of the most interesting books in the New Testament appear under the title "Epistles of John," listed within Bibles usually as 1 John, 2 John, and 3 John. Generally attributed to John the Apostle, the books were no doubt written toward the latter part of the first century to assure Christians of their life in Christ. They encouraged disciples to combat errors then present and instructed them in practical results of proper faith, that is, what their manner of life would be when following the Lord properly. One eminent scholar remarks that this work is ". . . a studied composition, and deals with the weightiest questions of doctrine and the largest concerns of practice."[1]

A brief outline given by Merrill F. Unger gives a worthwhile synoptic glimpse into the contents of 1 John:

Family fellowship and the Father, Chap. 1-3;

Family fellowship and the world, Chap. 4-6.[2]

"The entire development of the argument of the Epistle is based upon the single fundamental conviction of the antagonism subsisting between the 'world' and 'believers.' Whilst the former are under the power and dominion of the devil, the latter are in fellowship with the children of God. Those who belong to the world are the children of the devil, the others are the children of God."[3] Thus one can see the study of these epistles will give much enlightenment about fellowship.

Several great themes of "faith," "light," "love," "fellowship," "abiding in Christ," and "knowing God" interweave throughout the book. One theme may begin early, re-entering within another chapter or paragraph and receiving repeated mention. These are recurrent ideas, not hard-and-fast divisions. They are chains of thought, never once broken throughout the entire epistle, and coming into focus again and again.

SEVEN CONTRASTS

Many students of the epistle note that seven contrasts appear in succession, highlighting a dominant theme of the book: truth versus error. Each is begun by statements like "Hereby we know," "By this we know," or "Hereby shall we know." Note these contrasts:

1. Light versus darkness 1:5 - 2:11
2. Father versus the world 2:12 - 17
3. Christ versus the antichrist 2:18 - 28
4. Good works versus evil works 2:29 - 3:10
5. Spirit of truth versus the spirit of error 4:1-6
6. True love versus false love 4:7-21
7. Begotten versus unbegotten 5:1-21[4]

SEVEN TESTS

Baxter also points out several distinguishing traits of true disciples, which are seven tests of integrity as a Christian.[5] They are tests of honesty, consistency, reality, and perhaps even self-knowledge. Each begins with a claim that someone might make.

1. 1:6: "If we say we have fellowship with him and walk in darkness. . . ."
2. 1:8: "If we say we have no sin. . . ."
3. 1:10: "If we say we have not sinned. . . ."
4. 2:4: "He that saith, I know him, and keepeth not his commandments. . . ."
5. 2:6: "He that saith he abideth in him, ought to walk. . . ."
6. 2:9: "He that saith he is in the light and hateth his brother. . . "
7. 4:20: "If a man say, I love God, and hateth his brother. . . ."

Honesty in each of these claims is called for in the one who wishes to be a true disciple of the Lord Jesus. In the first, one would lie to others about fellowship with God. In the second, third, and fourth, one would be lying to himself. In the fifth, one would not be honest with the world. In the sixth, a Christian would be dishonest with a brother, and in the last test, a Christian would be dishonest toward associates.

The author, John, seems to feel that there are impending dangers to the faith of these Christians and strives to show them the paths of true piety. A large portion of the book is given over to this, and one would do well to use these great teachings as continual tests of faithfulness to Christ. To identify true followers of the Lord, study these books carefully.

AUTHENTICITY

It is remarkably clear these books have been treasured from the earliest years as authentic books to be a part of the canon of the New Testament. There are two major sources of information: external and internal.

1. **External information.** Men who were personal disciples of the apostle John—Polycarp (c. 110), Papias (c. 140), and perhaps Justin (c. 50) as well—attest in their writings to the genuineness of these General Epistles of John.[6] If one assumes the date of writing to be the last decade of the first century, then evidence of genuineness leaps back almost within twenty years of John himself!

Iranaeus (c. 180) quotes the First Epistle of John twice in his work, **Against Heresies,** ascribing it to John. And it is useful to remember Iranaeus was a pupil of Polycarp. Some therefore conclude, "If Polycarp were John's spiritual son, then Iranaeus was John's spiritual grandson"! Clement of Alexandria (c. 185) quotes John frequently, as do Tertullian (c. 195) and Origen (c. 200). Thus Eusebius (c. fourth century) is well justified in including these books as genuine. Other information comes from Dionysius of Alexandria, Cyprian, Athanasius, Cyril of Jerusalem, and Epiphanius.[7]

It is of note that these books are included in the Muratorian Canon[8] and Syria Version, generally afforded to be from the first century.[9]

Such is the external evidence about 1 John, and mostly also for the other two epistles, that rarely are they ever called in question. If the student is interested in such research, there are plenty of reputable sources.[10]

2. **Internal information.** Internally, vocabulary, topics, expressions, phrases, recurrence of themes, and grammatical style are too similar to the Gospel of John to ignore.

As Albert Barnes notes, "There is nothing in the epistle that would particularly remind us of the Gospel of Matthew, or Mark, or Luke; but it is impossible to read it and not be reminded constantly of the Gospel by John."[11] Barnes then lists fifteen major teachings current in both the Gospel of John and the First Epistle.

In addition, Ross observes that, "The following words and phrases are common to both writings: **abide, advocate, believe on, children of God, darkness, do sin, do the truth, eternal life, keep His word, lay down one's life, life, light, love, murderer, new commandment, witness,** etc."[12] He further points out twenty-nine coincidences of language in the first two chapters alone.

Finally, Woods notes that, "Inasmuch as much of the form and content of the Gospel of John is reproduced in the Epistle, those who regard that work as a production of the apostle have no difficulty in attributing the Epistle to the same author. . . . Inasmuch as the author never names himself, this conviction of writers both ancient and modern cannot be satisfactorily explained save on the ground that it is true, and that it began with the first readers who received the Epistle from the author who was known to them personally, and who thus became competent witnesses of its apostolic origin."[13]

INTEGRITY

Only two passages within the first epistle have ever come under serious question, 2:23 and 5:7-8. "Whosoever denieth the Son, the same hath not the Father: he that confesseth the Son hath the Father also." The last clause, **he that confesseth the Son hath the Father also,** is not included in the **Textus Receptus** and is thus italicized in the Authorized Version (KJV). Later evidences support this passage well, and it is included in the American Standard Version and others of later date.

As to the second passage in question, "For there are three that bear record in heaven, the Father, the Word, and the Holy Ghost: and these three are one" (5:7 in the KJV), world-wide controversy rose in the early science of translation and still rages. The weight of opinion seems to hold this part of the record as spurious.[14]

AUTHOR

As internal information has already shown, it is almost certain that the apostle John was the author of these epistles. Such weighty evidence of similarities cannot go ignored; neither is the charge of forgery likely to be found valid under the scrutiny of scholarship.

Tradition surely corroborates the thrust that the apostle John penned the books. The evidences offered by Polycarp, Papias, Clement, and the other early writers are too much to ignore. The author claims to be an eyewitness: "heard, seen, beheld, handled, seen, manifested, seen, heard" (1:1-4). Further, he is given to the use of "I" and "you," though no name is given for him. On the other hand, the authenticity of the letters does not depend on authorship by the apostle John, since the author could have been another inspired John. Nevertheless, the enormous weight of early evidence and acceptance nearly overwhelms those studying the subject carefully.

A BRIEF LOOK AT JOHN THE APOSTLE

John was the son of Zebedee (Mark 1:20) and Salome (Matthew 27:56) and the brother (elder brother most likely) of James (Matthew 4:21). His name in both Hebrew and Greek means "Jehovah is gracious." He is thought to have lived in Bethsaida since his partners in fishing, Andrew and Simon, lived there (John 1:44; Luke 5:10).

He was known to be an influential man with friends in high places (John 18:15), and it is implied that he owned his own home, into which Mary was taken after the death of Jesus (John 19:27). John was rebuked by the Lord for intolerance when he told the Lord he had forbidden a man to cast out demons when he was not in company with the apostles (Mark 9:38; Luke 9:49). His personality had two sides, for as one said later about his epistles, "The apostle of love, as he is, is a real son of thunder, when Gnosticism shows its head."[15] This apostle, along with his brother James, is also mentioned as wanting a chief seat alongside Jesus in glory, another incident when he was rebuked (Mark 10:35-45). Matthew records that John's mother made the request (Matthew 20:20).

John is most often paired with Simon Peter during travels with Jesus; and later when they were both apostles, John must have been a leader among the apostles themselves. He was included at the transfiguration of Christ (Matthew 17:1), was arrested along with Peter early in the history of the Church (Acts 4:3,13), was sent to Samaria to help impart the Holy Spirit to the new converts (Acts 8:14), and was later named among those called "pillars" (Galatians 2:9).

He had a special relationship with Jesus, being called five times within the New Testament "the disciple whom Jesus loved" (John 13:23; 19:26; 20:2; 21:7,20). He was one of the more visible apostles, having been at the trial of Jesus (John 18:16) and evidently at the foot of the cross during the crucifixion (John 19:26). In addition, he was the first of the men to arrive at the grave after the resurrection (John 20:4), and late in life he was imprisoned on the Isle of Patmos (Revelation 1:9). He was surely very close to the heart of Jesus with his loving personality and ways.

Tradition holds John to have moved to Ephesus later in the first century, many commentators referring to him as "the Bishop of Ephesus," though nothing within Scripture justifies his being referred to as an overseer.

Iranaeus records an interesting event in John's relationship with Cerinthus, the famous false teacher and founder of Gnostic Docetism. In his work **Against Heresies,** Iranaeus recalled, "There are also those who heard from him that John, the disciple of the Lord, going to bathe at Ephesus, and perceiving Cerinthus within, rushed out of the bath-house without bathing, exclaiming 'Let us fly, lest even the bath-house fall down, because Cerinthus, the enemy of truth is within.' "[16]

Another tradition, this one mentioned in Scripture (John 21:21-23), held that John was to live until the Parousia of the Lord. John records that he did not hold to that view, and subsequent events have substantiated that Jesus said no such thing.

One other dear and sweet tradition is worth noticing. When very aged and too weak to teach or preach, even too weak to stand alone, he would be carried to the meetings of the saints. He would rise on his cane with the aid of others; with the voice of firm conviction, though feeble in volume and tone, he would say, "Little children, love one another!"

DATE

Nothing is claimed within the book about a date, and very little positive evidence is known. Hints are given that help one to conclude that the writing was at the latter part of the first century, perhaps about 90-95 AD.

The writer mentions "the last time" (1 John 2:18); and the message seems to come from an aged person, since the author often refers to his readers as "children" (1 John 2:1, 12, 28; 3:7, 18; 4:4; 5:21). The tone of endearment lends itself to this same assumption that an old Christian is addressing younger ones. It seems obvious that these books antedate the Gospel of John; and as many point out, it also seems the author presumes that his readers have that work in hand and available when reading the epistles.

TO WHOM WRITTEN

No mention is made of an address to any person or church. It is probable the work was intended to be a circular letter, as was the book of Colossians (Colossians 4:16). The author writes as if the readers know him well, and he seems to know them also.

The letter is well adapted to all Christians who might read it; but since John warns of idols, it is felt the readers must have included many Gentile converts (1 John 5:21).

OBJECT OF THE LETTER

The great themes of the book deal with the importance of developing faith and love and avoiding the corrupting influences of false teachers.

Faith and Love

The main scope of the book centers on belief in the name of the Son of God and the eternal life that ensues: "These things have I written unto you, that ye may know that ye have eternal life, even unto you that believe on the name of the Son of God" (1 John 5:13). Assurance of salvation, eternal life, occupies much of the writing. Three great themes can be found throughout: faith, light, love. John wants the disciples to know that faith does not go unrewarded.

A secondary scope of the book would include the importance of love in the life of Christians. If properly ensconced within the daily actions of followers, love would lead them to follow the commands of the Lord. In true fact, ". . . the doctrine of 'love' does not exclude or ignore faith and obedience as constituent parts of love."[17]

Dealing with False Teachers

A second purpose of the letter is to show members of the various congregations how to deal with false teachers. They seem to fall into several categories:

1. Destructive teachers. They are such as will "lead you astray" (1 John 2:26; 3:7). They will deny the Christ (1 John 2:22; 4:2-3), especially the idea of incarnation, God coming in the flesh (1 John 4:2; 2 John 7). If Jesus were not both Deity and humanity, He could not be the Christ. Denial of either facet of His unique self would destroy one's faith.

2. Seceding teachers. "They went out from us, but they were not of us" (1 John 2:19) indicates that certain of these teachers were leaving the congregations. They were insincere, for the language implies that they never had the proper stance toward the Lord. They wished to lead faithful ones astray (1 John 2:26), but John calls for them to "abide in him" (1 John 2:27-28).

3. Worldly teachers. They were "of the world," spoke as "of the world," and were heard (appealed to) "of the world" (1 John 4:5). So John cautioned his readers to avoid loving and serving the world (1 John 2:15-17).

4. Proud, self-righteous, arrogant teachers. They thought they could live any way they wished, fulfilling any desire of the mind and body, and still be in fellowship with God. John reminds them that to be in fellowship with God, one must walk in the light, not darkness (1 John 1:5-6). They felt they could ignore the commands of Jesus and still have a proper relationship with Him, but John said the opposite (1 John 2:3-6; 5:2-3). Their attitudes betrayed them for what they were.

5. Traveling teachers. As they came into various communities, these teachers claimed to have the Holy Spirit and to be divinely directed in their teachings (1 John 4:1-2). In subsequent writing, it is evident they traveled throughout Asia, desiring the hospitality and support of the Christians; but they were to be denied (3 John 6-8, 9-11). John is clear that faithful followers of Jesus were to cut off support and to deny the hospitality of their homes to false teachers, lest Christians participate in false teaching by such encouragements.

These teachers represented a number of different philosophies present during the first century. Sometimes these philosophies could be distinguished easily; at other times there might be mixtures in the work of any one teacher.

Judaizers. These were Jews in the early Church "who accepted Christianity, but adhered to the Mosaic Law."[18] Perhaps they were the best known group of all the false teachers, as evidenced by early actions in the days of the apostles (Acts 15); and much teaching is done on these problems (Galatians, Romans, Hebrews).

Docetae. This group was ". . . an early heretical sect of Christians whose chief tenet was that Christ's body was a mere phantom, or, if real, of celestial origin."[19]

Gnostics. These teachers were an "admixture of paganism and corrupt Christianity."[20] They are defined as "mystical religions and philosophical doctrines combining Christianity with Greek and Oriental philosophies. . . [a] class of rationalists in the early church."[21]

Nicolaitans. This group, mentioned twice within the pages of Scripture (Revelation 2:6, 15), bears mentioning here because its members must have had strong influence throughout Asia when these epistles were written. The Nicolaitans were a ". . . group in the early church who sought to work out a compromise with paganism. . . [to] enable Christians to take part without embarrassment in some of the social and religious activities of the close-knit society in which they found themselves. . . ."[22] They were thought to be linked to the followers of "Balaam"; and if so, then Peter (2 Peter 2:15), Jude (v.11), and John (Revelation 2:6,15) have somewhat to say.

Dealing with False Doctrines

A third objective of these epistles was to correct errors in doctrine creeping into the early churches.

1. There were the errors afforded by Gnostics and Docetics. Though some observe certain distinctions between the two classes of teachers, it seems likely that a mixture of the two might have been the prevailing strain of error. It was perhaps early for some of the crystallized argumentation that was later known, but the errors were already prevalent. This early form of "Dualism" was fought by Ignatius (c. 115) and Iranaeus (c. 180). Cerinthus is thought to be the author of many of the falsities, and it is known he was a resident of Ephesus.

There were two major thrusts to this error: (a) the supremacy of intellect over matter, and (b) matter as inherently evil. The first perhaps led to the name "Gnostics," as these teachers claimed a superior intelligence.

"Gnosticism. . . professed to give its approval and patronage to the gospel. The gospel was very good, as far as it went; but the Gnostics had 'a more excellent way.' They understood the gospel better than the apostles themselves. It was a mistake to suppose that the historical facts and moral precepts of the Scriptures were to be taken literally. It was a still greater mistake to suppose that the Scriptures contained all that was necessary for man's spiritual well-being. There was a high knowledge, a more profound gnosis; and this the Gnostic could attain to and impart. Illumined by this, men would see that everything else was comparatively of unimportance. . . .

"Gnostics also taught the Oriental doctrine that matter, with everything material is evil. This principle also entailed a complete subversion of Christian doctrine and Christian ethics. (1) If the material universe is utterly evil, it cannot have been created by the supremely good God, but by some evil, or at least some inferior, power. (2) The supremely good God must be utterly removed from such a universe. (3) The Incarnation is impossible; for the Deity could never consent to be united to a material body, innately and incorrigibly impure.

"In morals opposite conclusions were drawn from this Gnostic premise of the inherently impure character of everything material. (1) If the human body is utterly evil, it must be subdued and chastised to the utmost, that the enlightened spirit may be freed from the burden of so vile an instrument. (2) If the human body is utterly evil, it is a matter of indifference what it does; and so worthless an instrument may be made to commit any act from which the spirit can derive additional knowledge."[23]

With these thrusts, two major dilemmas arise: (a) What about the body of Jesus? And (b) what about our own bodies? If one says the body of Jesus was composed of real flesh and blood, then did not Jesus partake of something inherently evil? This position would have to be unthinkable. If the body of Jesus were not real flesh and blood, then what about incarnation, crucifixion, and the giving of His blood? This doctrine would have to say that the sufferings and death on the cross were mere illusions. Some later adherents claimed that the physical body of Jesus was inhabited only from His baptism to the crucifixion by the Christ-spirit, thus denying true Deity.[24] The atonement is lost in accepting either of these errors.

Regarding the bodies of Christians, there appear two dilemmas also. Since (a) the body was felt to be evil inherently, the more one afflicted his body, the more righteous he could become. Or (b) since the body was evil anyway and was given to man by God, then man surely could not be judged by any actions done in the body. Only those things of the spirit of man would be subject to judgment. Ascetism was one philosophy that came to the fore, and Paul had warned the Colossians earlier about just such false teaching (Colossians 2:20-23). Licentiousness also came to the fore, since those taking the view that deeds of the body were not to be judged felt free to do anything that came to mind. Physical desires and mental lusts could be satiated safely without having to answer for them in the Judgment Day, so they thought.

2. There were the errors of aloofness from guilt and responsibility. Regenerated Christians were being taught that the spirit of man was unaffected by any deeds of the body, so there was the danger of unrestrained sin, indul-

gence of enormous proportions; and orgiastic lifestyles were to be the norm. The choice of an ascetic lifestyle or a licentious one leaves little doubt as to which of the philosophies was the more prevalent.

Here, the influence of the Nicolaitans could be well seen. Remember they encouraged a lifestyle that caused no embarrassment in accepting the culture of the day (shades of the twentieth century!), compromising and accommodating to any circumstance. It was truly "first century situation ethics" or "existentialism" in its embryo stage.

John argues just the opposite: Those who act right are right, and those who act sinfully are sinners. They bear the guilt and pollution of sin and will be judged as sinners. Individual responsibility for one's actions in the body is real to John, subject to control in the present life and judgment by God in the next life.

JOHN'S STYLE OF WRITING

J. W. Roberts gives some valuable information about the stylistic features, which is of interest to avid students.[25] He lists these characteristics as follows:

Antithetic parallelism, two lines balanced for contrast of thought (1 John 1:5; 2:4, 7).

Antithesis, true contrast that joins one concept to its opposite (1 John 3:7-10; 4:4-6; 5:18-19; 3 John 11).

Recapitulation, introducing a word or a thought and developing it in successive clauses and sentences, as he does in "sin" (1 John 3:4) and also "old commandment" (1 John 4:7).

Word parenthesis, using a thought unit between the first and last use of the same word: "last hour" (1 John 2:18), "abide" (1 John 2:27), and "love" (1 John 4:7-8).

Anaphora, beginning successive clauses with the same word, "If we say" (1 John 1:6,8,10), "the one saying" (1 John 2:4,6,9), and "I write" (1 John 2:12,13a,13b; 2:14).

Duadiplosis, introducing a new theme by an incidental clause at the close of the previous section. He says, ". . . because he has given us of his Spirit" (1 John 3:24) prior to a fuller treatment of the Spirit (1 John 4:1-6). Again, he says, ". . . the one not loving his brother" (1 John 3:10) prior to the fuller section on love of brethren (1 John 3:11-24).

Variation, using synonymous words in succeeding passages: "we have seen" with "we have beheld" (1 John 1:1), "be in him" with "remain in him" (1 John 2:5), and "have fellowship" with "know him" (1 John 1:6; 2:3).

---

[1]James Hastings, *A Dictionary of the Bible,* (T. & T. Clark, Edinburgh, Scotland, 1910), Vol. II, p. 728.

[2]Merrill F. Unger, *Unger's Bible Handbook,* (Moody Press, Chicago, Illinois, 1967), p. 817.

[3]John Ed. Huther, *Critical and Exegetical Handbook to the General Epistles of James, Peter, John, and Jude,* (Funk & Wagnalls, Publishers, New York, 1887), p. 437.

[4]J. Sidlow Baxter, *Explore the Book,* (Zondervan Publishing House, Grand Rapids, Michigan, 1960), Vol. 6, p. 323.

[5]Baxter, *Explore the Book,* Vol. 6, pp. 327-328.

[6]I. H. Marshall, *Illustrated Bible Dictionary,* (Inter-Varsity Press, Leicester, England, 1980), Vol. II, p. 798.

[7]Albert Barnes, *Notes on the New Testament, James, Peter, John and Jude,* (Baker Book House, Grand Rapids, Michigan, 1949 reprint), p. 272.

[8]Alexander Ross, *The New International Commentary on the New Testament, the Epistles of James and John,* (Wm. B. Eerdmans Publishing Co., Grand Rapids, Michigan, 1954), p. 108.

[9]Barnes, *Notes,* p. 272.

[10]J. W. Roberts, *The Living Word Commentary, the Letters of John,* (R. B. Sweet Co., Inc. Austin, Texas, 1968), p. 12;
Ross, *NIC,* pp. 11-14;
John M'Clintock and James Strong, *Cyclopedia of Biblical, Theological, and Ecclesiastical Literature,* (Harper & Brothers Publishers, New York, New York, 1894), Vol. IV, p. 951ff;
William A. Smith, *A Dictionary of the Bible,* (John Murray, London, England, 1893), Vol. I, Part II, pp. 1764.

[11]Barnes, *Notes,* p. 272.

[12]Ross, *NIC,* p. 109.

[13]Guy N. Woods, *A Commentary on the New Testament Epistles of Peter, John and Jude,* (Gospel Advocate Co., Nashville, Tennessee, 1954), p. 199.

[14]M'Clintock and Strong, *Cyclopedia,* Vol. IV, p. 951.

[15]A. T. Robertson, *Word Pictures in the New Testament,* (Broadman Press, Nashville, Tennessee, 1933), Vol. VI, p. 201.

[16]Roberts, *Living Word,* p. 6.

[17]Wm. A. Smith, *Dictionary,* Vol. I, Part II, p. 1765.

[18]Noah Webster, *Webster's New Twentieth Century Dictionary Unabridged,* (World Publishing Co., Cleveland and New York, 1940, revised by Jean L. McKechnie, 1968), p. 989.

[19]Webster, *Dictionary,* p. 539.

[20]Woods, *Commentary,* p. 205.

[21]Webster, *Dictionary,* p. 781.

[22]E. M. Blaiklock, *Illust. Bible Dict.,* Vol. 2, p. 1085.

[23]A. Plummer, *The Pulpit Commentary,* (Wm. B. Eerdmans Publishing Company, Grand Rapids, Michigan, 1950), Vol. 22, *Epistles of Peter, John & Jude, The Revelation,* pp. iv, v.

[24]Ross, *NIC,* p. 115.

[25]Roberts, *Commentary,* pp. 13, 15.

1 JOHN OUTLINE

INTRODUCTION 1:1-4

I. THE CHRISTIAN AND GOD: Walking in the Light
   1:5-2:29
   A. Things to Do for Fellowship with God
      1:5-2:11
      1. Walk in the light 1:5-7
      2. Accept, repent, confess one's sins 1:8-10
      3. Trust in the Advocate 2:1-2
      4. Walk in obedience 2:3-6
      5. Love the brethren 2:7-11
   B. Things to Avoid for Fellowship with God
      2:12-29
      1. Love of the world 2:12-17
      2. The antichrists 2:18-23
      3. Forsaking the promise, anointing, and life of
         righteousness 2:24-29
II. THE CHRISTIAN AND THE WORLD: Walking in Love
    3:1-5:13
    A. Reminders of Proper Relationship to God 3:1-4:6
       1. God's example of love 3:1-2
       2. The Christian response to purity 3:3-12
       3. Love and hate; life and death 3:13-24
       4. Truth and error 4:1-6
    B. Response to Love 4:7-21
       1. Accepting God's love 4:7-11
       2. Confessing God's love 4:12-15
       3. Abiding in God's love 4:16-19
       4. Practicing God's love 4:19-21
    C. Tests of Love 5:1-12
       1. Overcoming the world 5:1-4
       2. Faith in the witness God gives 5:5-12

1

CONCLUSION 5:13-21
- A. Boldness in the Assurance of Eternal Life 5:13-15
- B. Boldness in Prayer 5:16-17
- C. Boldness in the Things Christians "Know" 5:18-21

Chapter 1
Introduction 1:1-4

¹*That which was from the beginning, that which we have heard, that which we have seen with our own eyes, that which we beheld, and our hands handled, concerning the Word of life ²(and the life was manifested, and we have seen, and bear witness, and declare unto you the life, the eternal life, which was with the Father, and was manifested unto us); ³that which we have seen and heard declare we unto you also, that ye may also have fellowship with us: yea, and our fellowship is with the Father, and with his Son Jesus Christ: ⁴and these things we write, that our joy may be made full.*

John sets forth a basic statement in this introduction, reminiscent of that of the Gospel of John (John 1:1-3). Several expressions and words are common to both:

beginning vs. 1 and John 1:1
Word vs. 1 and John 1:1-3,14
life vs. 1 and John 1:4
we beheld vs. 1 and John 1:14 ("we beheld his glory")
manifested vs. 2 and John 1:14 ("light shineth")

There seem to be three major purposes for writing this epistle: (1) that his readers may have fellowship with the apostles, and even further, with the Father and His Son Jesus Christ; (2) that his readers may accept the facts given by eye witnesses about Jesus Christ; (3) that his readers might accept John's personal testimony about the Christ for his fullest joy and pleasure in these "children" (chap. 2:1).

Notice the verbs that John uses in stating his case stressing the actuality of the God-man, Jesus Christ:

verse 1: **heard** (AKEIKOAMEN), . . .**have seen** (EORAKAMEN), . . .**beheld** (ETHEASAMETHA), . . .**handled** (EPSEILAPHEISAN);

3

Verse 2: **was manifested** (EPHANEROTHEI), . . .**have seen** (EORAKAMEN), . . .**bear witness** (MARTUROUMEN), . . .**declare** (APANGELLOMEN), . . .**was with** (HAIN PROS), . . .**was manifested** (EPHANEROTHEI);

verse 3: **have seen** (EORAKAMEN), . . .**heard** (AKEIKOAMEN), . . .**declare** (APANGELLOMEN).

Such power in words and phrases is neither accidental nor incidental to John. These verbs rise in crescendo and power of intensity. The fact that John uses both the aorist and perfect tenses underscores the importance of noticing the grammar of the original language. Greek is extremely expressive in its use of verb tenses, far more so than our common English is today. John builds to a climax thusly:

have heard (from AKOUO) - Perfect Tense

have seen (from ORAO) - Perfect Tense

beheld (from THEAOMAI) - Aorist Tense

handled (from PSELAPHAO) - Aorist Tense

This sequence is cumulative and additional in its structure. In using the perfect tense, John is stating what has happened in the past and what continues to be true even today. In using the aorist tense, John emphasizes an accomplished fact, a completed action, an actuality of historical record. There is hardly any other way John could have said it with more emphasis. Jesus was a man with whom the apostle John companied, seeing Him also as the Christ of God. He experienced these times and events with Him and was willing to testify to any and all who wish to know the truth about Him! Jesus Christ is both God and man; He is Very God, but also fleshly man. He is both Divine and human; He manifested every attribute of Deity but partook of flesh and blood. He is the Incarnate One; He is the God-man.

Verse 1 That which was from the beginning, that which we have heard, that which we have seen with our own eyes, that which we beheld, and our hands handled, concerning the word of life.

That which was from the beginning - No doubt John refers to the Person of the Son of God, much the same as he did in the introduction to the Gospel (John 1:1-3). Four times John here used the neuter gender word (HO - "That which" rather than "He") instead of a masculine word,

4

which has puzzled many. Albert Barnes argues this neuter word was used to emphasize the proofs and evidences of the Son;[1] Lenski proposes the neuter allows not only a reference to Jesus as the Son of God, but also all "he was and is and will ever be for us."[2] Woods states it is "an affirmation of the eternal character."[3] Such usage of the neuter would certainly include all one could think of this God-man: a flesh-and-blood man with all attributes of Deity, or Deity in all its splendor yet having all the flesh and blood characteristics of humanity. Say it either way; this unique person compassed both time and eternity, earth and heaven, God and man. The use of "Word" (LOGOS) both here and in the Gospel will have much of the same connotation, a comprehensiveness, an entirety of Jesus' earth-bound experiences being told by John and his associates.

from the beginning - can refer to eternity past, as in John 1:1, "In the beginning," even though John often uses "beginning" (ARCHE) to refer to other things also. See 1 John 2:7 (. . .old commandment which ye had from the beginning) and 1 John 3:8 (. . .devil sinneth from the beginning). One remembers the first verse of Genesis, "In the beginning," and this use supports the stronger idea that John has reference to eternity, a glimpse backwards out of time to Him who has always been. The Son of God was not created, He never began to be, He never came into existence; He was, He is, He will be. These are important declarations of the eternity of the Word, the Son, the one later using the human name of Jesus:

". . .through whom he made the worlds" (Hebrews 1:2).

"Thou, Lord, in the beginning didst lay the foundations of the earth" (Hebrews 1:10).

"Jesus Christ is the same yesterday and today, yea and for ever" (Hebrews 13:8).

"In the beginning was the Word. . .the Word became flesh and dwelt among us. . ." (John 1:1,14).

"Before Abraham was born, I am" (John 8:58).

"Christ. . .God blessed for ever" (Romans 9:5).

". . .in him were all things created. . .he is before all things. . ." (Colossians 1:16-17).

". . .existing in the form of God. . ." (Philippians 2:5).

"I am the Alpha and the Omega" (Revelation 1:8).

"I am the Alpha and the Omega, the first and the last, the beginning and the end" (Revelation 22:13).

John is therefore affirming that anything and everything about this One, all of which is true from all eternity, and that which is expressed in His earthly life, is that of which He is a personal witness. He was a willing companion and now an outspoken witness.

that which we have heard. . .seen. . .beheld. . . handled. . .heard - John was in company with Jesus as much or more than most of the other disciples. He is mentioned almost as prominently as Peter, though Peter was the more outspoken of the two. Three sensory perceptions are brought into John's proof statements: hearing, seeing, and touching. Sixty years have now passed since those times, but the indelible stamp of His teachings and life are still blazing in the heart of this aged disciple—his sermons, parables, rebukes, defenses against railing Jews, tender words to sinners, compassionate acts among the ill and afflicted, the encouragements to the contrite of heart. All of these John remembers as if they happened only yesterday.

seen - John mentally records with vividness the healing of the sick, raising of the dead, feeding the thousands, teaching the throngs. John saw all these marvels, and the world could not contain the writing of the whole of them (John 21:25). But these events in the life of this One will lead to faith and life eternal, the reason why John had written the Gospel (John 20:30-31).

beheld - Here is a more intensive word, one that suggests steady and deliberate gazing. It includes comprehensive and full consideration, not just briefly viewing an incident. It was not a passing glance at events, but a serious, fixed, steady study of the man and the actions throughout His life.

handled - John affirms he did actually handle and touch Jesus after the resurrection. This person was not a phantom, a ghost, exclusively spirit. Touching was not uncommon among the apostles ("Reach hither thy finger. . .thrust it into my side. . .," [John 20:27]; and ". . .handle me and see: for a spirit hath not flesh and bones, as ye see me have," [Luke 24:39]). John is insistent on the reality of the fleshly Jesus. Since the Docetics denied God ever came in the flesh, John is tenacious in such insistence, giving detailed witness and corroboration to meet this error directly. Remember that the aorist tense here (EPSELAPHEISAN) suggests an accomplished fact. John adds to the verb by saying "our hands," thus further substantiating what his "eyes" had seen.

What had Cerinthus heard, seen, beheld, or handled? What had any Docetic experienced about this man Jesus? What had any other person to bring forth in first-person denial? It is clear that John and other inspired writers were saying something in clear terms: "We have. . .but you have not"!

Word of life - Where did John come by the use of this nomenclature, "Word" (LOGOS)? Was it a common expression among the people of his day? Was it a word in current use among the educators and teachers? It is easy to document the philosophic idea of "word," plentiful among Philo, Aristotle, Plato, and the Stoics. It evidently was a topic of common discussion.

It also was not uncommon to Jewish backgrounds, for it is used limitedly in the Old Testament: **by the Word of Jehovah were the heavens made** (Psalm 33:6); **He sendeth his word and healeth them** (Psalm 107:20). Such personification was not unknown among the Jews, and the abstract idea that "Word" and Deity were synonymous may have been well developed.

Does John have here in mind some sermon the Lord preached, perhaps the parables He taught? Or does John have in mind the entirety of His teachings? It is doubtful that is what John had in mind by his use of "Word." Rather than reference to statements made by the Lord, John speaks of the Lord Himself. The term refers to the complete description and expression of Deity in the person of the one who **became flesh and dwelt among us, full of grace and truth.** John thus uses an expression that would not have been missed by those first century people of the common class, and certainly not by those teachers and philosophers either. It is right and proper, therefore, for this expression "Word" to be capitalized, though later translations seem to tend not to do so. That He is the "Word of life" refers to the fact that life emanates from Him, abides in Him, and is

7

given by Him. He is the "bread of life" (John 6:35,48), the "light of life" (John 8:12), and "the life" (John 14:6). His law brings life out of death, where there is no condemnation (Romans 8:1-2).

Verse 2 (and the life was manifested, and we have seen, and bear witness, and declare unto you the life, the eternal life, which was with the Father, and was manifested unto us);

and the life was manifested - This expression shows a progressive emphasis when one notes the verbs used: **manifested. . .seen. . .bear witness. . .declare.** Incarnation accomplished this progression, as there was first the manifestation, followed by the disciples' seeing Him and then bearing witness to those incidents, and finally by their declaring Him and His work. The Gospel had so stated this also: **. . .made flesh. . .beheld his glory. . .** (John 1:14), **. . .beginning of his signs. . .manifested his glory. . .** (John 2:11). John and all the other apostles were able to see and understand what was previously a mystery, unknown and unrevealed.

we have seen - John claims personal eye witness events similar to Peter's claim, "we were eye witnesses of his majesty" (2 Peter 1:16), speaking of the time they were with Him "in the mount," the mount of Transfiguration.

and bear witness - (KAI MARTUROUMEN) that is, testimony of eye witnesses is now given, since eye witnesses are competent to testify. This idea is often restated throughout the book (4:14; 5:9).

and declare unto you the life, the eternal life - Here John affirms (1) the eternal nature of the Son, and (2) the Son as the source of all life, especially human life. Notice He was said to be "with the Father"; therefore, it is essential to understand that Jesus had a pre-existence in relation to the human birth to Mary. This external existence, this pre-human existence can be seen easily in the instances of the appearances of "the Angel of Jehovah" in the Old Testament. A Person called "the Angel of Jehovah" appeared to Hagar, One who was also referred to as "God" and "Jehovah" (Genesis 16:7-13). A Visitor called "the Angel of Jehovah," along with two other visitors, appeared to Abram to announce the doom of Sodom (Genesis 18:1ff).

When two of these visitors went into Sodom, it is said Abram "stood yet before Jehovah." When Abraham was told to offer Isaac in sacrifice, it was "the Angel of Jehovah" who stayed his hand; yet this Speaker is also called "God" and "Jehovah" (Genesis 22:11-18). Again, when Jacob wrestled with a "man," a later prophet said it was "the angel," going on to refer to Him as "Jehovah, the God of hosts; Jehovah is his memorial name" (Genesis 32:22-32; Hosea 12:3-5). Moses was visited by "the Angel of Jehovah" in a flame of fire coming out of a bush; yet the presence of this One was so awesome that the place was called "holy ground" (Exodus 3:1-15). This same Angel said, "I am the God of thy father, the God of Abraham, the God of Isaac, and the God of Jacob" (v.6). And even more revealing is the statement that this Person was "I AM THAT I AM" (vv. 14-15). One may look into other incidents of this Personage, "the Angel of Jehovah" (Exodus 23; Joshua 5,13), but suffice it to say they add to one's amazement at the pre-human existence of the Lord Jesus.

Using the term "Word," John lends emphasis to such pre-existence, even as he did in the Gospel (John 1:1-3,14). "Eternal" (AIONIOS) is used here for best emphasis, for "everlasting" (AIDIOS) might not convey this pre-existence as well to readers.

manifested unto us - There is the undeniable fact of real existence prior to Jesus' life on earth, as well as real bodily presence while on earth. Remember John is writing to those who might be afflicted with false teachers who deny the real fleshly existence of the Lord.

V. 2 is parenthetical, repeating the gist of v. 1 for emphasis, explaining and qualifying the claims already made.

Verse 3 that which we have seen and heard declare we unto you also, that ye may also have fellowship with us: yea, and our fellowship is with the Father, and with his Son Jesus Christ:

that which we have seen and heard declare we unto you - The author resumes now the main thought of v. 1, in order to proceed to speak about fellowship. Calling attention to all that was seen and heard while with Jesus, John places a qualifier on any fellowship with Jesus. Non-believers, rejecters, deniers have no way to enjoy any fellowship with Jesus.

that ye also may have fellowship with us. . .our fellowship is with the Father - To have fellowship (KOINONIA) is "fellowship, partnership, . . .participation, communion. . . ."[4] Additionally, the word ". . .implies more distinctly the idea of community with others. . .always used of active participation, where the result depends on the cooperation of the receiver as well as the action of the giver."[5] John wishes all the blessings of salvation and peace, that he himself enjoys, could come to his readers. An early expression of these common bonds was given in the unity of worship within the early Church (Acts 2:42). Such unity is first dependent upon holding valid beliefs and convictions, as well as being obedient to valid instructions.

and with his Son Jesus Christ - Proper relations for man are based on a proper God-man connection. This is not a sharing of divine nature, but rather a sharing of beliefs, views, hopes, joys, and aims. God calls us by the gospel (2 Thessalonians 2:14) to a proper fellowship in Jesus Christ, ". . .called into the fellowship of his Son Jesus Christ our Lord" (1 Corinthians 1:9). God has never had agreement with false gods, idols, but rather calls for separation from them, ". . .come ye out from along them and be ye separate. . ." (2 Corinthians 6:17). John now hints at, or introduces, a vital truth to be developed later in the book: True spiritual fellowship must be with both God and fellow men. Without proper relations with either one, the other also fails (vv. 6ff). Also, this fellowship is equally shared with both the Father and the Son. One cannot follow the Father properly without following the Son. One cannot believe accurately in only one; both Father and Son must be believed and trusted, else faith is invalid. There is an inseparable and unfathomable union between them, ". . .even as thou, Father, art in me, and I in thee. . ." (John 17:21). This premise introduces a vital argument to answer the Gnostics and Docetae, who claimed that Jesus was a "lesser" personage.

Verse 4 and these things we write, that our joy may be made full.

and these things we write, that our joy may be made full - The expression "these things" (KAI TAUTA) refers to what John previously described and will continue to enunciate through the epistle. "We" is common among writers, not necessitating more than one author, rather an idiom of modesty claimed universally by authors. How fortunate are later generations for such writing! By inspired "God-breathed" scripture (1 Corinthians 2:13; 2 Timothy 3:16-17), and in such simplicity that common folks can read and understand (Ephesians 3:1-4), God provided that succeeding generations would be able to know these precious truths. Vital to man's salvation, such truths will free one from sins and afford a proper lifestyle, or "abiding," for "If ye abide in my word, then are ye truly my disciples; and ye shall know the truth, and the truth shall make you free" (John 8:31-32).

Whether it is "our joy" (ASV) or "your joy" (KJV) makes little difference (HINA HEI CHARA HEMON). Essential it is to produce this book for full and complete views, bringing full and complete joy. If it be John's joy (ASV), it coincides with other statements that he could have "no greater joy than this, to hear of my children walking in truth" (3 John 4). If it be the joy of the readers (KJV), it would emphasize such joy is found only in the Savior and that such joy could come only by precise and accurate testimony of such epistles as John's.

I. The Christian and God: Walking in Light 1:5-2:29

A. Things to Do for Fellowship with God 1:5-2:11

1. Walk in the Light 1:5-7

Verse 5 And this is the message that we have heard from him and announce unto you, that God is light and in him is no darkness at all.

And this is the message - This is the essence of communication by God to man. God reveals Himself, using inspiration to communicate (HA ANGELIA) the truths through human vessels (2 Corinthians 4:7). Such men as John then wrote the truths for all future generations.

that God is light - Light (PHOS) is often a symbol of purity, righteousness, knowledge, peace, joy, and happiness. God is light (James 1:17), a source of light. It is often used when it is ". . .applied metaph. to those who impart life. . ."[6] God's very being is absolute light, ". . .who is the blessed and only Potentate, the King of kings and Lord of lords; who only hath immortality dwelling in light unapproachable; whom no man hath seen nor can see. . ." (1 Timothy 6:15-16). Scriptures strive to describe the Indescribable and can give only one window at a time through which to look from paltry human eyes. This light, as with all other attributes, is limitless, infinite, and incomprehensible to man. Notice God is not said to be "a light" or "the light," but **light itself.** He is perfectly pure with no blots, stains, errors, mistakes, or sins. He is perfectly knowledgeable, all wise, with no imperfection of ignorance. He is perfectly composed and happy, with nothing miserable about Him. He is perfectly righteous, with nothing unholy or impure.

This major affirmation is one of three that John makes about Almighty God: (1) God is Spirit [John 4:24]; (2) God is light [1 John 1:5]; and (3) God is love [1 John 4:8]. Without

12

the writings of John, man would be bereft of precious insights into the personality and nature of Jehovah.

in him is no darkness at all - John now states the negative for the sake of emphasis. Not even one small shadow, absolutely nothing is ever present to blot or dim God's light. "Darkness" (SKOTIA) is often used to indicate evil, ". . .delivered us out of darkness. . ." (Colossians 1:13); and the works of the devil, ". . .against the world-rulers of this darkness. . ." (Ephesians 6:12), and the kingdom of Satan, ". . .how then shall his kingdom stand. . ." (Matthew 12:26). Jesus often taught such truths, ". . .men loved darkness rather than the light. . .everyone that doeth evil hateth the light" (John 3:19-20). Christians were ". . .once darkness, but are now light in the Lord. . ." (Ephesians 5:8) and will have no fellowship with the "unfruitful works of darkness. . ." (Ephesians 5:11). The structure of the Greek grammar John used here could not be more emphatic: "the darkness in him not is none" (KAI SKOTIA EN AUTO OUK ESTIN OUDEMIA). It signifies that not even one tiny particle of darkness is in God.

Verse 6 If we say we have fellowship with him and walk in the darkness, we lie, and do not the truth:

If we say we have fellowship with him and walk in the darkness - If we count ourselves, profess ourselves, claim ourselves, in partnership and joint participation with Jehovah God, yet continue a walk in darkness, we are wrong.

John begins six conditional statements with the word "if" (EAN, used with the subjunctive):

verse 6	**If we say we have fellowship with him**
verse 7	**If we walk in the light**
verse 8	**If we say we have no sin**
verse 9	**If we confess our sins**
verse 10	**If we say we have not sinned**
verse 2:1	**If any man sin**

Each time John uses "If we say," he hurls a thunderbolt denunciation for such falsities! The first is a false claim of fellowship; the latter two are false claims of living without or above sin. How pungent this must have been to the Gnostics and the Docetae! The very heart of all their claims is being ripped out by the truths presented by John. The

"Apostle of Love" is loving enough in this early part of the epistle to correct false doctrine and emphasize doctrinal accuracy, something many moderns disdain.

The other three conditional "if" clauses, (walk in the light, confess our sins, and if any man sin) are majestic statements of God's grace and its results:

verse 7 **Condition: if** we walk in the light (PERIPATOMEN, present subjunctive, i.e., continue walking in the light)

Grace: we have fellowship (KOINONIAN ECHOMEN, present indicative active, i.e., continue to have fellowship), and the blood cleanses (KATHARIZEI, present indicative active, i.e., continues to cleanse).

v. 9 **Condition: If** we confess our sins (HOMOLOGOMEN, pres. subj., i.e., continue to confess)

Grace: He is faithful and righteous to forgive and cleanse (ESTIN, pres. ind. act., i.e., He presently is, and continues to be faithful and righteous to forgive and cleanse).

2:1 **Condition: If** any man sin (HAMARTEI, aorist subjunctive, i.e., commit any sin, referring to completed pinpoint action, not a continuance of sins)

Grace: we have an Advocate (ECHOMEN, pres. ind. act., i.e., we now have and continue to have an Advocate).

The one who is contrary to all these conditional statements has three problems:

v. 6   he lies and does not the truth.
v. 8   he deceives himself and the truth is not in him.
v. 10   he makes God a liar and his word is not in him.

All of these are unthinkable conclusions, so the adverse of each condition is the choice for Christians to take: Do not claim fellowship with God while walking in darkness, do not claim to be without sin, and do not claim never to have sinned.

walk in darkness - Again the verb tense (SKOTEI PERIPATOMEN, pres. subj.,) lends emphasis to the fact that John is speaking about a continual walk in darkness, not a brief stumbling or falling through weakness and human frailty. "Walk" refers to continual practice, a way of life, and is so used elsewhere: "walk in newness of life" (Romans 6:4), "walk not after the flesh" (Romans 8:1), "wherein you once walked according to the course of this world" (Ephesians 2:2). It is said by some to be the "summation of one's life." The man claiming fellowship with God (light), but walking in sinful ways (darkness); has no fellowship with God. Cerinthus, the famous heretic of John's time, claimed this very thing. He and his followers claimed fellowship with God while indulging in all manner of fleshly sins (see Introduction). Thinking actions of the fleshly body would not be accountable in Judgment Day was fatal then and is fatal now, ". . .each one may receive the things done in the body, according to what he hath done, whether it be good or bad" (2 Corinthians 5:10).

lie and do not the truth - this is literally "not living in truth," (OU POIOUMEN TAN ALETHEIAN) or "not continuing to do truth." One cannot separate ethics and actions, theory and practice. Men who thus walk in darkness and claim fellowship do two things: (1) they profess a lie, and (2) they live continually in lying actions.

Verse 7 if we walk in the light as he is in the light, we have fellowship one with another, and the blood of Jesus his Son cleanseth us from all sin.

if we walk in the light, as he is in the light - On the other hand, one who walks in (keeps doing and practicing) the light (righteous, God-imitating practices) can accurately claim fellowship with God.

we have fellowship one with another - Here is an additional blessing now introduced, the fellowship (KOINONIAN) with one another. Besides fellowship with God, the walking-in-light person also has fellowship with all others who are walking in the light. There is a common bond brought on by a common walk, and this establishes a common relationship. Paul expresses the same principle in his use of the metaphor "body" and "members" (1 Corinthians 12:20,26-27). No one in darkness has such fellowship, either with the Father or with any fellow man who is a Christian. Only those walking in the light can claim such exclusive fellowship.

and the blood of Jesus his Son cleanseth us from all sin - This blood, the cleansing blood of Jesus, is the very thing the Gnostics denied. They theorized one of two things:

15

(1) Either the Son never became real flesh and blood, that he only appeared to have such, or (2) if he did have an actual flesh and blood body, it was inhabited only for a while by the Son, who left that body prior to the crucifixion. These two theories effectively deny the reality of the shed blood of the Lord. John declares in the strongest of terms the specific blood of Jesus as the cleansing agent. It alone has merit to cause God to justify man. It is the only **meritorious cause** man could ever claim.

The present tense "cleanseth" (KATHARIZEI) in the Greek is deeply significant. It states that which goes on continuously, constantly for the benefit of man. With the conditional clause already stated, "If we walk in the light," it is easy to realize how long the blood is effective: just as continual as is one's walk in the light! It might also be noted that such "walking" would have to include the "confessing" stated in v.9. It would be unthinkable that one could walk properly but refuse or neglect to confess his sins properly. God's word does not have to state every detail in every descriptive passage in order for the detail to be necessary.

Laying a foundation statement here, John will build many other conclusions throughtout the letter, which are based on the efficacy of Jesus' blood. If He were merely a man, His blood was worth only that of Himself, or the same as any other one man. Yet, being the Son of God, He was able with His blood to redeem all mankind as Peter succinctly wrote, "knowing that ye were redeemed, not with corruptible things, with silver or gold, from your vain manner of life handed down from your fathers; but with precious blood, as of a lamb without blemish and without spot, even the blood of Christ" (1 Peter 1:18-19). The vast importance of the doctrine of propitiatory blood in the New Testament should be evident to all:

". . .the cup of blessing. . .a communion. . .of the blood of Christ" (1 Corinthians 10:16);

". . .how much more shall the blood of Christ. . .cleanse" (Hebrews 9:14);

"This is my blood of the covenant poured out for the remission of sins" (Matthew 26:28);

"in whom we have redemption through his blood, the forgiveness of our trespasses" (Ephesians 1:7);

". . .having made peace through the blood of his cross. . ." (Colossians 1:20);

". . .according to. . .the sprinkling of the blood of Jesus Christ" (1 Peter 1:2).

2. Accept, Repent, and Confess One's Sins 1:8-10

⁸If we say that we have no sin, we deceive ourselves, and the truth is not in us. ⁹If we confess our sins, he is faithful and righteous to forgive us our sins, and to cleanse us from all unrighteousness. ¹⁰If we say that we have not sinned, we make him a liar, and his word is not in us.

Verse 8 If we say that we have no sin, we deceive ourselves, and the truth is not in us.

If we say that we have no sin, we deceive ourselves - This kind of error was showing itself even as John made this doctrinal statement, denying any such false assertion. Through Christians surely were cleansed of all their past sins at baptism, still none could claim sinless perfection since that time. Possibly there were those in the early churches who succumbed to the Gnostic theory that God would not hold one accountable for sins done in the fleshly body. Nothing could be farther from the truth. Past sins are forgiven truly; present sins still must be accounted for by all men. "Purification from sin presupposes the existence of sin even in believers; the denial of this is self-deception."[7]

In more modern times, some might brashly deny their mistakes; others might deny God has any law to which one is amenable. Still others are prone to deny sins are laid to one's account. The idea of "imputation of sins" and "imputation of righteousness," mistakenly assumed from Paul's statements about Abraham (Romans 4:3-8), has given later religionists false concepts and false hopes. The righteous character of Christ is never given or "imputed" to anyone upon becoming a Christian. The **justification** offered by Christ is given to all who become Christians. And that is exactly what Paul means throughout the book of Romans when he uses the terminology "God's righteousness." This "righteousness" in Romans does not refer to an

17

attribute of the Holy One; rather, it refers to an act done by God for the benefit of man and is synonymous to the idea of justification. Many other times the term "righteousness" does refer to God's own character of holiness and purity; but throughout Romans it nearly always refers to "justification," and that justification is what is "imputed" or counted to man when he becomes a Christian.

In modern times also, men have not argued so much that sins in the fleshly body do not contaminate a Christian; rather, they argue that sin is not a reality. Some say that sin (1) exists only in the minds of legalists and those who are guilty of "Bibliolatry," those who cling to the fundamental study of the Bible so much that they "worship the word"; (2) is not actually evil enough in God's sight to merit all the attention it gets, that which is a little consequence, a small matter; (3) depends upon one's circumstances, environment, education, and culture; (4) is simply a mistake of good, honest folks, and a loving God surely will not condemn them for such; (5) is not necessarily a sin in all cultures and centuries, since mores and values change so much in varying times and cultures; (6) will not be counted to a Christian anyway, since Christ's blood is supposed to "look forward" as well as backward in its cleansing power. All these foregoing claims are untrue.

Sad and pitiable it is that so many in modern times are listening to these false arguments and claims. Those who would place their hopes in these false claims would also have listened gladly to Satan in the Garden!

and the truth is not in us - Such a man claiming holiness, which belongs only to the Lord, must not know his own heart. When one considers the vast possibilities of omission, it is non-sensical to hoist oneself into the domain belonging only to God. Such crass egotism is unthinkable!

Verse 9 If we confess our sins, he is faithful and righteous to forgive us our sins, and to cleanse us from all unrighteousness.

If we confess our sins, he is faithful and righteous to forgive us our sins - One of the requisites of this "walk in the light" (v. 7) is that a Christian will confess his sins as he is able to comprehend and repent of them. God's pardon has ever required a confession by the sinner of his sins: "He that covereth his transgressions shall not prosper; but whoso confesseth and forsaketh them shall obtain mercy" (Proverbs 28:13).

Three kinds of confession are noted in the New Testament: (1) **confession of personal actions of sin** as did those baptized of John (Matthew 3:6; Mark 1:5), as did the Prodigal Son (Luke 16:18), as do all Christians to those whom they have wronged (James 5:16); (2) **confession of faith in Jesus as the Christ, the Son of God** as a prerequisite to baptism (Romans 10:9-10; Acts 8:36-38; 1 Timothy 6:12) and which many Jews refused to do (John 12:42); (3) **confession as a way of life, a profession,** as did the twelve when they were sent out on the first limited commission (Matthew 10:32; Luke 12:8). The confession used by John in this verse is obviously the first one, a confession of one's sins.

This confessing (HOMOLOGOMEN pres. subj.) has the force of "if we keep on confessing"; this would be consistent with having light in us (v. 6), walking in light (v. 7), and having the truth in us (v. 8). Further, this confession (literally "to speak the same") is not mere acknowledgment of error. Rather, it is a full acknowledgment of errors, mistakes, and wrongs, with pious and humble appeal to God for mercies.

faithful and righteous - This expression refers to God, the One upon whom man can ever depend to be true to promises. God cannot lie or break a promise, the two "immutables": ". . .that by two immutable things, in which it is impossible for God to lie. . ." (Hebrews 6:18). Even if man breaks his word, God remains faithful: "If we are faithless, he abideth faithful; for he cannot deny himself" (2 Timothy 2:13). These are attributes of the Great God who must uphold his own personal justice while justifying sinful man (Romans 3:26).

Forgive. . .sins and cleanse. . .all unrighteousness - Sins (HAMARTIAS, missing the mark) are forgiven; iniquities (AKIKIAS, "unrightness") are cleansed. Forgiveness (APHEI, from APHIEMI) carries the idea of "to send away, dismiss, suffer to depart; to emit, send forth. . .to remit, pardon. . ."[8] one's debts or sins. Cleansing (KATHARISEI, from KATHARIZO) means "to cleanse, render pure. . .purify by expiatory offering, make expiation for. . . ,"[9] or ". . .to make clean, to cleanse. . .in a moral sense, from the defilement of sin, ..."[10] So the Faithful and Righteous One sends away from us our failures and removes all our defilements, **as we come to him confessing these things.**

Verse 10 If we say that we have not sinned, we make him a liar, and his word is not in us.

If we say that we have not sinned - V. 8 spoke of "having no sin" to point out the **present** condition of men; now John points out man's **past** condition, i.e., "have not sinned." The perfect tense (HAMARTAKAMEN) emphasizes the full force of the statement: "have not in the past and have not now." The perfect tense states the present result of past action. In this case, men are covered up with miserable sins, regardless of their foolish claims. Man just cannot claim errorless life, either past or present, and be accurate and truthful. More and more John is refuting the errors of his day, like Gnosticism, that denies the reality of sin. Past or present, no one can claim that no stain of sin belongs to his soul. Such a one makes out God to be a liar, certainly an unthinkable conclusion to any believer.

we make him a liar - The man who denies personal sins "accuses God of lying."[11] Perhaps this is done ignorantly or carelessly, but John makes it so no longer to his readers. Far stronger than John's previous words, "we lie" (v. 6), "we deceive ourselves" (v. 8), John now comes to the worst possible conclusion and consequence—the blasphemy of making God a liar! Totally to the contrary ring the words of Paul as he wrote, "Let God be true and every man a liar" (Romans 3:3). No amount of dodging, extemporizing, or philosophizing can erase this grievous and heinous error. This is a sin of all sins—blasphemy. And those who deny their need of the blood of God's Son are well on their way to the state of mind that would trap them in such a shameful and degrading declaration.

his word is not in us - Truth, the word of God (John 17:17), is not resting in this heart. No welcome mat is out for such a man in the presence of the angels. No discipleship is near for this one, since one must "abide" in His word to be a disciple (John 8:31). In this kind of "abiding," a disciple will know and live in the paths of truth taught by Jesus' precious word (John 8:32). The treasuries of revelation from the mind of God have bypassed the one who denies the Christ (Colossians 2:3).

John will emphasize this dedication to truth throughout this epistle: "know the truth" (2:21), "we are of the truth" (3:19), "keepeth his word" (2:5), "word of God abideth in you" (2:14), and God's "witness" that he "gave unto us eternal life and this life is in his Son" (5:11). Most might assume readers would understand such a simple and basic principle; John keeps on reminding his readers, since this was one place where Christianity was under attack in the first century (an attack that has continued throughout every century since).

---

[1]Albert Barnes, *Notes on the New Testament, James, Peter, John and Jude,* (Baker Book House, Grand Rapids, Michigan, 1949 reprint), p. 278.

[2]R. C. H. Lenski, *The Interpretation of the Epistles of St. Peter, St. John, and St. Jude,* (Augsburg Publishing House, Minneapolis, Minnesota, 1963), pp. 370-371.

[3]Guy N. Woods, *A Commentary on the New Testament Epistles of Peter, John and Jude,* (Gospel Advocate Co., Nashville, Tennessee, 1954), p. 210.

[4]Samuel Bagster, *Analytical Greek Lexicon,* (Samuel Bagster & Sons, London, England, 1852, Revised Edition by Moulton, Harold K., Zondervan Publishing Co., Grand Rapids, Michigan, 1978), p. 235.

[5]James Hope Moulton and George Milligan, *The Vocabulary of the Greek New Testament,* (Wm. B. Eerdmans Publishing Co., Grand Rapids, Michigan, 1960), p. 351.

[6]Moulton and Milligan, *Vocabulary,* p. 680.

[7]Joh. Ed. Huther, *Meyer's Commentary on the New Testament, Critical and Exegetical Handbook to the General Epistles of James, Peter, John and Jude,* (Funk & Wagnalls, Publishers, New York, 1887), p. 485.

[8]Bagster, *Lexicon,* p. 62.

[9]Bagster, *Lexicon,* p. 206.

[10]W. E. Vine, *An Expository Dictionary of New Testament Words,* (Riverside Book and Bible House, Iowa Falls, Iowa, 1952), p. 187.

[11]Joh. Ed. Huther, *Critical and Exegetical Handbook,* p. 490.

3. Trust in the Advocate 2:1-2

¹My little children, these things write I unto you that ye may not sin. And if any man sin, we have an Advocate with the Father, Jesus Christ the righteous: ²and he is the propitiation for our sins; and not for ours only, but also for the whole world.

Verse 1 My little children, these things write I unto you that you may not sin. And if any man sin, we have an Advocate with the Father, Jesus Christ the righteous:

My little children - there is no break in the thought of a Christian walking in the light (1:5-2:29), for now there is an introduction to what such a walk would entail: absolute trust in the Advocate.

The aged apostle John, now ninety years plus, uses the tender words "my little children" (TEKNIA MOU), the plural diminutive of child (TEKNON). Thus he introduces a poignant and tender note into his admonitions and warnings. Only in this verse is the use of the word "my." "Children," however, is used seven times in John's epistle (2:1,12,28; 3:7,18; 4:4; 5:21), a term he no doubt learned at the table while reclining on the breast of the Lord (John 13:23,33). John does not identify the persons addressed; he simply invites readers to feel there is the closest possible relation existing between the author and his readers.

these things I write unto you that ye may not sin - the preceding things about sin (confession, lying, walking in the light, walking in darkness, and fellowship) all have one purpose; to warn John's spiritual little children about any act of sin. "I write" evidently refers to the previous things, plus the things yet to come in the entire epistle.

Note that when the purpose was stated, "that ye may not sin," John uses an ingressive aorist. This is significant, for it emphasizes that John wants them not to be guilty of even one sin! Perhaps there could have been several errors in the minds of the readers. (1) Since they have been baptized for the remission of their sins and understanding that all previous sins had been forgiven, they might now be puzzled as to what happens to sins committed after one is baptized. (2) Since sin is certainly present in all persons, even those baptized into Christ, why even strive for holiness (from Gnostic influence)? (3) Since cleansing by the blood of Christ, through confession and prayer is so readily available, why not let God's grace cover all such sins; why worry one's head about it all?

Such errors no doubt were present in the thinking of the First Century Christians, perhaps the latter two under the influence of the Gnostics, and John is about to take care of any and all such notions. The last error, number three, is perhaps the forerunner of modern "eternal security" error. It is that some believe that the blood of Jesus not only remits past sins at conversion to Christ, but also is applied automatically to any future sin! Some take this so far as to say forgiveness is automatic whether or not there is ever repentance. This pernicious doctrine may be based on the false idea of "imputed righteousness," as if the perfections of the character of Christ could be transferred to the newly converted brother (see under 1:8).

John speaks of inadvertent sin, ignorant sin, sins of frailty, sins of weakness, and not the practice of sin, or the rebellious sin. He states later, "every one that hath this hope set on him purifieth himself even as he is pure" (3:3). Peter repeated the often present argument from the Old Testament, testifying the same thing, when he wrote, "but like as he who called you is holy, be ye yourselves also holy in all manner of living; because it is written, Ye shall be holy; for I am holy" (1 Peter 1:15-16). Yet, the Christian who finds himself in such sin is not without hope.

And if any man sin - sometimes "and" (KAI) is used adversatively and then it is usually translated "but" (see NIV). The goal of a Christian is a consistent walk in light, but provision is made for inconsistencies. The gospel is surely "good news" to frail humans. There is a proper remedy.

we have an Advocate with the Father, Jesus Christ - "we have" is present indicative plural, with the force of "we keep on having." There is always a present remedy for one's mistakes, for Christians keep on having an Advocate.

This Advocate (PARACLETE) refers to "one who is called alongside to help." It is in the passive sense, as God's grand scheme of things did, in effect, call Him alongside to help.

23

There are two major ideas of what such a helper might represent: (1) a lawyer, or (2) a friend willing to help. The first, the forensic sense, as a lawyer, would entail His pleading our case before the judgment bar of God. He would stand before the bar as one fully qualified to represent mankind. Albert Barnes shows his to be a most unusual work of a lawyer: (1) he admits the client's guilt, (2) he then offers himself as security if the crime could go unpunished, (3) he has already suffered and paid the price for such guilt.[1] The second meaning, that of a friend, might show some other insights into the work of this One. As a friend above all friends, (1) he is always at home with the Father, (2) he is the Eternal Son of God, a unique and special relation, (3) he is also true man, man in every sense of the term, (4) he is the Anointed King - Messiah - Christ, (5) he is our High Priest, (6) he is the Righteous One, fit for the presence of the Almighty Judge. Either of these two senses of advocate only serves to show the grandeur of the one who represents us in heaven!

In other uses PARACLETE is sometimes translated "comforter," and applied both to Jesus and the Holy Spirit (John 14:16,26; 15:26; 16:7). Jesus speaks of the Holy Spirit as "another comforter" whom He will send to the apostles (John 14:16). He uses the term "another" (ALLOS), denoting "another of the same sort." It has a numerical meaning, showing a difference in number of comforters. Jesus is one of the comforters; the Holy Spirit is another, an additional comforter. Thus Jesus and the Holy Spirit share the chores and role of comforter to the apostles. Perhaps Jesus comforted in a special sense by pleading their case before the throne of the Father, while the Holy Spirit subsequently pleaded the apostles' case before the world. The apostles spread the gospel to the world, aided, inspired to do so by that very Holy Spirit. That Spirit aided, comforted the apostles in such work.

the righteous - is used by Peter both as a Messianic title (Acts 3:14) and as the quality of His person, His character (1 Peter 3:18 - KJV translates DIKAIOS as "just"). John refers to Jesus again as righteous (2:29) and related to all who practice such purity of life. It is as John later says, "he that doeth righteousness is righteous, even as he is

24

righteous" (3:7). Three things are suggested by John's statement here: (1) "Jesus," the human name given at birth - Matthew 1:21; (2) "Christ", as Deity and Messiah - "made to be both Lord and Christ" - Acts 2:36; (3) "righteous" as essential Deity, inherent Deity, an eternal attribute of flawless self in perfection, thus surely a proper sacrifice for the sins of the world. He, being righteous, suffered for the sins of the unrighteous (1 Peter 3:18), was denied by the Jewish nation out of whom He sprang and to whom He came first (Acts 3:14), and was betrayed and murdered by His own people (Acts 7:52). Jesus can properly be called "righteous" for ". . .by the epithet DIKAIOS, Christ is held up before the HAMARTANOUSI as one who by His nature is fitted to be the Paraclete of sinners, i.e., as one who perfectly satisfies the will of God; who is 'just and stainless, and without sin' (Luther). 'Only as the Holy One, in whom the holy ideal of manhood is seen realized, can He intercede for sinners with the heavenly Father' (Neander)."[2]

Verse 2 And he is the propitiation for our sins; and not for ours only, but also for the whole world.

and he is the propitiation for our sins - the word propitiation (HILASMOS) occurs only twice in the New Testament, here and in 4:10. Other forms of the same root word occur: "whom God set forth to be a propitiation" (Romans 3:25); "overshadowing the mercy seat" (Hebrews 9:5); "God be merciful to me a sinner" (Luke 18:3); and "to make reconciliation for the sins of the people" (Hebrews 2:17). The root word (HILASKOMAI) is one that means "to cause one to be gracious." Commentators and Greek scholars are careful to point out that God is never propitiated or appeased in the sense of appeasing a capricious, idolatrous god. Such a false picture would have Jehovah sitting on His throne, irritable, angry, wrathful, and offended by man, waiting to be placated and persuaded. Such was thought to be the nature of the idols whom men served in these times. Since they worshipped so many things within the universe and nature, it is not hard to see that they felt angry gods had to be appeased: storms, lightning, earthquakes, floods, etc., would, to their mind, be punishment from unpredictable wrathful gods for their unfaithfulness. Not so the true picture of Jehovah.

Many men use another term to avoid such a false concept: "expiation" (RSV). To expiate is to "pay a penalty, atone, propitiate, make amends or reparation for."[3] This would place the emphasis, not on God's feelings, but on the sins and what is done with them. These sins and their guilt are made ineffective by the offering of Jesus. Sins are set aside in God's sight; proper reparation has been made. Sins are robbed of any validity before the throne, for atonement has been offered. God can now be favorable toward the sinner. Lenski says, "The abstract is more significant than the concrete since it combines the person with his act of 'expiating' and 'we prefer expiation' because of 4:10: in His love God commissioned His Son as expiation regarding our sins. The thought is not that this expiation propitiated, placated God, for he was full of infinite love when he sent his Son; we needed expiation, needed it regarding our sins; needed it regarding them every day when we still sin."[4]

On the other hand, most versions use "propitiation" (KJV, ASV, NASB), with others adding: "personal atonement" (Phillips, Knox, Williams), "remedy for the defilement" (NEB), "the way our sins are taken away" (Simple English, Easy-To-Read New Testament). The emphasis is on man's stance before God as that which is changed. God is not changed!

The view of secular Greek about HILASMOS is about the same as the Biblical view, that is, a diversion of wrath. In the Bible it is Divine wrath, holy indignation, God's perfect hatred of sin. It is not petty irritability, or arbitrary anger. This anger, calling for propitiation, may be perfectly justified. The moral governance of the universe is at stake, as it demands justice and wrath for those who violate God's laws. Remembering that "sin is transgression of God's law," "lawlessness" (1 John 3:4), one can understand that God's consistency would inevitably call for punishment of those who thus violate His law. David speaks of "perfect hatred" in saying, "Do not I hate them, O Jehovah, that hate thee?" (Psalm 139:21-22). Again, David says, "Through thy precepts I get understanding, therefore I hate every false way" (Psalm 119:104, see also veres 128). Further he declares, "O, Ye that love Jehovah, hate evil" (Psalm 97:10).

It is well to note a number of things that God is said to

hate: idolatry (Deuteronomy 16:22); workers of iniquity (Psalm 5:5); wickedness (Psalm 45:7); evil (Psalm 97:10); vain worship in new moons and feasts (Isaiah 1:14; Amos 5:21); robbery for burnt offering (Isaiah 61:8); false oaths and evil in hearts against a neighbor (Zechariah 8:17); and divorce (Malachi 2:16). Barnes states four notable things about this definition: (1) God's will has been disregarded, His law has been violated, and He has reason to be offended, (2) God cannot overlook consistently such offenses, (3) God must either show displeasure to us or use some other way that answers to the same purpose, (4) the means of propitiation enters the problem here so that it is proper to treat us as if we had not sinned.[5]

The idea of propitiation therefore is a satisfaction of divine justice. God's righteous character demands perfect governance of the universe and is conditioned by His grace. Satisfaction for sins must be shown, yet grace is freely bestowed. Divine wrath is diverted from the sinner to God's Son, given in love to satisfy the just demands for death punishment for sins. God is not a reluctant Deity, one who needs to be begged to forgive. Rather,He is the loving and gracious Provider of what His own law and justice demand (4:10). This is singular in history: (1) man offends God by his sins, (2) God permits a substitute to pay the penalty for man's sins, (3) God Himself provides this substitute, (4) God substitutes Himself in the Person of the Son. Can anyone ever doubt that God is serious about sin?

The use of "concerning sins" (PERI), which is used both in 2:2 and 4:10, should also be noticed. If the idea were only expiation rather than propitiation, one might expect a different Greek grammatical construction, i.e., "of sins," putting the emphasis on man's sins rather than on God.

A further argument for using propitiation is that the context has mentioned that our Paraclete appears to speak before the offended party. Now the just and proper principle for winning the offended party over can be given consistently: the satisfactory offering made by Jesus of Himself.

In understanding Jesus as our propitiation, one must exercise care about several things:

1. The dire need of man to be reconciled must not be avoided; it is the first and greatest need of man.

2. Any concept of sin that compromises or downplays the horrendous nature of sin is to be avoided: sin is the grossest of all things a man could do in his relationship to God.

3. Any attempt to portray God as changing must be avoided. He has ever been merciful, compassionate, loving, ready to forgive man whenever man makes a change called repentance.

4. All ideas that there may be other ways to appear before God as cleansed and suited for heaven must be avoided. There is no other sacrifice that would suffice; only the Innocent One could be adequate, "just for the unjust" (1 Peter 3:18).

5. Even one claim that the propitiatory blood is already applied to all mankind as an accomplished fact must be met and defeated at all points. The blood has been offered before the Throne, but it must be accepted individually by every man. It has not been automatically applied.

6. That one can learn about this propitiation any other way than through the Gospel is another pernicious lie that must be expunged. Conscience, life experience, emotions, dreams, or visions cannot bring one to the proper knowledge of Christ. This can be found only through His Word.

Thus, such an offering is perfect, in that it (1) removed all obstacles that could prevent full and free forgiveness, (2) maintained the honor and integrity of God and His law for man, and (3) met all the demands for God to be just as He engages in justifying man from his sins (Romans 3:26).

and not for our sins only, but also for the whole world - the scope and extension of this propitiation is not limited to one race, one class or one culture; rather, it extends to the entire world (KOSMOS). There is no limit to the bounds of atonement with respect to mankind; Jesus "tasted of death for every man" (Hebrews 2:9), "one died for all" (2 Corinthians 5:14), was the "ransom for many" (Matthew 20:28), and "ransom for all" (1 Timothy 2:16). "World" is used here similarly as it was used in "God so loved the world. . ." (John 3:16).

Such a statement by John emphasizes that the propitiatory offering of Jesus is applicable to all men (Titus 2:11), adequate for all men, sufficiently meritorious (Romans 1:16-17), addressed to all men in the gospel (Matthew 28:19; Mark 16:15), able to be administered to all men through faith (Romans 3:25), appealing to all men who can be constrained by the goodness of God (Romans 2:4).

4. Walk in Obedience 2:3-6

The student now comes to the fourth of five things John mentions for fellowship with God: walking in obedience. Prior actions already discussed are: (1) walking in light, (2) accepting, repenting, and confessing one's sins, and (3) trusting in the Advocate. Now one comes to another re-emphasis: walking in obedience is the same as walking in light.

³And hereby we know that we know him, if we keep his commandments. ⁴He that saith, I know him, and keepeth not his commandments, is a liar, and the truth is not in him; ⁵but whoso keepeth his word, in him verily hath the love God been perfected. Hereby we know that we are in him: ⁶he that saith he abideth in him ought himself also to walk even as he walked.

Verse 3 And hereby we know that we know him, if we keep his commandments.

And hereby we know that we know him - The antecedent of "Him" is Jesus our Savior. The last person mentioned in verse 1 is Jesus, and verse 2 has the first pronoun "He," which must refer to Jesus. Thus the thought continues in verse 3. "Hereby" brings us to a conclusion almost the same as saying "therefore" or "in this way." John now uses a favorite expression, "know," (GINOSKO) which he uses twenty-five times in this epistle alone, and over sixty times in the Gospel. The emphasis of this word is to perceive, to understand completely. It means far more than just recognizing facts about Jesus or a mere acquaintance with the person. It involves the complete acceptance of God's sovereignty and subsequent yielding to His divine will. It is properly a true, full, and just view of Jehovah accompanied by active compliance to His will, i.e., "keeping his commandments." Jesus previously stated this idea in His prayer, "And this is life eternal, that they should know thee the only true God, and him whom thou didst send, even Jesus Christ" (John 17:3). John also uses another word for know (OIDA) fifteen times. This word emphasizes knowing from observation.

This seems to combat false knowledge of Gnostics which presently threatened believers. Since they boasted of superior knowledge, yet did not attempt to keep His commandments, here was sure proof that their claimed knowledge was false.

The use of the perfect tense, "that we know Him," prompts the idea "we have known Him in the past and continue to know Him in the present." Ever since the Gospel was first presented to these readers, they have thus "known Him."

if we keep his commandments - these commandments are simply equal to the "truth," that which came by Jesus Christ (John 1:7), was embodied by Him (John 14:6), could make men free from sins (John 8:32), could effect sanctification (John 17:17), and pleases God to know it is such in which His children walk (2 John 4; 3 John 4). This keeping of commandments is equal to "walking in light" (1:6-7), and "doing righteousness" (2:29; 3:7).

Verse 4 He that saith, I know him, and keepeth not his commandments, is a liar, and the truth is not in him;

He that saith, I know him, and keepeth not his commandments - a conclusion can now be drawn safely from the previous verse: The man claiming knowledge and fellowship with Jesus, but denying Him by an ungodly life, is not truthful. The present indicative verbs are used here: "continues saying," and "continues not keeping commands." A practice of life, continuous course, or deliberative direction is indicated here. This is not a weakness or mere mistake; this is a continual walk in disobedience.

is a liar - this is the second of five times the word "liar" is used in the letter. This shows a deliberate direction of one's life, deeply ingrained and embedded. This person is not one that is simply contradictory, not one that is simply deceived, not one honestly mistaken; this man's very character is flawed.

truth is not in him - the truth is viewed as a dynamic that would cause this one to live differently or claim differently. Truth would cause him to cease one of the two! Again, the emphasis is that such a one has not escaped corruption, though the Gnostics of the antinomian lifestyle were claiming their libertine ways were not viewed by God as defiling their souls.

Verse 5 but whoso keepeth his word, in him verily hath the love of God been perfected. Hereby we know that we are in him:

but whoso keepeth his word, in him verily hath the love of God been perfected - "Keepeth his word" is equal to "keeping his commandments" (verses 3-4), and the "truth in us" (1:8). Shades of difference can be shown between commandment, word, and truth; but for John's purposes, he equates them in practical Christian life. "Whoso" ("anyone" - NIV) shows that a relationship with God is not limited to the elite few with superior knowledge, but is available to all persons of real faith.

love of God - John now advances beyond "knowing God" to a higher concept of "loving God." Much disputation has taken place among commentators as to whether this use of the genitive is God's love for man (subjective genitive), or man's love for God (objective genitive). Context is helpful here, for John has been speaking of walking in the light (1:7), confessing sins (1:9), keeping commands (2:3-4), and now keeping His word (verse 5). All of these are actions by man. So, it is best to apply this love to man's obedience and love toward God. In line with this is a later statement, "For this is the love of God, that we keep his commandments. . ." (1 John 5:3), and a previous statement, ". . .if a man love me, he will keep my word. . ." (John 14:23).

been perfected - John previews his later teaching that love is incomplete if it does not include deeds of love (3:13-24). This perfected love does not mean without any flaw; rather it means a mature love that brings about consistency in practice. This kind of man completes his faith-directed life by keeping God's word.

Hereby we know that we are in Him - by keeping God's word, we prove that we are in the proper stance, or relationship, with Him. Just as John previously advanced from knowing God (2:3) to loving God (2:4), he now advances from knowing Him to being "in Him." This amplifies what it is to know Him; i.e., it is to have the highest intimacy of all spiritual relationships: being in fellowship with God. "In Him" is also a favorite expression of Paul (Ephesians 1) and encompasses the same idea that John uses. Union with God is real to those keeping God's commandments, His word.

Verse 6 he that said he abideth in him ought himself also to walk even as he walked.

he that saith he abideth in him - Here is the summation, conclusion, final test of one who graduates as a Christian. John perhaps draws from Jesus' use of "abide" in the Lord's teaching about the "vine and branches" (John 15:1-8): "branch in me," "abide in me" are used freely there — six times. Here, as well as in John 15, the word "abide" (MENEIN) means more than simply to be in Him. It includes the idea of remaining in Him, and is so translated by some.[6] The essence of the word is a permanent and intimate association, not temporary or superficial. This union lasts.

ought himself also to walk even as he walked - Now, as in every case of blessings to man from God, there comes a corresponding obligation: "ought also to walk even as he walked." In the Garden, blessings plus obligations were announced to the first pair (Genesis 3), to Abraham also (Genesis 12:1-3), to Moses (Exodus 3), and to all others whom God had fellowshipped. There have always been expectations of God for man to fulfill if he accepts God's blessings and privileges. So also today, those blessed with this union with Christ are obligated to fulfill actions consistent with that union. "Ought" (OPHEILEI) in the present indicative shows continuing "oughtness," a moral obligation, a debt, a behest. This, incidentally, is an appeal that can be made to one, and only one, of God's creatures: man. No other creature of God has within itself such a sense of oughtness.

As we are to keep walking in the light (1:7), keep on keeping His commands (2:3-4), John here says the same things in another way to emphasize continual action: keep on walking as Jesus walked. This is indicative of all activities in which a Christian might participate with equanimity. This characterizes the course of the Christian life. Often used also by Paul, one is said to be able to walk in adultery or fornication (Colossians 3:7), good works (Ephesians 2:10), love (Ephesians 5:2), after the Spirit (Romans 8:1), and newness of life (Romans 6:4). "Walking in" simply means continual practice.

And this walk of a Christian follows the "snapshot" portrait of Jesus. Looking at His life in almost a glimpse, as a completed whole (aorist tense), John points Christians to Him after whom they are named. Peter called also upon Christians as sojourners and pilgrims to "follow in his steps," the steps of His exemplary life (1 Peter 2:11,21).

5. Love of the Brethren 2:7-11

7Beloved, no new commandment write I unto you, but an old commandment which ye had from the beginning: the old commandment is the word which ye heard. 8Again, a new commandment write I unto you, because the darkness is passing away, and the true light already shineth. 9He that saith he is in the light and hateth his brother, is in the darkness even until now. 10He that loveth his brother abideth in the light, and there is no occasion of stumbling in him. 11But he that hateth his brother is in the darkness, and walketh in the darkness, and knoweth not whither he goeth, because the darkness hath blinded his eyes.

Verse 7 Beloved, no new commandment write I unto you, but an old commandment which ye had from the beginning: the old commandment is the word which ye heard.

Beloved, no new commandment write I unto you, but an old commandment which ye had from the beginning: - "Beloved" occurs first here, supported by the Alexandrian Text (KJV has "brethren" - ADELPHOI, supported by the Byzantine Text), and the word will be found five more times in the book. It will appear four times in 3 John. It is particularly appropriate to be used for the brethren when one remembers what love (AGAPE) in this sense is. It includes (1) man's mind as he scrutinizes intelligently, (2) man's will as he chooses objects to be loved, (3) man's emotions as he then involves objects of his love in deliberate fashion. How different this is from turning loose rampant and rampaging emotions, letting them run free. When this happens, man's mind is clouded and his will is overrun.

This is the fifth and last in John's list of things required for fellowship with God (see Outline): love the brethren. **First,** this is not a new command in the sense that they had not been informed previously about such brotherly love. It had been theirs from the "beginning" (ARCHE) and could bring to mind several different times: (1) their own conversion, (2) the time the Gospel began to be preached, about sixty years previous (Acts 11:15), (3) the creation of mankind, as Augustine maintained it meant, (4) or the beginning of the Law of Moses. In regard to the last, it might be remembered Jesus called the concept of brotherly or neighborly love one of the two greatest commands (Matthew 22:34ff), quoting from the Old Testament. The second meaning, the beginning of the gospel message, is preferred.

Second, this command was not new in the sense that it originated with John. As false philosophers of the day were prone to propose new and novel precepts, it might also have been attributed to John that he was beginning something new. John is careful to include that this command could not be tied to him alone. There was nothing singular about his stating this command; rather, these were old and familiar teachings. Gnostics had been proposing antinomianism, the divorce of morality from religion (John answers such in 1:5-7). They proposed a denial of sin (answered in 1:8-2:2). And they claimed a freedom from consideration and love of the brethren. Iranaeus, living just beyond John's time, showed what was already beginning to be proposed and practiced in John's day:

"And committing many other abominations and impieties, they run us down (who from the fear of God guard against sinning in thought or word) as utterly contemptible and ignorant persons, whilst they highly exalt themselves, and claim to be perfect, and the elect seed."[7]

Third, this command was not new in the sense of another kind, for KAINOS is the word used. It means a "qualitative other," perhaps stressing all the more that this command was not novel to them or different from what they already knew. If John were speaking of that kind of new command, he could have used another word, indicating "numerical new" (NEOS).

the old commandment is the word which ye heard - Right on target with his thought, John identifies the authority as the word (HO LOGOS), the apostolic message originating in Jesus Christ. Two things of note might be valuable: (1) the word preached is to be recognized as proper and true authority, since they had "heard" it, (2) since they had heard it, credence is then given to when the "beginning" might be: evidently when they heard the gospel preached. "From the beginning," in this part of the text is not likely (as in the KJV), since it is not supported by most of the latest and best manuscripts.

Verse 8 Again, a new commandment write I unto you, which thing is true in him and in you; because the darkness is passing away, and the true light already shineth.

Again, a new commandment write I unto you, which thing is true in him and in you - John now, paradoxically, claims this command is both old and new. He is in effect taking a second look at the same command from a different perspective. From another viewpoint, whatever is new in this command is new both in him (Christ) and in you (believers). The example is of Christ and will help one to know what can be considered "new." This can only spark memories of Jesus' statement, "A new commandment I give unto you that ye love one another; even as I have loved you, that ye also love one another. By this shall all men know that ye are my disciples, in that ye have love one to another" (John 13:34-35).

Two major things are of note about such a new command: (1) this love would go beyond any previous extent, (2) this love would be a **badge of identity** for disciples. The extent would be to the point "even as I have loved you." Never before had man ever been called to practice love to such an extent toward his fellowman. It is obvious that God has ever expected man to love others even from the creation, but now a **limitless** extent is exemplified. Christ gave Himself for others (John 15:13), and John later calls for a similar laying down of one's life "for the brethren" (1 John 3:16). Additionally, this would be the one identifying feature of God's people. All other men have ways to be identified, whether they be businessmen, politicians, military, rulers, etc.; now disciples will have a peculiar mark of distinction: they will be lovers of each other to a Jesus-like extent.

"The grace of love is so basic that he who lacks it is deficient in all the virtues of Christianity. Where it does not exist, no other can."[8]

because the darkness is passing away, and the true light already shineth - "darkness is passed" is the reading of the KJV, but it is not the preferred reading. The present indicative tense is used here, with the force of "is passing away." It is coupled in this verse with "shineth," literally "is shining." While darkness is now passing away, the true light is in the process of continuing to shine. John's repeated use of darkness and light is most expressive. Jesus was Himself the "true light" (John 1:4,5,9), and His disciples may be cast accurately as those who walk where this light shines.

The more the light shines in the life of the believer, the more the darkness in his life recedes. "He that followeth me shall not walk in darkness, but shall have the light of life" (John 8:12). Isaiah also comes to mind, "the people that walked in darkness have seen a great light" (Isaiah 9:2).

The word "true" (ALETHENON) is also common to John, being used for times in this letter, once in 3 John, eight times in the Gospel, and ten times in Revelation. This adjective is used to re-affirm that this light is right and darkness is wrong. This light is true and darkness is false. This light will be victorious and darkness will be defeated. Light is thus certain to conquer darkness, for it is "true."

Verse 9 He that saith he is in the light and hateth his brother, is in the darkness even until now.

He that saith he is in the light and hateth his brother - Here is another test, a character test, stated both in the negative and affirmative. What a man claims is tested by his actions toward his brother. These actions show the exact sphere in which a man is walking: either darkness or light. The hypothetical claim of a darkness-walker is quickly put to rest by the inconsistencies seen in his actions.

"Hateth" can have more than one meaning: (1) Jesus used this same word in the sense of "loving less," a milder term showing mere preference [Matthew 6:24], (2) John uses it here in its worst sense, as he later enlarges on the same concept, "whoso hateth his brother is a murderer" [1 John 3:15].

"Brother" can be several things also: (1) blood kin, (2) any human being, or (3) brother in Christ. Since this is still called a "new commandment," it refers back to the teaching of Jesus that the disciples were persons who had singular love among themselves. So, the third meaning, brother in Christ, is preferred.

is in the darkness even until now - Regardless of the claimant's idea that he is walking in the light and is in fellowship with God, John says he is not just casually mistaken; he is actually walking in darkness. He really has no fellowship with light, regardless of his claim. He adds "even until now," which is an emphatic prepositional phrase evoking the idea "even until now, this very moment." There is no middle ground, no neutral place in these delineations; it is love or hate, it is light or darkness, it is truth or a lie. Jesus did not offer a suggestion about brotherly love; rather He said, "These things I command you, that ye love one another" (John 15:17). A man can fool himself no more destructively than to enjoy holding a grudge, to delight in downgrading his brother, or to harbor hatred in his heart.

Verse 10 He that loveth his brother abideth in the light, and there is no occasion of stumbling in him.

He that loveth his brother abideth in the light, - Now comes the positive and affirmative side of this test: the one who abides in the light will act another way. This brother is not tainted by darkness; his love is clear proof of this. Notice that John does not begin this statement with "he that saith," as he did in verse 9; rather, this man's progression is real, not just claimed. He makes no claims about it; he simply does what is true and right and lets those actions speak for him.

and there is no occasion of stumbling in him - This "stumbling" (SKANDOLON) seems only to occur in Biblical Greek and is found in the New Testament fifteen times. It originally referred to the stick used to snare wild game and is also properly used in reference to a trap. Here it seems to express a block over which one could stumble, which is somewhat different from its original meaning. Just to whom this would be a stumbling block is also a matter of difference. It could mean a stumbling block to others or to one's self. Since this is a statement of a test of Christian character, the context would lead one to think it refers to the latter. This seems most natural to what John is proposing: let a man learn to love his brother and he is less likely to stumble out of the light and walk in darkness. Jesus said, "If a man walk in the day, he stumbleth not, because he seeth the light of this world. But if a man walk in the night, he stumbleth, because the light is not in him" (John 11:9-10).

Verse 11 But he that hateth his brother is in the darkness, and walketh in the darkness, and knoweth not whither he goeth, because the darkness hath blinded his eyes.

But he that hateth his brother is in the darkness, and walketh in the darkness, - Here is the man evincing actual ill will toward a brother. Who could be more blind? Who could be more helpless to attain true spiritual maturity? John uses the adversative word "but" to contrast boldly with verse 10, the one who loves his brother.

and knoweth not whither he goeth, because the darkness hath blinded his eyes. - Three things are said of this hating man: (1) he walks in darkness, (2) he is in the darkness, and (3) he is blinded by this darkness and does not know where he is going. In John's repetition, or what some commentators call his "spiral style," he enlarges some of the thoughts as to what might be the results of foolish ways of life. Now we are told darkness will blind a man, so that he can only grope about, unable to know anymore just which way he is going. Such is all the more apt to be fatal and final, for this one can no longer see; this one can no longer distinguish between right and wrong! Since the god of this world can blind unbelievers to the truth (2 Corinthians 4:4), can he also blind backsliding believers? Jesus claimed Isaiah spoke about a kind of blindness (John 12:39-40), and we know Israel had similar problems

38

(Romans 11:7-8). In addition, Jesus issued dire warnings about letting blind guides lead us about (Matthew 15:14). So such blindness is not going to be a surprise.

This blindness also is not a recent state or a temporary state; it is a matter of long standing in John's thinking.

How sad when one fails to learn love for his brethren. He puts himself into darkness and stumbles deeper and deeper into the clutches of Satan, finally entering into a state where he can no longer recognize spiritual and beneficial activities. He who would enjoy hating and hurting his brethren is headed into more disaster than he ever thought possible.

B. Things to Avoid for Fellowship with God 2:12-29

1. Love of the World 2:12-17

¹²I write unto you, my little children, because your sins are forgiven you for his name's sake. ¹³I write unto you, fathers, because ye know him who is from the beginning. I write unto you, young men, because ye have overcome the evil one. I have written unto you, little children because ye know the Father. ¹⁴I have written unto you, fathers, because ye know him who is from the beginning. I write unto you, young men, because ye are strong, and ye have overcome the evil one. ¹⁵Love not the world, neither the things that are in the world. If any man love the world, the love of the Father is not in him. ¹⁶For all that is in the world, the lust of the flesh and the lust of the eyes and the vainglory of life, is not of the Father, but is of the world. ¹⁷And the world passeth away, and the lust thereof: but he that doeth the will of God abideth for ever.

This section is a passage for assurance and exhortation. John is writing **to** them, not **about** them. He is writing about some errors that must be recognized, errors that are well known to them, and errors that are a present danger to them. Some of these errors have come out of them, that is, from those who formerly were among them. In all, this is a passage of encouragement and hope in the midst of dangers.

There is a most curious and intriguing construction here by John that brings up several questions. He writes to children, to fathers, and to young men. He uses two different Greek words, TEKNIA and PAIDIA, in addressing children. He uses two different tenses of "write," present indicative and aorist, to convey this message to his readers. And he repeats several things in his exhortations to these classifications. Thus, several questions come to mind about this entire section: (1) Are these three classifications to be understood literally or figuratively? (2) Why this order, an order seemingly in juxtaposition, since one normally thinks of child-young men-fathers, a progressive order of address? (3) Why are two different words used to address the youngest classification, the children? (4) Why does John say both "I write" and "I wrote" when it is the same message being sent?

In this passage, there are two triplets. Each of the three classifications is addressed twice, with some variance as to the exhortation. The organization of this material might be easier to see this way:

1. Children:
   a. sins are forgiven for his name's sake - 12
   b. ye know the Father - 13
2. Fathers:
   a. ye know him who is from the beginning - 13
   b. ye know him who is from the beginning - 14
3. Young men:
   a. ye have overcome the evil one - 13
   b. ye are strong, word abides in you, you have overcome the evil one - 14

To the first triplet, John says "I write" (present indicative). To the second triplet he says "I have written" (aorist). It is interesting that in the NIV, this section is put in poetic form, and no change of tense is recognized, with each of the six usages of "write" simply "I write." There is a reason for this change of tense, perhaps subtle, and one that has produced no little disputation among commentators.

In order to treat this section cogently, note the answers offered to the above questions. As to **Number 1** (three classifications), whether these classifications are to be taken literally or figuratively, it seems best to understand them as representing classifications of their spiritual state, not their chronological status. John seems to be speaking to fathers and young men in a sense of spiritual development, not to literal fathers and young men. Reasons for this include:

(1) A literal usage would eliminate mothers and young women, also older men and women who might not have

children, etc.;

(2) that which is said to the fathers, repeated exactly the second time, is something usually characteristic of aged, mature Christians; and the victories of the young men, while not stated to these fathers, must have also occurred previously in their lives;

(3) what is said to the young men is something normally thought of as being what happens in the recent lives of newer converts, but they have not yet attained to the maturity spoken of as being in the fathers;

(4) John has already spoken of his readers as "children," and this is a common term throughout the book (2:1,14,18,28; 3:7,18; 4:4; 5:21 as well as four times in 2 John and 3 John) that represents all Christians, not just those of tender years. So it is of more force to say these classifications refer to some spiritual differentiation.

As to question **Number 2** above (why this order), the order of address is somewhat unusual. Normally, one would expect John to address readers in chronological order, either children-young men-fathers, or fathers-young men-children. This would make a normal ascending or descending order by age. John, however, speaks twice in the order of children-fathers-young men.

A **first** possibility is that John uses "children" as an address to all his readers; then he classifies all the "children" into two age groups: "fathers" and then "young men."

Commentators propose a **second** possibility, that babies are in the Church since John includes little babies or infants. And so it might be if this were to be taken literally. It is easy to see, however, that he does not have small babies in mind as he is addressing those who can read his epistle, what he writes to them.

Yet a **third** proposal is that these children refer only to young "babes in Christ," the recent converts. This would make the "fathers" refer to the oldest converts and the "young men" to those converted a moderate amount of time back. This proposal has merit and may well be the answer. But (1) because of the unusual juxtaposition of the classifications and (2) the usage by John twelve times in this letter alone of the word "children," it seems the weightier position is that this order would mean that "children" refers to all the readers, who then will be addressed further as either "fathers" or "young men," older or younger Christians.

Question **Number 3,** then, about the two different words used for "children," will be easier to see. TEKNIA is used here and in 2:1,28; 3:7,18; 4:4; and 5:21. (A similar word, close to this is TEKNON, used in 3:1,2,10 and 5:2.) PAIDIA is used in 2:13,18. Some difference in meaning is seen when one considers that TEKNIA refers to the fact of childhood, or being born into a family. PAIDIA, on the other hand, refers to one's age as a younger person, and a person who is subordinate to the authority of the family. John probably is not noting any hard and fast distinction along these lines but is probably interchanging both these words as terms of endearment for all his readers. The aged Apostle John is pouring out his love to his dear children in the faith.

Last, question **Number 4** ("I write" and "I wrote") offers a precision of detail that is not unusual in John's writings or the writings of any of the apostles. This precision suggests, perhaps, why KOINE Greek was used. It later became a "dead language," its first century usage preserved. Such precision of language has proven a great boon to serious Bible students throughout the ages. John uses "I write" in addressing the first triplet and "I wrote" in addressing the second. The first is present indicative, the second is aorist. When using the present indicative, John speaks from **his viewpoint,** as he is presently in the process of writing the book. For variation and emphasis, he then uses the aorist, "I wrote," as the **readers' viewpoint.** By the time they read this letter, it could be said to them "I wrote." This is called the epistolary aorist and is not uncommon in the New Testament. Paul said he "counted it necessary to send Epaphroditus" (Philippians 2:25), and "I sent him therefore" (Philippians 2:28), though at this very time of writing he had not yet sent him. By the time Epaphroditus delivered this letter, it could be said he "had sent" him. Also Paul spoke of Onesimus, "whom I have sent back to thee" (Philemon 12), though at the time of the writing, Onesimus was waiting to carry the letter when Paul finished it. So when the readers receive them, the writing of these messages would have been in the past.

With these introductory matters before us, we can now regard this text as John's assurance and exhortation to his children in the faith concerning their fellowship with God. If they continue in the proper fellowship, they must avoid contamination from the world.

Verse 12 I write unto you, my little children, because your sins are forgiven you for his name's sake.

I write unto you, my little children - John is writing to all his readers as dear children whose sins have been forgiven. Reminding them now of the precious blessing of cleansing at the fountain of Messiah's blood, John speaks of two categories of sin: (1) those forgiven at baptism into Christ and (2) those forgiven at confession and cleansing [1:9]. Since sin is a transgression of the law (5:3), the idea of "future sins" cannot be here. Only those things that are in reality sins, past actions of a transgressing nature, can be understood as forgiven. The verb tense of "forgiven" is perfect, indicating a past action of forgiveness continuing even until the present.

because yours sins are forgiven you for his name's sake - Mention of "his name's sake" presents three ideas: (1) "For" is used in a causal sense, on account of His name; (2) the name stands for the person Himself, another major emphasis of the One whom the Gnostics were denying, Jesus the Christ; and (3) the name of Jesus Christ is one of the most powerful principles in the New Testament. As to its power, one should remember the apostles were to preach in this name (Luke 24:47), Paul was to declare this name before the Gentiles (Acts 9:15), baptism for the remission of sins was in this name (Acts 2:38; Matthew 28:19; Acts 8:16), salvation was in this name (Acts 4:11-12), this was the name on which sinners might call for salvation (Romans 10:15; Acts 22:16), sinners are justified in this name (1 Corinthians 6:11), thanks is to be given in this name (Ephesians 5:20), disciples who suffered in this name could glorify God (1 Peter 4:16), and someday in Judgment this name will be confessed by all men, even by sinners (Philippians 2:10).

Verse 13 I write unto you, fathers, because ye know him who is from the beginning. I write unto you, young

men, because ye have overcome the evil one. I have written unto you, little children, because ye know the Father.

I write unto you, fathers - fathers (PATERES) here seems to refer to the older Christians among John's readers. It is not limited to men alone, but would include all Christians who have had the time to mature, or age, in their relationship with the Lord. They might be of varying ages; possibly some as young as about forty might have been Christians for over twenty years, and thus be among the "fathers." The term does not exclude men or women who have no children; rather, it includes any and all who have strong points of experience in Christ. At the time of this writing by John, it has now been over forty years since Paul was in Ephesus. Thus, numerous ones could well be aged in the faith. "Know him" is in the perfect tense, indicating present continuance of a past condition. They are persons who perceive and understand in fullness as to their relation with Jesus, in the habit of keeping His commands (2:3).

him who is from the beginning - Since the first reference by John to Jesus Christ (1:1) was "from the beginning," it is seen that he continues to fight the Gnostic heresy. This does not necessarily demand personal acquaintance, though it might include it in the case of some. It simply speaks about a long opportunity to understand the One whom they serve.

I write unto you, young men, because ye have overcome the evil one - These young men (NEANISKOI) are the more recent converts, some babes in Christ. They have conquered the pull of the fleshly world in turning to the Lord. These are in the prime and vigor of their youth in the Lord, i.e., life in Christ, as opposed to the fathers. If this word for young men were to be used literally, it would refer to those between the ages of twenty and forty. To overcome the "evil one," perfect tense again used, means they enjoy presently a victory that was accomplished earlier in their life. They continue to enjoy this victory. "Overcome" is a common term with John, as readers will remember he used seven promises to "overcomers" in Revelation 2-3.

The victory over the evil one is one that may be appreciated all too little by members of the church. Later John speaks of them as having "overcome the world" (4:4). In another setting, Jesus said, "I beheld Satan fallen as lightning from heaven" (Luke 10:18) upon the conclusion of the mission of the seventy, and again said, "the prince of this world hath been judged" (John 16:11). Paul spoke of Jesus in His resurrection and ascension as being one who "led captivity captive" (Ephesians 4:8) and also of one who "despoiled the principalities and powers, he made a show of them openly, triumphing over them in it" (Colossians 2:15). John later speaks of Christians being those who "overcame him" (Revelation 2:11) and of the time when Satan was "bound for a thousand years" (Revelation 20:2). The victory has already been won by Jesus, and the same victory is given to any Christian. God sees to it that Satan and his forces will not overpower any faithful child of God, for temptations will never test the faithfulness of God (1 Corinthians 10:12-13). Man can prevail in Christ.

The evil one is Satan, a person, not just an influence or an abstract principle. He is one who is active and vicious in his campaign for recruits. He is the archenemy of mankind. The evil one (PONARON) is far stronger than another word for evil (KAKOS), which means only the absence of good. This one not only has no good in him, he is the father of lying and murder (John 8:44).

I have written unto you, little children, because ye know the Father - PAIDIA is used here for children and, for all practical purposes, is synonymous to TEKNIA in v. 12. He again refers to the entire Christian community as his dear children. Previously, he had stated their sins were forgiven; now he adds they know the Father. They know Him in the sense that they understand He is one who, in every way, loves, forgives, provides, and cares for the children who may need Him.

Verse 14 I have written unto you, fathers, because ye know him who is from the beginning. I have written unto you, young men, because ye are strong, and ye have overcome the evil one.

I have written unto you, fathers, because ye know him who is from the beginning - John repeats the statement about the fathers of verse 13. This repetition emphasizes all the more their knowledge and maturity in Christ. They

46

know Him who changes not (Hebrews 13:8).

I have written unto you, young men, because ye are strong, and the word of God abideth in you, and ye have overcome the evil one - Strength is a characteristic of youth, and two statements emphasize their spiritual vigor; the word abides in them, and they have overcome the evil one. This "word" is the message of truth, but additionally, it is the message of truth that has been communicated to them. Truth has been truth eternally, but until it is communicated to sinners, it can do no good. This truth must be communicated, taught, and applied in life. "Word" can often refer simply to the message, but this is a message which has been taught to learners. This is "communicated truth," not just abstract truth. This message is now in them, permeates them, controls them, and directs their actions. Is there an implication they will in turn use their youthful vigor in the Lord to communicate this to others?

Verse 15 Love not the world, neither the things that are in the world. If any man love the world, the love of the Father is not in him.

Love not the world - "Love" is the present imperative tense, forbidding a course of action that would be continuing. "Love not now, and keep on loving not the world" is the sense of the tense. This love (AGAPE) includes intelligent and purposeful devotion, not just a warm-hearted affection (PHILIA would then have been used). James uses PHILIA (James 4:4) when he says friendship (PHILIA) with the world is enmity with God. He adds, however, the idea of deliberate intention when he says, "whosoever would be a friend" (literally, "resolves a friend to be"). This shows AGAPE is the stronger word, for within itself is the idea of intention; it does not have to be added in further statement. The usual sense of AGAPE includes the sense of "placing a higher value on." The Christian must not place a higher value on the world or its things.

neither the things that are in the world - "World" (KOSMOS) has several possible uses in the New Testament: (1) the universe, the totality of creation [John 17:24]; (2) the inhabited earth [Romans 1:8]; (3) dwellers upon the earth, the people themselves [1 John 2:2]; (4) the evil order of the earth and its inhabitants, under the control of Satan [James

47

4:4; 1 John 5:19; John 15:18-19]. It is the last sense in which John now uses the word. This is an ethical usage that refers to anything dominated by the evil one. Thus this world is "with John eminently an ethical conception — mankind, fallen away from God, and of hostile disposition towards Him, together with all that it lives for and has made its own; . . . ."[9]

The "things of the world," in line with this usage, would not be just material things alone; the idea would include anything that partakes of the evil and worldly nature of Satan, the prince of this world. Clarke claims, "Covetousness is the predominant vice of old age. . . . The things that are in the world, its profits, pleasures, and honours, have the strongest allurement for youth: . . . ."[10] This will be shortly expanded in the following verses, for John goes on to explain what he includes. He is speaking of "Dangerous D's and Pernicious P's." The "D's" include deceptive treasures, deceptive pleasures and and deceptive honors of this world. The "P's" are those things that pamper one's worldly appetites, promote distraction from the Lord, and prevent spiritual growth and activity.

If any man love the world, the love of the Father is not in him - "Love of the Father" could mean one of three things: (1) the love of the Father, as the source of all love, (2) the Father's love to the person, or (3) the person's love to the Father. Since John here speaks of the possibility that one may love the world and has previously spoken of one who walks in darkness (1:6; 2:11), and those who keep not the commands of the Lord (2:4), and one who has even discounted and disregarded his heinous sins (1:8,10), the context might point us to the third, or last, meaning given above. This person would block any proper affection and regard for the Father by his choices already made. He directs his love to the world, another way, and not to the Father. Many, however, argue similarly that actions like those stated in the context have already blocked off the Father's love from being effective. Either way the force of the passage is the same: The right fellowship between a man and the Father cannot continue if the man's love is world-directed.

Verse 16 For all that is in the world, the lust of the

flesh and the lust of the eyes and the vainglory of life, is not of the Father, but is of the world.

For all that is in the world, the lust of the flesh, the lust of the eyes and the vainglory of life - The following three phrases explain what John means when he says, "Love not the world," in the previous verse. These are not exhaustive explanations; they are illustrative of what he means. They describe three attitudes, covering broad principles, that will destroy a Christian. These three are the typical forms of evil, three deadly enemies of believers who want the fellowship of God. Some see here three broad general areas, covering all possible types of sins. They draw parallels between these three and the temptations in the Garden (Genesis 3), as well as the formal temptations of the Lord at the beginning of His ministry (Matthew 4). Such parallels are fine to draw and teach, but whether John intended for this to be an exhaustive and all-inclusive list of categories is not quite that clear. Many lessons can be drawn, but care should be exercised in emphasizing John's intentions.

lust of the flesh - lust (EPITHUMIA) denotes strong desire, whether it be good or evil desire. The word is used both ways in the New Testament, with the great preponderance of its use given over to evil desire. It is used in the good sense only three times: (1) "with desire I desired to eat the Passover" [Luke 22:15]; (2) "having the desire to depart and be with Christ" [Philippians 1:23]; and (3) "endeavored the more exceedingly to see your face with great desire" [1 Thessalonians 2:17]. All other times (thirty-five in all) it is used in a bad sense. Thus, one reads about "passion of" (1 Thessalonians 4:5), "foolish and hurtful" (1 Timothy 6:9), "youthful" (2 Timothy 2:22), "divers" (2 Timothy 3:6; Titus 3:3), "of defilement" (2 Peter 2:10), and "ungodly" (Jude 18) kinds of lust. This lust carries the idea of "anxious self-seeking," a seeking that, if not quickly fulfilled, would be painful. This lust demands satisfaction, and any deployment away from immediacy is most frustrating. This is the lowest form of worldly indulgence; it refers to animalistic appetites.

"Flesh" (SARX) refers to the animal propensities of man's nature, that which he has by being an animal creature. It comes from the animal nature and is expressed in fleshly actions. It is unlawful pleasure to the senses, that which springs only from the baser part of man, the flesh. This word SARX can mean several things: (1) the material of man's body, that which is involved with bone and sinew; (2) man's nature, with its opportunities and tendencies to sin; and (3) simply a human being. Literal flesh itself, covering the bones, is not sinful or evil. The desires that spring from uncontrolled fleshly appetites are what can be called sinful. Gnostics of John's day felt flesh itself was sinful, and any desires or actions emanating therefrom had to be sinful also. Paul taught otherwise, realizing there is a proper use of the body and there are proper desires which can be controlled. Paul spoke of (1) the body being for the Lord, "sanctification and honor" [1 Thessalonians 4:4]; (2) the fleshly body as a temple of the Holy Spirit [1 Corinthians 6:19-20]; (3) the fleshly body as reserved for the Lord [1 Corinthians 6:13]; (4) resurrection of the body like the body of Jesus [Romans 8:11; 1 Corinthians 6:14; 15:22ff.]; and (5) the fleshly body as a "member of Christ" [1 Corinthians 6:15]. It would be wise, therefore, to understand that the flesh itself, the physical body of man, is moral, capable of both holy and sinful actions. When the body is turned over to uncontrolled and evil desires, raging rampant over the intelligence and will of man, then what is produced is classified as "works of the flesh" (Galatians 5:19ff.), or "members which are upon the earth" (Colossians 3:5ff.).

lust of the eyes - This is some sense literal, for it refers to what one can see with the organs of sight. Man may "feast his eyes" on something, or he may see the avid desire to obtain. Sins may come about from yielding to what he first saw. One example of literal use would be the warning of the Lord about looking on a woman to lust after her and committing adultery in one's heart (Matthew 5:28). Another example that comes to mind quickly is that of Achan: "I saw. . .I coveted. . .I took. . .I hid. . . ." (Judges 7:21). Without literal sight, it is hard to image what the examples would mean. After all, "when the devil has trained the eye, what will it not see to keep the furnace of ungodly emotions and imaginations aglow? The world shouts 'artistic,' 'beautifully realistic,' freighted with 'beautiful moral lessons,' etc., and thus it gilds vileness."[11]

vainglory of life - This is the boastful pride of life, from ALAZONIA, which means arrogant display. Two things might be involved in this vanity: (1) things of which man might boast; and (2) a way of controlling one's own life independent of God. The word itself is related closely to braggart, but goes much further in assuming an arrogant independence from God. It is called by one "the braggadocio of life."[12] A man might boast of things that he has obtained or which he controls. These might include material possessions of wealth, land, houses, automobiles, jewelry, stocks, bank accounts, businesses, etc. A man might also boast of a certain lifestyle, culture, education, honors attained, etc. Or a man might boast of being able to order his own life any way he chooses. Such attitudes as these come not from the Lord, but are devilish, emanating from him who is the prince of this world (John 12:31). The man who is caught up in these concerns is out of self-control in the worst way; the devil has control of his life, not himself, not the Lord. Peter warned "promising them liberty, while they themselves are bondservants of corruption; for of whom a man is overcome, of the same is he also brought into bondage" (2 Peter 2:19). Paul said, "Know ye not, that to whom ye present yourselves as servants unto obedience, his servants ye are, whom ye obey; whether of sin unto death, or of obedience unto righteousness?" (Romans 6:16). The man who boasts of his ability to order his own life is in the worst of all possible slaveries!

So a progression is now seen in John's line of thought: (1) God condemns the desire for immediate self-satisfaction in the "lust of the flesh," (2) God condemns selfish, inordinate visual desires in the "lust of the eyes," and then (3) God condemns haughty prideful boasting of possessions, life-style, or mastery over one's life.

is not of the Father, but is of the world - Such desires cannot have originated in the Creator of all mankind, for every unlawful desire is destructive to mankind. He made us in His image and for His glory. Why would there be any desire on His part to complicate man's life with everything that would destroy him and keep him from eternal fellowship with his Creator?

51

Verse 17 And the world passeth away, and the lust thereof: but he that doeth the will of God abideth forever.

And the world passeth away, and the lust thereof - This "world" that passes away (see v. 15) is right now in such a process. "Is passing away" is the literal translation, since it is present tense. Such passing away is now going on, so it would be well to understand the transitory nature of the material sphere on which man lives. Evil is self-destructive. It is on a time clock that is ticking rapidly to the close; one day the alarm will sound and the end will be. The "fashion of this world is passing away" (1 Corinthians 7:31). Its very nature is not to last; it is designed to destruct. "A thousand wrecks lie strewn along its path, and it shall be altogether wreck and ruin."[13] Those whose main employ is only for this life will lose all, for there are no treasures for them over yonder (Matthew 6:19-21). They have laid none up, and none shall be supplied them by God or anyone else. All this world will some day burn up (2 Peter 3:10,12). What will happen to all the houses we have built? What will happen to all the magnficient church buildings we say we have built for the use and glory of the Lord? Material earth and all its treasures will pass away. All earthly, devilish passions and controls will pass away from man's environment also. What will be left?

but he that doeth the will of God abideth for ever - This is "unto the ages," or "remaining for the eon." Its emphasis is of a nature unending. The one that "doeth" (present tense) is the one that "abideth" (present tense). The continuous practice of the will of God will culminate in the continual fellowship with God. These present tense usages emphasize continuancy, permanency in a given state. Something "is passing away," something else "is abiding." This is the contrast of impermanency and permanency. Something is temporary; something is forever. John is quite clear about this and intends his readers to know just what value to place upon each state in which a man has a chance to live. This reminds one of the Hebrew writer who spoke of the quaking of Mt. Sinai, of the promise of God to shake "yet once more" this old earth, and preeminently of Christians who receive the "Kingdom that cannot be shaken" (Hebrews 12:28).

2. The Anti-Christs 2:18-23

[18]Little children, it is the last hour: and as ye heard that anti-christ cometh, even now have there arisen many anti-christs; whereby ye know that it is the last hour. [19]They went out from us, but they were not of us; for if they had been of us, they would have continued with us: but they went out, that they might be made manifest that they all are not of us. [20]And ye have an anointing from the Holy One, and ye know all things. [21]I have not written unto you because ye know not the truth, but because ye know it, and because no lie is of the truth. [22]Who is the liar but he that denieth that Jesus is the Christ? This is the anti-christ, even he that denieth the Father and the Son. [23]Whosoever denieth the Son, the same hath not the Father: he that confesseth the Son hath the Father also.

In addition to avoiding the love of the world with all its lusts, there is now introduced the second thing to be avoided in order to have fellowship with God — the anti-christs and the anti-christ. There are some general observations about a proper approach to this section of John's epistle that must be given prior to the study. There are varied beliefs about the things found in this section, and these topics are much disputed. One can approach this section from several different viewpoints; and depending upon the viewpoint, the conclusions drawn will be in line only with that particular viewpoint. It is much the same with any scripture that is apocalyptic in nature, or even close to being apocalyptic. When one reads the book of Revelation, it is seen easily that one's approach colors the understanding placed on the entire book. Once persons get into a certain vein of thought, they will have to stay in the vein till the very end, lest they lose consistency. So it is with the section dealing with the anti-christ.

There are four questions of note in this section: (1) What is the "last hour"? (2) What or who are the many anti-christs? (3) What or who is the single anti-christ? (4) What is the "unction" (KJV) or anointing from the Holy One?

Varying opinions, one about the "last hour," will include

53

(1) the end of the Jewish state, (2) the last hour immediately preceding the Parousia, the Second Coming of the Lord (those who take this literally, such as Plummer, usually say John turned out to be mistaken; i.e., he was wrong in thinking this was the last hour, as history has proven subsequently that Jesus has not yet appeared), (3) the time from the appearance of the anti-christs until the Second Coming, and (4) the Christian Dispensation, the time of the Church, the last era in which man will live on this earth.

The opinions about the anti-christ are just as varied. They include (1) false teachers who foretold the second coming of the Lord at the destruction of Jerusalem (MacKnight), (2) the Gnostics and Docetics who were then opposing Christ, (3) one who puts himself in the place of the reigning Christ, identical then with the "man of sin" described by Paul in 2 Thessalonians 2:1-5, and thus being the "Papacy" of Rome, and (4) a principle or group of teachers and their teachings, all of which oppose Christ in some special way.

Then, when one comes to the "unction" or anointing, it is just as much a matter of disputation. Major ideas set forth as to the meaning of this include (1) the gifts of miraculous abilities known to be working in the churches of the first century as the apostles laid their hands on members and imparted the gifts, (2) the truth, the word that is presently contained in our written Bibles, as it was being written then and taught orally, (3) the indwelling of the Holy Spirit in each Christian upon his baptism into Christ, and (4) the illumination, supposedly coming from the indwelling of the Spirit, that enables one to know exactly the teaching of the Bible.

Verse 18 Little children, it is the last hour: and as ye heard that anti-christ cometh, even now hath there arisen many anti-christs; whereby we know that it is the last hour.

It is the last hour - "Last hour" is used only by John in the New Testament, twice here in this verse, four verses in all (2:22; 4:3; 2 John 7). John uses another term, "last day," (four times in John 6; 11:24; 12:48). He meant, obviously, something different from that which Paul and Peter meant when they used the plural "last days" (Acts 2:17; 2 Timothy 3:1; Hebrews 1:2; 2 Peter 3:3). The plural refers to a period of time, an era, an epoch, perhaps described well when as a "dispensation." The singular "last day" used by John evidently did not refer to a period of time but to **the very last day of time!**

No plural of John's "last hour" is to be found, so it is not quite so easy to fix it with such certainty. It no doubt refers to the approaching end of something. God has given His final message through Jesus Christ His Son (Hebrews 1:1-3; Jude 3), the last message ever to be given from the portals of heaven to mankind. It is the word of God's grand Scheme of Redemption for humanity. Next in line of events will be the coming of Christ. The time of the Church, the time of Christianity, is the last period of time this earth shall know. Beyond this will be only eternity. God has thus dispensed the last effort of His grace.

The fact that John does not use a definite article has led many to conclude he is speaking not of the single last hour of all time, but rather, of a category, a period of time (Westcott thus argues.). Others demur from this: "The linguistic remark that the article is omitted in the predicate is incorrect, for it is not omitted when the subject and predicate are identical and interchangeable."[14]

The double use of this phrase in verse 18 does show that the coming of the anti-christs signals the "beginning of the end." It is doubtful the phrase could refer to Number 1 above, since the destruction of Jerusalem had already taken place prior to the penning of this book. Neither could it refer to Number 2 above, as Jesus did not come in the first century to execute judgment. History has proven this. Perhaps it could mean Number 3, from the appearance of the anti-christs until the second coming. There is little difference between this argument and the one for Number 4, with only the time of the beginning of the period in dispute. Did it begin at Pentecost or at the coming of the anti-christs?

Vine points out three major words used in the New Testament for "time": (1) CHRONOS, a space of time, short or long; (2) KAIROS, a fixed or definite period, a season; (3) HORA, hour or time. He states that HORA can mean "primarily, any time or period fixed by nature."[15]

"Last hour" used by John, then would be synonymous to

"last days" as used by Paul and Peter. It is used figuratively for a fixed period of time preceding the second coming of Christ.

as ye heard that anti-christ cometh - "Anti" (ANTI) can be used for two meanings: either it can mean something "opposed to," or it can mean something "instead of." It cannot mean both in the same single usage or passage. It must mean only one or the other. Jesus had warned of "false christs" (PSEUDOCHRISTOS) that would come claiming to be the Messiah (Matthew 24:24; Mark 13:22). John now speaks of anti-christs (ANTICHRISTOS), something different from that of which Jesus spoke. If Jesus spoke of men who claimed to be the Messiah, then it stands to reason that John was speaking of the other meaning of "anti," of those opposed to Christ. He was speaking not of those who would be "instead of" Christ but of those who opposed Him. We are thus limited to understanding this by reading John, for he is the only one to use this term. Of course, someone claiming to be the Christ, becoming a "false-christ," would qualify for this use of "instead of" the true Christ. He would also offer opposition to the true Christ and in that sense be a part of the anti-christ. But it is doubtful that John means to refer to men who were false claimers to being the Messiah.

Later, John goes further into detail about this anti-christ by saying he is "the liar" who "denies the Father and the Son" (v. 18). Additionally, he said this one refuses to "confess" Jesus (4:3), and still later he adds that this confession is that he came in the flesh (2 John 7). Whether John is speaking of men personally or a principle of false teachings is hard to distinguish. It seems he is giving a broad and progressive principle here about any dangerous denial of the Son of God, as none of John's four passages are decisive. The Gnostics and Docetics were already spreading abroad their pernicious denials of Jesus. They were saying He was not born as a man, nor did He die as one. This was certainly a denial of what John taught about Christ, and no known commentator would deny that these men were included in whatever John means by anti-christs.

Many commentators teach that this anti-christ is synonymous to the "man of sin" mentioned by Paul

(2 Thessalonians 2:3-4). Barnes gives four statements of such conclusion: (1) considerable numbers would claim to be the true Messiah, (2) a great apostasy was coming, (3) this would ultimately be concentrated in a single leader, and (4) prior to this there would be many partaking in the same general spirit opposing Christ.[16] Another, somewhat more forceful in stating his views, says, "To the candid mind the conclusion is irresistible that the 'man of sin,' whom Paul describes, is identical with the 'antichrist,' to which John refers. And in the centuries which have passed since these words were penned, no character in history so nearly conforms in minute detail to the representation here given as **the pope of Rome!** To deny that these prophecies find fulfillment in him is to close one's eyes to the facts in the case, utterly to ignore the evidence which obtains, and to reduce Biblical exegesis to mere caprice."[17] Lenski is also blunt, as he writes, "The great Antichrist is the papacy."[18] Yet he continues and points out there are many other varied oppositions fulfilling the plural "anti-christs" used by John, and names numerous other religions and leaders. It is doubtful how he can connect these, as many of the other opposing religions were equally negative about the papacy. So how could they all be in the same business of being anti-christs? Then, McGarvey writes, "The man of sin is identical with the antichrist of 1 John 2:18. . . . The antichrist will be antagonistic to God, and will exalt himself as a rival to everything that is worshipped. . . ."[19]

Several problems arise in being this dogmatic about limiting the anti-christ to the papacy, either in a single leader, or the entire system itself. It seems John is speaking about a particular false system that had begun already in his day and would include any and all systems that would oppose the truths about the Son of God. John's use of "anti-christ" is broad enough to include Paul's "man of sin," but to say they are exactly synonymous is perhaps too narrow and limiting a concept.

even now hath there arisen many anti-christs - Many teachers following this principle or teaching have arisen to deny vital truths about the Christ. Many have the same characteristics, teaching that Jesus was an imposter, or that he only appeared to be the Messiah. These teachers already present and prolific; John therefore was issuing a warning about them all.

It seems therefore some conclusions can be drawn about "the anti-christ."

1. They (he) were already there in John's time and that is why John is issuing the warning presently. It is not sufficient to say Gnosticism or Docetism led to something; this problem was already among them. They needed to exercise due caution then. The letter certainly is applicable to modern day Christians, but John wrote also of a present problem, as well as an impending and continuing one.

2. Gnosticism and Docetism did not lead to the digression into the papal system. The beliefs of those early philosophers were at the opposite end of the spectrum from views of Catholics through the centuries.

3. The anti-christ is a liar, denying the Son of God (v. 22), and the papal system has not been guilty of this.

4. This anti-christ denies that Jesus came in the flesh, denied true Incarnation; the papacy has never done this.

5. This was a spirit of lawlessness and error, a spirit of dissent, a spirit of denial of essential facts of the gospel. It is hostile to all ideas of submission and obedience to the Christ. It embodies the actions of those who would undermine basic truths about Jesus the Son of God and overthrow the faith of those following Him.

6. This spirit, or attitude, can be present in any age. It is a valid warning to all generations. Any who would deprecate the deity of Jesus in any way, who would deny His miracles, His miraculous conception, His resurrection and ascension, His advocating and interceding continually for the saints would come under the blanket of John's description. Close to these would be all who would set themselves against the will and laws of the Lord.

Verse 19 They went out from us, but they were not of us; for if they had been of us, they would have continued with us: but they went out, that they might be made manifest that they all are not of us - These broke the fellowship of which John is presently speaking. They may not have broken it the first way he mentioned, loving the world (vv. 12-17), but they were breaking it by opposing the Lord. They are seceders, they are apostates, they were formerly members in fellowship; now they are "out from us." "They" evidently refers to the anti-christs; "us" (note that this word is used here five times for emphasis) refers to the saints.

To go "out from us" ("out" is EK, source or origin) necessitates first of all being a part of "us." Barnes says this was a "humiliating statement that those who showed themselves to be so utterly opposed to religion had once been members of the Christian church; but this is a statement we are often compelled to make."[20] This concept of apostasy from the truth eliminates Islam, Buddhism, Judaism, Hinduism, satanic cults, etc. from being categorized as the anti-christ. They did not go out from the Church; they did not "fall away from the faith" (I Timothy 4:1-4). Neither could one classify paganism, atheism, agnosticism or any such philosophies as the anti-christ. This anti-christ represented those who once were Christians. "By the emphatic position of EX HAMON it is brought out that the antichrists were previously METH HAMON, and belonged therefore to the Christian Church."[21] Further, the idea that this anti-christ is some political power of any generation (in WW II it was heralded to be Germany, Japan, and Italy while some decades later it was claimed to be Red China, Russia, North Korea, North Vietnam, etc.!) is just as foolish and untrue. All opposers of all kinds are not necessarily the anti-christ. And it is sad but humorous to see how succeeding generations of preachers try to be prophets about such applications!

This passage is often used by false teachers who claim the doctrine of "eternal security." They place particular emphasis on the phrase "but they were not of us," taking it to mean these were never true converts. The idea continues in the vein that if they had ever been truly converted, they could not fall away. It would be well to note several points of consideration: (1) There is an ellipsis here, and the word "still" is understood, so that the passage would read, "for if they had been **still** of us, they would have continued with us." Somewhere along the line they had lost the commitment they had at first to the Christ. (2) They went out (EK) from us, which preposition emphasizes origin. They originally were with us, i.e., the Body of the

Lord, the Church. (3) These may never have imbibed deeply of the same spirit of obedience and compliance as the remaining ones, but they still once had been a part of Christ. They had begun the journey; they just did not complete it. (4) This is illustrated by Jesus' story of the four soils (Luke 8:4-15). There were two of the soils in which the seed took root but never came to harvest — stony and thorny. Believers in "once saved always saved," impossibility of apostasy, would have us believe that the seed never took root or sprouted. John thus speaks here to apostate members, those who once had been converted, but then became a part of the movement of the anti-christ.

Verse 20 And ye have an anointing from the Holy One, and ye know all things.

And ye have an anointing from the Holy One - The KJV uses "unction," which comes from Middle English terminology meaning "ointment or unguent." The Greek term, CHRISMA, is used only three times, all by John (vv. 20,27). It is a term used by John with high symbolism. He uses it figuratively, by metonymy, to refer to something given from the Lord to Christians.

Four possibilities of what this anointing might be are referred to in the preliminary remarks above. However, it is suggested that one quickly eliminate the fourth position, the doctrine of illumination, for such cannot be supported at all by the scriptures. Paul argued that what he received by inspiration was written down in such simple communicative language that it could be understood (Ephesians 3:1-4). He further argued that the inspired scriptures afforded all one needs to be complete as a full-grown man in Christ (2 Timothy 3:15-17). Coupling these with many other such passages, one can conclude that Christians today do not need any special illumination, or light, from the Holy Spirit in order to understand the scriptures. The misuse of 1 Corinthians 2:14-16, the "natural" and "spiritual" man, gives no credence to this error. Paul speaks of inspired and uninspired men, not men of the world and Christians with special Holy Spirit illumination, as these false teachers would have one believe. Besides, if Christians are receiving special help from the Holy Spirit to understand the Bible, why are there so many divided opinions and conclusions about what it teaches? This doctrine therefore must be dismissed from this discussion.

Anointing one to be a king or priest was common in the Old Testament (Aaron and sons [Exodus 29:7]; David by Samuel [1 Samuel 16:14]). The Seed of David was to be the anointed one (Isaiah 61:11), the Messiah (Hebrew term meaning anointed). Jesus claimed to fulfill this in His career (Luke 4:18) and Peter verified this in his preaching (Acts 4:27; 10:38). The Septuagint Version (LXX) of the Old Testament used the term CHRISTOS to refer to this coming Messiah.

There may be a play on words here by John, as he is speaking of the anti-christs, but Christians are the CHRISMA. He suggests that they oppose the Anointed One, but you have anointing. There is a sense in which one could make such a play on words thus: "There are many anti-christs, but ye are christs also."

Christians are anointed by God (2 Corinthians 1:21). Yet that next verse speaks of the Holy Spirit, who is a seal and an earnest. The seal is of the new identity as a Christian (Ephesians 1:13). The earnest is of the inheritance or "day of redemption" (Ephesians 1:14; 4:30). It is a proper conclusion, therefore, that the Holy Spirit accomplishes all these things within those two verses — anointing, sealing, and being an earnest of final redemption.

It would be proper to note at this juncture that Christians are considered priests (1 Peter 2:5,9) and in some sense reign in the Kingdom of Christ (Revelation 1:6; 5:10). Paul spoke also of us as "reigning in life" (Romans 5:17; 1 Corinthians 4:8), while John pictured saints as reigning with Christ a thousand years (Revelation 20:4,6).

Therefore, the heavier weight of argument rests on the side of those who believe that John spoke of an anointing given to each Christian, not just the ones inspired to work miracles. This anointing would refer to the indwelling of the Holy Spirit given at one's baptism into Christ (Acts 2:38) to those that obey Him (Acts 5:32). This indwelling puts a special connotation thence forward on the physical body of a Christian, as it is now the habitation, temple, of God (1 Corinthians 6:12-20). It offered nothing miraculous to the recipients, empowered them to do nothing special, nor imbued in them any special knowledge or understanding of the truth. It did serve as a seal of identity and a down payment on eternity. This conclusion is based on the following:

1. The anointing of each disciple fits the teaching that all Christians are priests and reign in some spiritual sense now in life.

2. The anointing of each convert fits the teaching that all Christians are consecrated, set apart, devoted to the service of God. It fits in with the many uses of "saint" and "sanctification."

3. The Holy Spirit is connected with another use of anointing, and such usage is very limited within the New Testament (2 Corinthians 1:21-22). It obviously means the Holy Spirit has anointed the same ones who are established in the faith, sealed, and given the earnest. This cannot be limited to inspired teachers. These teachers were not the only ones to be established, sealed, and given a down payment on eternal life.

4. Christians are those who partake of holiness. Peter spoke of our being holy (1 Peter 1:15-16) and of partaking of the divine nature (2 Peter 1:4). Paul spoke similarly of being conformed to the image of the Son of God (Romans 8:29), of the new man as being created in righteousness and holiness (Ephesians 4:24), and of being partakers of his holiness (Hebrews 12:10). Such teachings echo the idea that every Christian is an anointed one.

5. The context is better served if each Christian receives the anointing, due to John's play on words. There are many anti-christs, but there are many anointed Christians.

6. The context is also best served in the understanding of John's use of "knowledge." He uses two major words (GINOSKO and OIDA) that are translated "knowledge" a total of thirty-five times in the epistle, and makes no distinction as to some knowledge as inspired and some as uninspired. In the immediate context, John speaks of their knowing (vv. 20,21,29), their having heard it from the beginning (v. 24), his writing to them (v. 26), their being taught (v. 27), the fact that those who have such knowledge are also those who are begotten of him (v. 29). John makes

no distinction that a few inspired men are the only ones who thus know; rather, it seems the path of wisdom to understand that John addresses all the Christians.

and ye know all things - as stated in the introductory remarks to this section, this could mean (1) you know everything, (2) all of you know everything, (3) all of you know enough to resist the anti-christ errors. There is a textual problem here, as a question arises on whether "all" comes from PANTA or PANTES, as manuscripts differ. The latest and most reliable evidence seems to point to the use of PANTES.[22] In line with the conclusion that the anointing comes to each Christian, it would make this part of the verse mean that each Christian has been taught enough of the truth to resist and defeat the anti-christs among them. " 'Ye all know it.' This anointing is open to all Christians, not just a select few."[23] It would not mean that the Holy Spirit is giving special knowledge, but that as a result of the teachings they have already heard from the Holy Spirit and their inspired teachers, they should handle this problem of apostasy. It ought to be noted, however, that it makes little practical difference as to whether one believes this anointing and knowledge are miraculous or non-miraculous. Either way, no claim can occur that one is able to know anything above, beyond, or outside the Bible today. That is God's final, last, and complete message to man through His Son (Jude 3, Galatians 1:6-9).

Verse 21 I have not written unto you because ye know not the truth, but because ye know it, and because no lie is of the truth.

I have not written unto you because ye know not the truth, but because ye know it - Here again is the epistolary aorist when John uses the past tense "written." He can say this, even while doing the actual writing about which he speaks; for when his readers see the letter, the action will be past history. When he speaks of knowing "it," the antecedent is "truth." But what truth? It is the truth about the anti-christs and their false claims. John speaks particularly here of the denials of the Incarnation. They are denying the God-man concepts of the dual person of Jesus of Nazareth. He must be understood as true man, but also

63

true God.

and because no lie is of the truth - One of John's favorite terms is truth (ALETHEIA). He uses it here to embrace a body of facts about this Jesus. Any claims, conjectures, fantasies, syllogisms, philosophies, or doctrines contrary to plain facts would have to be part of a category of non-truths, or lies. Truth is distinctively Christian. It is all within the Word as revealed through Jesus Christ and his apostles, yet how sad has been the case of the gullibility of men down through the years. Ever since the Garden, men and women have seemed to want to hear something different, new, unique, daring, etc. John now goes on to say exactly what the central core of this lie is.

Verse 22 Who is the liar but he that denieth that Jesus is the Christ? This is the anti-christ, even he that denieth the Father and the Son.

Who is the liar but he that denieth that Jesus is the Christ? - This lie is from the liar of all liars. He is the liar par excellence; he exceeds all other liars. This is the master falsehood. The use of the definite article, "the" anti-christ, points up the unique character of this deceiver. There is no one else like him; there is nothing to compare with his deceit and falsity. The literal translation here also adds emphasis to this: "who is a liar if not the one who denies. . . ." The words "if not" (EI MA) are translated "but" in our text, as well as in the KJV.

The use of the present participle (denieth) three times in both this and the following verse has continuous force. It is literally "denying" and carries the force that this anti-christ is presently denying and continues to deny Christ as the Son of the Father.

These teachers admitted that a man called Jesus lived. They denied that He had any connection to Deity. They denied that the man Jesus was the Christ (Messiah), the Son of God. Cerinthus taught the concept that "Christ" was merely an aeon, an emanation from Deity. This emanation came upon the man Jesus at His baptism but left Him sometime prior to the crucifixion, probably in the Garden of Gethsemane. Thus it was taught that Jesus was merely Joseph's natural son, upon whom a brief emanation came, resulting in His amazing three-year career of teaching and

64

miracles. If true, such claims by Cerinthus would necessarily void the virgin birth, the incarnation, the propitiation, and the efficacy of the blood given. The very foundation of all faith is thus voided by such teaching. Actually, such claims must have been close to a form of idolatry. These apostates seemed to worship their own ideas, knowledge, and postulations.

John has said these anti-christs were coming (v. 18), also that many were already there. Now he offers specific identity: they would deny Jesus as the Christ. These are deniers, not a sinister rival. And anyone who denies Jesus as the Messiah (Christ) also denies Jesus as the Son of God. John equates the two. The Gospel was written to show proofs for men's belief in this One (John 20:30-31), and such belief included that "Jesus is the Christ, the Son of God." Martha confessed both truths, "I have believed that thou art the Christ, the Son of God" (John 11:27). Nathaniel included both ideas in his use of "Son of God" as being the "King of Israel" (John 1:49), remembering that kings are the anointed ones. John continues this vital connection later in this First Epistle when he writes, ". . .that we should believe in the name of his Son Jesus Christ" (1 John 3:23). Paul, in the synagogue at Antioch of Pisidia, said God had fulfilled what was written in the second psalm, "Thou art my Son, this day have I begotten thee" (Acts 13:33). Then Paul also wrote of this second psalm as being fulfilled (Hebrews 1:5), but by one whom he called "Christ as a son over his house" (Hebrews 3:6). Again, Paul wrote about the one "born of the seed of David, according to the flesh, who was declared to be the Son of God by the resurrection from the dead, even Jesus Christ our Lord" (Romans 1:3-4). Further, Paul wrote about "the Son of God, Jesus Christ" (2 Corinthians 1:19). Thus, Paul connected the Son of God with Christ, as well as did John.

denieth the Father and the Son - To deny one is to deny the other. Incorrect views of the Son of God bring incorrect views of the Father. Jesus said, "He that honoreth not the Son honoreth not the Father that sent him" (John 5:23). Again he taught, ". . .he that receiveth me receiveth him that sent me" (John 13:20). And he also maintained, ". . .no one cometh unto the Father, but by me" (John 14:6).

Verse 23 Whosoever denieth the Son, the same hath not the Father: he that confesseth the Son hath the Father also — Here is a cancellation of fellowship. The denier of Jesus as the Christ, the Son of God, has no fellowship with either the Father or the Son. He is now a spiritual orphan. He has no family connection to heaven. This conclusion can now be drawn from the previous statements, as fellowship is impossible to those who believe and promote this gross error. Believers are the only ones given the power (right) to become the sons of God (John 1:12). The only way people can come to Jesus is from the drawing power of the Father: "No man can come to me, except the Father that sent me draw him" (John 6:44). That power to draw one to Christ is then delineated to be teaching, hearing, and learning (v. 45). John here has two groups in mind — anti-christs who deny essential doctrines, and believers who accept essential doctrines. One has fellowship with the Father; the other does not.

The believer, the confessor, has fellowship with both the Father and the Son. "Confesseth" (HOMOGLOGON) is a present participle showing continuous action. Such continual confession is akin to the same idea Jesus expressed to the twelve as He sent them out on a brief and limited commission (Matthew 10:32-33). This confession related to a complete entirety of life, not just a statement made prior to baptism (Romans 10:9-10).

The last part of the verse in the KJV, "but he that acknowledgeth the Son hath the Father also," is put in italics as if there were no proper basis in the manuscripts. Actually, this last part is included in the Sinaiticus, Alexandrinus, Vaticanus, Ephraemi, and Porphyrianus manuscripts.[24]

3. Forsaking the Promise, Anointing and Life of Righteousness 2:24-29

[24]As for you, let that abide in you which ye heard from the beginning. If that which ye heard from the beginning abide in you, ye also shall abide in the Son, and in the Father. [25]And this is the promise which he promised us, even the life eternal. [26]These things

have I written unto you concerning them that would lead you astray. ²⁷And as for you, the anointing which ye received of him abideth in you, and ye need not that any one teach you; but as his anointing teacheth you concerning all things, and is true, and is no lie, and even as it taught you, ye abide in him. ²⁸And now, my little children, abide in him; that, if he shall be manifested, we may have boldness, and not be ashamed before him at his coming. ²⁹If ye know that he is righteous, ye know that every one also that doeth righteousness is begotten of him.

We now see the third thing to avoid for fellowship with God — forsaking the anointing, the promise, and the life of righteousness. This is the last section of John's writing about the Christian and God (see Outline) and is also the third thing to avoid lest we lose our fellowship with God.

Verse 24 As for you, let that abide in you which ye heard from the beginning. If that which ye heard from the beginning abide in you, ye also shall abide in the Son, and in the Father.

As for you - A personal pronoun in the beginning of this verse emphasizes a contrast: You are not among the deniers, so you will have different actions and responsibilities.

let that abide in you which ye heard from the beginning - "You heard" is aorist tense and seems to view the entire period of their learning as once completed action. It is spoken of as a single occurrence, though it may have covered many years. It began when they first heard the gospel and continues even until now. "At the beginning" has already been used two ways by John in this book: (1) from eternity in his description of Christ [1:1; 2:13-14] and (2) from the inception of the gospel and the church [2:7]. Here it will refer to the latter of the two, the time the gospel began to be preached, or even perhaps limited to the time these disciples first accepted the gospel and believed the truth.

"Let that abide" (MENO) is present indicative again, meaning to settle down, remain, and stay. It is used six times in these five verses in various forms and is most important in John's writing. This is powerful language and grammatical construction. John speaks of "confessing" in the present tense; now "abide" is in the present tense. Both enforce the idea of continuity. The King James Version misses the point of this construction by changing the translation as if it were three different words (abide. . . remain. . .continue). The point of this whole section is to abide in the fellowship of God. Thus our version uses the same word three times to accomplish John's emphasis.

If that which ye heard from the beginning abide in you - This shows the conditionality of salvation. What ye heard is now abiding, but it may not continue to abide. "If" (EAN) plus the aorist subjunctive of "abide" (MEINA) shows grammatically that the possibility is that such might not remain abiding in the Christian.

Verse 25 And this is the promise which he promised us, even eternal life - This promise is what you have heard from the beginning, the sum and substance of which is eternal life. It is all about how to obtain this eternal life; this is the object of the whole exercise of one's Christianity. This is the divine life within the person. Several things equate this relation: (1) fellowship with the Son equals eternal life [5:11-12,20]; and (2) fellowship with the Father equals eternal life [2:24-25; 1:2]. This is why there is no way to separate fellowship with one and the other, for to fellowship the Son or the Father is to be in fellowship with both.

Eternal life is spoken of in both qualitative and quantitative ways. In quality it is the same kind as that of Deity. In quantity it is everlasting, eternal. This "eternal life" is used two ways in the New Testament — (1) the life the Christian possesses now and (2) the life the Christian will inherit after Judgment Day. That the Christian presently possesses this life ought to be without question, but many deny this for some reason, perhaps fearful of denominational error that claims Christians presently have this life and can never lose it. The Bible does not so teach that the life one now possesses can never be lost, but neither does it lack teaching that eternal life is now a part of one's discipleship.

Jesus spoke of passing out of death into life (John 5:24), that life eternal is to know the Father and Son whom He sent (John 17:3). He also said eating the Bread of Life (highly figurative wording) brought eternal life (John 6:51), and this was not presently possessed by those who did not eat (John

6:53), but the one who does "hath eternal life" (John 6:54). Thus the one who eats can be raised up with Him in the last day, for he already participates in the life that extends beyond the judgment. Paul wrote that baptized believers would rise in a new life (Romans 6:3-6) and contrasted the disobedient Gentiles who were alienated from this life in God (Ephesians 4:18). Paul also wrote that the Holy Spirit in the Christian was the "earnest of our inheritance" (Ephesians 1:13-14; 2 Corinthians 1:21-22). Connecting this with the birth of the water and of the Spirit (John 3:1-5), one would be hard pressed to deny that this rebirth, this rising to walk in newness of life, this indwelling of the Spirit, is but the present participation in eternal life. Peter speaks of being granted "all things that pertain to life and godliness" (2 Peter 1:3); and if the godliness is now, the life is now. Then John makes it specific and clear: "These things have I written unto you, that ye may know ye have eternal life" (1 John 5:13).

Yet the Bible also speaks of eternal life as a promise. Jesus spoke of life that is in the world to come (Mark 10:30), and a well of water, the water that Jesus gives, that will spring up to such life (John 4:14). Paul wrote of reaping life everlasting (Galatians 6:8), the hope of eternal life (Titus 1:2), and the future prospect of laying hold on life eternal (1 Timothy 6:12,19). James wrote of receiving a crown of life, that is, a crown that will consist of eternal life (James 1:12).

Just as salvation is viewed two ways within the New Testament (present forgiveness of past sins [Acts 2:38] and a salvation yet to be revealed [1 Peter 1:5] , so also can eternal life be viewed in two senses. To do so is not to weaken one's argument about the possibility of losing this life, for the New Testament is equally clear on that.

Verse 26 These things have I written unto you concerning them that would lead you astray.

These things have I written unto you - "These things" are not just the two previous verses, rather, the entire epistle. All the warnings are included in this general statement. "I have written," referring to this present writing, is again a use of the epistolary aorist. When the readers read this letter, it may be said that John had written (past tense).

lead you astray - is translated "seduce" also (KJV), but it literally means "to cause to go astray." This is classified as a tendential present tense, which refers to actions attempted but not actually taking place.[25] This participle shows continuing purpose of those who are enemies, and clearly there is a continuing danger to the faith of John's readers. Warnings about false teachers are voluminous (Acts 20:29; 1 Timothy 4:1-4; 2 Timothy 4:3-5; 2 Peter 2:1-3). John's closing of this book reiterates the dangers (4:1ff.). Safety in Christ can be found by doing as John has said: (1) Ye know the truth [v. 21], (2) recognize the lie and the liar [v. 22], (3) remember all who follow the lie will lose God's fellowship [v. 23], (4) abide in the truth and fellowship will continue [v. 24], and (5) this will bring about life for the obedient [v. 25).

Verse 27 And as for you, the anointing which ye received of him abideth in you, and ye need not that anyone teach you; but as his anointing teacheth you concerning all things, and is true, and is no lie, and even as it taught you, ye abide in him.

Anointing which ye received of him abideth in you - This anointing (see v. 20) is another safeguard. The influence of the Holy Spirit on our hearts and lives, by the use of His holy Word, can let us continue to abide in Christ. This is the safeguard — continuing in the life of obedience as taught in the Scriptures that the Holy Spirit has provided. This anointing teaches only the truth, never a lie; and man has the possibility of abiding in such truth. This anointing refers not to the mere act of anointing, the sending of the Holy Spirit into our hearts because we are His sons (Galatians 4:6). Instead, it refers to the results of such anointing, the life produced by the teachings of the Holy Spirit (Romans 8:14), the fruit of the Spirit (Galatians 5:22-24). Jesus also said the reception of such truth would make one free from the slavery of sin (John 8:32).

ye need not that anyone teach you - There is an ellipsis, perhaps two, here. John is saying, "Ye have no need for **additional** teachers (Gnostics) to teach you." He is also saying "Ye have no need that anyone teach you **anything else** than the truth about Jesus Christ." The context speaks rather clearly to these facts; thus, John is not saying that they have no need for any human teachers or any continuing teachings. He is saying they do not need the Gnostics who would teach something other than the truth about Jesus the Christ. Since these Gnostics claimed superior knowledge, John is all the more insistent that these babes in Christ did not need such teachers with all their pretended knowledge. Lenski has a pointed barb about this: "You are not a group of ignoramuses that need to be taught over and over again by the apostles and by Christian teachers."[26]

John could not be negating human teachers within the Church; it is too clear that such are within God's plan and providence. God ordained human teachers in the church (Ephesians 4:11-12), provided for prophets, ministers, teachers, and exhorters (Romans 12:6-8) and wanted teachers to train others who could continue such teaching (2 Timothy 2:2). In fact, this epistle being written by John is additional testimony that continual teaching is needed by Christians.

The only way the Holy Spirit teaches man today is through His word (1 Corinthians 2:13; 2 Timothy 3:16-17; Romans 8:14,16). No Christian has a private line of communication or teaching from the Holy Spirit. No Christian today has any miraculous abilities; none has any "illumination" abilities in understanding the Scriptures. All that a Christian knows is what he has been taught from the Bible. John has emphasized such teaching (2:7,13,14,24), and the Holy Spirit who is responsible for such teaching is the anointing one has from God.

and is true and is no lie - Since God cannot lie (Hebrews 6:18) and the Holy Spirit is God (Acts 5:4), these things that have been taught from the Holy Spirit are things in which it is worth abiding. Anything originating with God is true.

Verse 28 And now, my little children, abide in him; that, if he shall be manifested, we may have boldness, and not be ashamed before him at his coming.

And now, my little children - "And now" seems to complete a line of thought and is a prelude to a conclusion. "Little children" (TEKNIA) is one of the words used by John in tender compassion for these disciples (see comments on

71

2:1). **If he shall be manifested, we may have boldness** -
"If" (EAN) refers not to any doubt as to the Lord's
manifestation, only an uncertainty as to the **time** of His
coming. It is certain to be; John just does not know when.
It is not **whether** He will come; it is **when** will He come?
Thus, the KJV has the preferred translation of this word.

"Shall be manifested" (aorist tense of PHANEROO, "to
appear") points to the suddenness and completeness of
such appearing. It will not be a process; it will be only a
moment. "Boldness" (PARRHESIA) is what completes
John's thought. He wants them to be able to have boldness
and confidence (KJV) at this manifestation, coming. They
can do so without shame or fear, for they have continued
in the right teachings, exhibiting the proper quality of faith.
This word originally was used for freedom of speech in the
assemblies of the democratic city-states, a privilege
accorded only to those of full citizenship status.[27]
Additionally, "it means especially the fearless trust with
which the faithful soul meets God."[28]

at his coming - John uses PAROUSIA, one of three words
used in the New Testament for the Second Coming of Jesus:
(1) APOCALYPSE — unveiling; (2) EPIPHANEIA —
appearing, (3) PAROUSIA — presence, or coming. The last
is used for the coming of the king, the presence of royalty.
Such will hold no fears or intimidation for the Christian.

**Verse 29 If ye know that he is righteous, ye know that
every one also that doeth righteousness is begotten of
him** - Who is "he" that is righteous? It is difficult to say
with certainty, for it has been speaking of Jesus Christ.
Jesus Christ would present the nearest antecedent to this
pronoun, but there are difficulties. The New Testament
never uses the phrase "born of Christ." It uses born of God
(1 John 3:9; 4:7; 5:1, 4), born of the Spirit (John 3:5,8), but
never seems to say "born of Christ." Some say one is born
of Christ in the sense that one is born of the entire Godhead,
and Christ is the fullness of the Godhead (Colossians 2:9).
Perhaps so, but that stretches the thought to produce a
clumsy problem. It is easier to remember that the context
has been repeating the closeness of the fellowship and
relation to the Son and the Father. To be in fellowship with
one is to be in fellowship with the other. To be out of

72

fellowship with one is also to be out of fellowship with the other. Thus, it is not unnatural for John to make a transition here to a reference to the Father. This transition takes place between verses 28 and 29.

he is righteous - This refers to conformity to a standard. God is consistent, infallibly so, and He is both the standard and the perfect example of the standard! "If we are faithless, he abideth faithful; for he cannot deny himself" (2 Timothy 2:13).

A family trait is now shown, that of being righteous. As the father in the family is righteous, so are the children. It is a family characteristic. This does not show how one gets into a family; it shows the family traits and characteristics that are passed on to the children. It serves as a family heritage, even a family identity. It is the child's life practice, not just a simple, one-time action. It cannot refer to the good morals practiced by many in the world, though the actions might be identical. Those in the world are in the wrong family, and though they might show some of the same traits, they show one fatal flaw. They have not submitted themselves to the Master, the Father; the good morals they are evincing exist because they have made the decisions to live that way. On the other hand, children in the family of God submit themselves because the **Father** has asked them to do so. There is much difference in motive between the two. Some are obeying the Lord, some are obeying themselves.

is begotten of him - That John is not describing the way one is born into the family of God, however, should be emphasized. Doing righteousness is not the same as the new birth. The New Testament shows clearly that those obedient to Christ in the first century rose to walk in newness of life subsequent to their baptism into Him (Romans 6:3-5). This baptism was subsequent to a proper faith and confession of Him (Romans 10:9-10) and genuine penitence (Acts 2:38; 3:19; 17:20-31). All the examples recorded by Luke in the Acts of the Apostles confirm this teaching.

John affirms the fact of a person's birth but does not tell how that birth came about. He uses the perfect tense of "begotten" (GEGENNATAI), which shows the action was completed in the past and is continuing in its effect until the present. The doing of righteousness is only shown to be in the present; it is not claimed by John that this doing of righteousness was in the past and caused the birth. After all, the fruit does not produce the tree; the tree produces the fruit.

[1]Albert Barnes, *Notes on the New Testament, James, Peter, John and Jude,* (Baker Book House, Grand Rapids, Michigan, 1949), pp. 289-290.

[2]Joh. Ed. Huther, *Meyer's Commentary on the New Testament, Critical and Exegetical Handbook to the General Epistles of James, Peter, John and Jude,* (Funk & Wagnalls, New York, 1887), p. 496.

[3]Noah Webster, *Webster's New Twentieth Century Dictionary Unabridged,* (World Publishing Co., Cleveland and New York, 1940, Revised by Jean L. McKechnie, 1968), p. 645.

[4]R. C. H. Lenski, *The Interpretation of the Epistles of St. Peter, St. John and St. Jude,* (Augsburg Publishing House, Minneapolis, Minnesota, 1945), pp. 399-400.

[5]Barnes, *Notes,* pp. 290-291.

[6]Alfred Marshall, *The Interlinear Greek-English New Testament,* (Zondervan Publishing House, Grand Rapids, Michigan, 1968, published by special arrangement with Samuel Bagster & Sons, Ltd., London), p. 707.

[7]Iranaeus, *Against Heresies,* 1.6.4., as quoted by Donald W. Burdick, *The Letters of John the Apostle,* (Moody Press, Chicago, Illinois, 1985), p. 152.

[8]Guy N. Woods, *A Commentary on the New Testament Epistles of Peter, John and Jude,* (Gospel Advocate Co., Nashville, Tennessee, 1954), p. 232.

[9]Joh. Ed. Huther, *Critical and Exegetical Handbook,* p. 518.

[10]Adam Clarke, *A Commentary and Critical Notes,* (Abingdon-Cokesbury Press, New York and Nashville), Vol. II, *Romans to Revelation,* p. 908.

[11]Lenski, *Interpretation,* p. 426.

[12]Alexander Ross, *The New International Commenatary on the New Testament, the Epistles of James and John,* (Wm. B. Eerdmans Publishing Co., Grand Rapids, Michigan, 1954), p. 165.

[13]Lenski, *Interpretation,* p. 427.

[14]Lenski, *Interpretation,* p. 429.

[15]W. E. Vine, *An Expository Dictionary of New Testament Words,* (Riverside Book and Bible House, Iowa Falls, Iowa, 1952), p. 1150.

[16]Barnes, *Notes,* p. 302.

[17]Woods, *Commentary,* p. 243.

[18]Lenski, *Interpretation,* p. 432.

[19]J. W. McGarvey & Philip Y. Pendleton, *Thessalonians, Corinthians, Galatians, and Romans*, (The Standard Publishing Company, Cincinnati, Ohio, 1916), p. 35-36.

[20]Barnes, *Notes*, p. 303.

[21]Joh. Ed. Huther, *Critical and Exegetical Handbook*, p. 531.

[22]Burdick, *Letters*, p. 198.

[23]A. T. Robertson, *Word Pictures in the New Testament*, (Broadman Press, Nashville, Tennessee, 1933), Vol. VI, *The General Epistles and the Revelation of John*, p. 216.

[24]Ross, *NIC*, p. 173, footnote 4;
Burdick, *Letters*, pp. 201-202;
Barnes, *Notes*, p. 308.

[25]H. E. Dana & Julius R. Mantey, *A Manual Grammar of the Greek New Testament*, (The Macmillan Company, New York, New York, 1948), p. 186.

[26]Lenski, *Interpretation*, p. 442.

[27]Burdick, *Letters*, p. 209.

[28]Ross, *NIC*, p. 176, in a quote from Plummer.

II. The Christian and the World: Walking in Love 3:1-5:13

A. Reminders of Proper Relationships to God 3:1-4:6

1. God's Example of Love 3:1-2

¹Behold what manner of love the Father hath bestowed upon us, that we should be called children of God; and such we are. For this cause the world knoweth us not, because it knew him not. ²Beloved, now are we children of God, and it is not yet made manifest what we shall be. We know that, if he shall be manifested, we shall be like him; for we shall see him even as he is.

Now John enters into the second major division of his First Epistle: The Christian and the World: Walking in Love. He has presented "The Christian and God: Walking in Light" in two major ways: (1) identifying things to do for this fellowship, and (2) naming things to avoid for this fellowship. He is now ready to describe the Christian and his relationship to the world, emphasizing the walk in love that a Christian must accomplish. He will speak of this walk in three major thoughts: (1) reminders of this proper relationship, (2) response to love, and (3) tests in this relationship of love.

In this chapter, John first explains that Christians are children of God. This helps one understand why the world looks on us as it does. Next, John shows in this sonship that purity is the practice. Last, he will deal with love and hate, life and death.

Verse 1 Behold what manner of love the Father hath bestowed upon us that we should be called children of God; and such we are. For this cause the world knoweth us not, because it knew him not.

Behold what manner of love the father hath bestowed - "Behold" (EIDETE) is translated by some other versions as "See" and it is an aorist imperative, calling for immediate action. It is John's way of saying, "Quick, look!" and "Take a look right now." Or it might be like saying, "See at once this great love." "What manner" shows amazement, awe, and wonder. There was a similar use of this word by one of the disciples as he spoke with awe about the great temple in Jerusalem (Mark 13:1).

"Love" (AGAPE) is not just a strong emotional term, as if the major import were passion. It is a love of knowledge, discernment, and intent, followed by devotion to one's good (see 2:7). Lenski mentions "AGAPE is the love of comprehension and full understanding coupled with adequate purpose."[1] God's love is all the more wondrous and amazing as one remembers He loved us when we were yet sinners and gave His Son for us (Romans 5:8). We were the most unlovely and unloveable of all of God's creatures. Man is the only one to thwart God's creative purposes, for all other animal life occupies the role for which it was created. Only man turns away and serves self and the devil! Paul uses the idea of "sons" who are adopted into the family of God (Galatians 4:5), but the wonder is still there. Knowing man's willful, sinful, selfish ingratitude, we are caused to pause all the more and consider the wonder of God's inexpressible love to us.

"The Father" is placed at the end of this clause in the original grammar ("Behold what manner of love has given to us the Father"), which is a tool of Greek writers for special emphasis. The Father has already been mentioned (1:2-3; 2:1), so this is not a new juncture for this point of the epistle. This is the only place in the New Testament where the idea of bestowing or giving love by the Father is mentioned. It is often the case that we are told the Father loved us, but here is a new thought of bestowing love. "Love" is often used as a verb: "God so loved the world. . ." (John 3:16), but here we have love as something the Father has bestowed (DEDOKEN), perfect tense. This perfect tense matches that used in the previous verse in the last chapter, "is begotten" (GEGENNATAI). Here the Father not only loved man, but has given something to him, bestowed and imparted something to him. It is a stronger way of expressing the love the Father has for those who obey His Son.

that we should be called children - The Father's love thus brings about a result: we can be transformed into children. This is a purpose clause and shows that the result of God's love is that man comes into a new relationship: childhood. It is not that man is just called a child: he in reality becomes a child of God. Because he becomes a child, he then has a right to be called a child. "Children" (TEKNA) stresses natural kinship, not legal status, else John would more likely have used "sons" (HUIOS). TEKNA is used more in conjunction with a begettal, which has just been stated previously (2:29). John used this same word in stressing the spiritual begettal of those who received Jesus (John 1:11-12). At that time he said that this begettal was not of blood or of the will of the flesh or man, but of God.

and such we are - this wording is found in the better manuscripts. Although it is left out of the KJV, there is plenty of evidence for including it. The expression exclaims again the assurance of this wonderful truth that God's love has exalted us to be His children.

For this cause the world knoweth us not, because it knew him not. Certainly so! Who would think otherwise? If the world did not know the Son or the Father, how could it recognize His children? Lenski mentions, "Let no true spiritual child of God count on recognition from the world. . . .The names of God's greatest saints are not engraved on the tablets of the world's temple of fame."[2] The "world" (KOSMOS) has different uses in the New Testament (see 2:15), and here it refers to the people of the world. These are men who take the characteristics of the world, i.e., sinners, unregenerate men. Only men of this world can "know" (GINOSKO); things in the world are not able to know. This knowledge by worldly men points up more than mere outward recognition. They also can recognize that Christians are different in actions, beliefs, lives, motives, and feelings. Yet they are not able to know this in any deeper sense. They cannot appreciate these differences, they do not understand why Christians are so different. They do experience the same deep spiritual feelings as do Christians; thus, they do not know as John describes knowing. People of the world can have the same depth of emotions, but not in true spirituality (consider Moslems, Jews, Hindus, etc., who do not have faith in Jesus Christ). Jesus said it best: "If the world hateth you, ye know that it hath hated me before it hated you. If ye were of the world, the world would love its own: but because ye are not of the world, but I chose you out of the world, therefore the world hateth you" (John 15:18-19).

Verse 2 Beloved, now are we the children of God, and it is not yet made manifest what we shall be. We know that, if he shall be manifested, we shall be like him; for we shall see him even as he is.

Beloved, now are we the children of God, and it is not yet made manifest what we shall be - Now we sustain this dignity and a designation of "children," regardless of what the world might know or think. "Beloved" is one of the four terms of endearment used in 1 John: (1) "little children" [TEKNIA], (2) "children" [PAIDIA], (3) "brethren" [ADELPHOI], and (4) "beloved" [AGAPATOI]. "Beloved" is associated so closely with love (AGAPE) that its meaning is clear (see 2:7). "Now" necessitates a present relationship of life with God, as children, though perfection and fulfillment come only in eternity. How can we be the children that have been begotten (2:29) if we do not presently participate in this eternal life in some fashion? This is the third time in two verses that John affirms this begettal. There is no other or further relationship ever to be established with the Father; we are now children, and there is nothing more to come. This relationship is eternal; we shall still be children. The physical and fleshly part will change, but we shall still have this spiritual relationship as children. We will only move to the last stage of this blessed relationship. This wording drives another nail into the coffin of error for those who miss the great Bible truth that we now possess in some manner eternal life. The major differences between now and then (time and eternity) are that we presently abide in the flesh and still could lose the inheritance. John will address this in the last part of this verse. "Now" is only the first part of the contrast being shown; "shall be" will complete the contrast. If we remain faithful, there is no doubt as to our future with whom and where; we just have not been shown the true and full glory.

It is expressed so well by one author, ". . .not yet has God made a public display of the glory that belongs to his children, of the inheritance incorruptible, unstained, unfading, reserved for us in heaven (1 Peter 1:4). Not yet do we wear the white robes of heaven; not yet does the crown of glory sparkle on our brow. The robe of Christ's righteousness, our crown of hope, the diamond of faith, the pearls of love, are invisible to physical eyes. We still wrestle with the flesh; in a sinful world and with a mortal nature we plod on wearily. A child of God is here and now, indeed, like a diamond that is crystal white within but is still uncut and shows no brilliant flashes from reflecting facets. . . . This shall be changed completely."[3]

if he shall be manifested - Again this is the use of "if" (EAN) as in 2:28: "when." It is not something of doubt, but of strongest expectancy. It is more in line with "whenever," as that is the only thing in question about His second coming. The KJV has the better wording here.

we shall be like him - We are now involved in transformation that can be accomplished in earthly life, "into the same image from glory to glory" (2 Corinthians 3:18). And we are "foreordained to be conformed to the image of his Son" (Romans 8:29). Thus, even our bodies will be changed to be like His body which ascended (Philippians 3:20-21). Christ is the "firstfruits of them that are asleep" (1 Corinthians 15:20), and when thus risen bodily from the tomb, was caught up incorruptible, glorious, powerful, and spiritual (1 Corinthians 15:42-44).

"Like him" is not the same as "equal" and never will be. We will have similar characteristics and qualities; we shall have similarity in our spiritual bodies. "Like him" (HOMOIOS) refers to similarity. If equality in form and substance were meant, the word would have been ISOS, as when Peter claimed "the like gift" that had come to the Gentiles in the house of Cornelius (Acts 11:17). It was the same Holy Spirit that came upon the apostles as came upon the house of Cornelius.

John's emphasis is on **what** we shall be, not **how** or **when** the transformation takes place. There is a Scottish paraphrase which portrays this truth beautifully:

80

High is the rank we now possess,
But higher we shall rise;
Though what we shall hereafter be
Is hid from mortal eyes.[4]

we shall see him as he is - There now appears a problem, for it is clear the actual substance of Deity is invisible. It is not able to be seen by human, fleshly eyes. God is invisible, "dwelling in light unapproachable, whom no man hath seen, nor can see" (1 Timothy 6:16). "No man hath seen God at any time" (John 1:18). Again, Jesus said, "Not that any man hath seen the Father, save he that is from God" (John 6:46). Paul said Christ was the "image of the invisible God" (Colossians 1:15). And John later will claim, "No man hath beheld God at any time" (1 John 4:2). Several temporary manifestations, anthropomorphisms, are known (such as Moses beholding the back, but not the face [Exodus 33:17-23]), but somehow in glory we shall be able to know, understand, be influenced, and "see" the Lord in a unique way. The pure in heart shall see God (Matthew 5:8), the sanctified shall see God (Hebrews 12:14), the servants in glory shall see his face (Revelations 22:4), and David in the long ago said, "I shall behold thy face in righteousness" (Psalm 17:15). So, it is not with the physical organ in our fleshly bodies that we shall see Him." "See" (HORAO) here can be used for either bodily vision or mental discernment. Undoubtedly John has in mind the latter. To say we shall see only the Son and not the Father is misunderstanding the nature of the Godhead. There is a singularity in nature and substance, and our finite minds can only struggle, mostly ineffectively, with understanding the Infinite. We shall see and know all we need to know and are capable of handling in glory!

2. The Christian Response of Purity 3:3-12

[3]And everyone that hath this hope set on him purifieth himself, even as he is pure. [4]Every one that doeth sin doeth also lawlessness; and sin is lawlessness. [5]And ye know that he was manifested to take away sins; and in him is no sin. [6]Whosoever abideth in him sinneth not: whosoever sinneth hath not seen him, neither knoweth him. [7]My little

children, let no man lead you astray: he that doeth righteousness is righteous, even as he is righteous: 8he that doeth sin is of the devil; for the devil sinneth from the beginning. To this end was the Son of God manifested, that he might destroy the works of the devil. 9Whosoever is begotten of God doeth no sin, because his seed abideth in him: and he cannot sin, because he is begotten of God. 10In this the children of God are manifest, and the children of the devil: whosoever doeth not righteousness is not of God, neither he that loveth not his brother. 11For this is the message which ye heard from the beginning, that we should love one another; 12not as Cain was of the evil one, and slew his brother. And wherefore slew he him? Because his works were evil, and his brother's righteous.

The second reminder of the proper relationship to God, after God's example of love, is the response of the Christian to purity. This is not an unnatural response, but one that ought to follow easily and logically.

Verse 3 And every one that hath this hope set on him purifieth himself, even as he is pure.

And every one - Though the Gnostics regarded themselves as being especially enlightened, and supposedly above moral restraints, John names the qualification of this special way of life in Christ: purity. "Every one" (PAS HO), without exception, will strive for purity who has such a hope.

this hope - This is the hope previously stated. We shall be like Him and see Him as He is. This New Testament use of "hope" (ELPIS) describes assured and confident expectation of something future. It is not just a mere wish or desire, as in common in the English language usage. Our God is a "God of hope" (Romans 15:12), and thus we can "abound in hope." "We have our hope set on the living God" (1 Timothy 4:10; 5:5). We are saved in hope and we "hope for that which we see not" and "with patience wait for it" (Romans 8:24-25).

purifies himself, even as he is pure - "Purifies" (HAGNIZEI, present tense) and "pure" (HAGNO) mean far more than sexual purity as used by Paul (2 Corinthians

11:2). In the LXX it had the connotation of integrity.[5] Both these words refer to freedom from any defilement and are close to the word used for "holy" (HAGIOS). Present tense shows continuous action, so it is a lifelong pursuit. Such purity is not yet an accomplished fact. If the false doctrine of "imputation of righteousness" (supposed ethical transference of Christ's character to the new child of God upon his conversion) were true, why then John's insistence on purity? If the character of the new Christian is already transformed into that of Christ, he would be pure already. Yet, John insists that the Christian be involved in a continual process of purification by the one who has this hope. This cleansing is not automatic. God may forgive, cleanse, redeem, justify, and remit our sins, but He expects man's efforts then to continue in a lifelong process. Man will never attain to the same purity as Christ, but he will always be in the stance of striving toward it. Man can have the same **kind** of purity, never to the same **degree.** Man is not claimed to live above and without sin; he is claimed to be on a different highway than the children of the devil. There are no exceptions among those who have this hope; all are striving for this purity. This is a mark of identity.

Note that John does not call for men to purify themselves as Christ is purifying Himself. Christ is pure already — pure totally and eternally. He is the standard, the goal toward which we strive. There is no trace of sin in Him, no stain. We are called to walk in His steps (1 Peter 2:21).

Verse 4 Every one that doeth sin doeth also lawlessness; and sin is lawlessness.

Every one that doeth sin doeth also lawlessness - "Doeth" (present tense participle POIOWN) entails one who practices (NASB has "practices sin") and continues in sin. In John's argument there are only two kinds of people — those who practice righteousness - (2:29) and those who practice sin. The KJV uses the translation "committeth" and is misleading. What is under consideration is not a single violation of the law of Christ but a habitual way of life. "Doeth" in 2:29 and 3:4 are the same word, and both are in the same tense — present. If "doeth" of 3:4 refers to one act and one act alone, then so would "doeth" in 2:29. That would have a Christian committing just one act of righteousness! Conversely, both refer to durative action, since they are in the present tense. Such is habitual, a general rule of one's life. Neither usage by John leaves out occasional lapses; he is describing the pattern of one's life.

Having in this context introduced that Christians know that God is righteous (2:29), John proceeds to other developments to show the mark of this childhood: (1) Those begotten will do righteousness continually (durative action of the present tense), (2) sin is the opposite of such righteousness, for it is lawlessness, (3) Christ came to deliver men from such lawlessness, (4) Christ is righteous and without sin, our example and standard, (5) those begotten again live consistent with His life, (6) the practice of sin aligns one in the other family, the family of those who are not begotten, (7) Jesus came to destroy such works, and (8) the begotten ones have seed abiding in them, thus they will not practice sin. The general development of this context is important in the judicious study of this difficult and oft wrested scripture.

This context shows clearly that sin is incompatible with the begotten ones: (1) because of **sin's nature** of lawlessness, (2) because of **Christ's nature** of sinlessness, (3) because of **sin's source,** the devil, and (4) because of **sin's end,** destruction.

The student enters now another much abused section. Some men claim they are above sin. Some claim men will not commit any sin if they are born again. Others claim any sins committed after conversion are wiped clean automatically and not counted against the Christian. Yet others claim this refers only to willful and rebellious sins. Behind all such abuse is the false premise of the doctrine of "eternal security," also sometimes referred to as "once-saved-always-saved." Men striving to defend this doctrine have asserted extremes in hermeneutics in this passage. They have striven mightily to espouse conclusions that are indefensible, and but few of them will ever rise to public defense of such patently ridiculous notions.

and sin is lawlessness - the KJV has "for sin is lawlessness," but there is no reason for such. "And" (KAI) can be also translated "indeed." "Sin" (HAMARTIA) at its root means "missing the mark," and is used throughout the

84

New Testament as a general word for sin. It has the idea of aiming at something but not being able to hit it. What this sin (HAMARTIA) is, however, is "lawlessness" (ANOMIA); and this is a much stronger term. Since the general idea of law in the New Testament is God's instructions for man, instructions to regulate man's life and actions, then lawlessness would be a major definition of sin. This is a purposeful disregard of God's law and is often translated "iniquity." The word means without law, not lawful, rejection of law, violation of law. All of God's instructions, law, are under consideration here. The one who may claim to be begotten, but who continues to practice sin, is asserting his rule above the rule of God. This suggests revolt and rebellion. The begotten one just must realize that sin and his begotten nature are incompatible. And these sins could be either of omission or comission. Remember that the Gnostics claimed to taste freely of all manner of sins without being affected in their spiritual status. They claimed immunity from sin, since they felt flesh and spirit were so separated as to allow for such. John delivers another death-blow to their false doctrine.

The grammar and word position here are interesting. "Sin" and "lawlessness" can be interchanged. Either could be the subject of the sentence and either could be the predicate nominative: sin is lawlessness, or lawlessness is sin. "The article with both subject and predicate makes them coextensive and so interchangeable."[6] Since both have the definite article "the" and thus could be translated either way, the preferred way seems to be as our text says.

Verse 5 And ye know that he was manifested to take away sins; and in him is no sin.

ye know that he was manifested - Jesus was manifested, or appeared (PHANEO) and this refers to the entire scope of Incarnation. That John would say manifested rather than "born" implies prior existence, or ". . .assumes the fact of a previous being."[7] John keeps up the constant barrage of truth, a veritable array of references to Jesus Christ that will defeat the Gnostic errors. This was the one that "shall save his people from their sins" (Matthew 1:21). "Ye know" (perfect tense OIDATE) refers to the present possession of such facts received in the past, and John spoke of such as common knowledge. The believer in Jesus Christ has this knowledge securely in his possession.

to take away sins - The use of the aorist subjunctive here refers to an act of Christ by which sins were removed. This could be a single reference to His death on the cross, or it could be the view of his entire life as a single act of grace that remitted sin for mankind. The same word is used when John spoke of Jesus as the one that "taketh away the sin of the world" (John 1:29). The footnote in the ASV adds "or, beareth the sin," and is similar to the footnote in the present text. This word (from AIRO) means "to take up, lift, raise; bear, carry; take away, remove; destroy, kill."[8] Thus John has a purpose to remind his readers that Christ expiates sins, bears them away. So if we profess to follow Christ, and Christ came to take away sins, why would we wish to practice sin?

in him is no sin - literally "and sin in him there is not." The word order is important and impressive here. It places emphasis on "sin" and asserts such sin is absent totally from Christ. He has no stain, blotch, taint of sin past, present or future. Sin and Jesus Christ just do not mix! They are not compatible in any sense. Sin in principle, or sin as an action are both foreign to the Son. He challenged men to convict Him of sin, "which of you convicteth me of sin?" (John 8:46); and no one took up the challenge. He "knew no sin" (2 Corinthians 5:21); He was the "Holy and Righteous One" (Acts 3:14); "who did no sin, neither was guile found in his mouth" (1 Peter 2:22); He was "holy, guileless, undefiled" (Hebrews 7:26); and He was "without sin" (Hebrews 4:15). If the One we serve is thus sinless, it follows those who serve Him will also refrain, restrain, separate themselves from sin. What was begun in their new birth (2:29) is continued in sanctification. The believer, follower of the Lord, continues to strive for purification (v. 3).

Verse 6 whosoever abideth in him sinneth not: whosoever sinneth hath not seen him, neither knoweth him. This now comes as a logical conclusion to the previous verse. The one who habitually abides in Christ will not continue in habitual sin.

whosoever abideth in him sinneth not - True to the

86

previous usages of "abideth" and "sinneth," John speaks of continuing practice. "Abide" (2:6,24,27,28) emphasizes remaining or dwelling in the proper relation with Christ as contrasted with remaining or dwelling in sin and the service of Satan. The KJV translation "sinneth not" again seems to place the wrong emphasis, suggesting that John was speaking of a single sin. The NASB also leaves this impression by saying, "No one who abides in him sins." Remember the verb tense is important. If John had intended to speak of even a single sin, he had the aorist tense that would have expressed that emphasis. This, however, describes a character being formed, family traits being followed, sanctification taking place. Some claim these distinctions in verb tenses and grammar are too subtle for John's readers to grasp, so conclude that John had no such intentions.[9]

Verb tense changes, however, were most important even to the Lord. He changed tenses for obvious reasons in some well-known and most important passages: "if any man would come after (aorist tense) me, let him deny (aorist tense) himself, and take up (aorist tense) his cross, and follow (present tense) me" (Matthew 16:24). To begin following, to deny self, and to take up the cross are completed actions, while following Christ is to be durative (present tense). Again, "But if I do them, though ye believe me not, believe the works: that ye may know (aorist subjunctive GINOSKO) and understand (present subjunctive GINOSKO) that the Father is in me, and I in the Father" (John 10:38). This latter change of tense, using the same word GINOSKO, was used by the Lord obviously to show the possibility of their first knowing plus their continued knowing of Him and the Father.

Barnes points out that if the doctrine of perfection is here taught, (1) a Christian is perfect, (2) such is not and cannot be true, and (3) it is not necessary to the proper understanding of this passage. Rather, he continues to point out that the Christian does not sin (1) habitually, (2) deliberately or by design, or (3) finally and thus fall away.[10]

Thus John states that abiding and sinning are both considered continuous and just cannot be in the same person at the same time. The one abiding in Christ will quit such sinning. The one continuing to practice sin is not the one abiding in Christ.

hath not seen him, neither knoweth him - Both verbs here are perfect tense (EIORAKEN and EGNOKEN); and when employed with a negative conjunction "neither" (OUDE), they declare a strong and full denial. This declaration is not now true, nor has it ever been true. One who still continues a life of sin has not seen or known him, **ever!** "See" means more than outward vision of the physical eyes. It reminds us of the "eyes of your heart" (Ephesians 1:18) and "light" that shines "in our hearts to give the light of the knowledge of the glory of God in the face of Jesus Christ" (2 Corinthians 4:6). This is the opposite of "the god of this world hath blinded the minds of the unbelieving" (2 Corinthians 4:14), the "blind guides" (Matthew 23:16,24) who will lead followers only into the pit (Matthew 15:14), or "he that doeth evil hath not seen God" (3 John 11).

"Knowing" Him again refers to inward spiritual knowledge. It is knowing, recognizing what He claims to be and is in truth. It is possessing familiarity with Him, experiencing a relationship with Him. This is a direct denial of what the Gnostics proclaimed so loudly. If they truly had superior spiritual knowledge of God, they would not advocate so much practice of sin.

Verse 7 My little children, let no man lead you astray: he that doeth righteousness is righteous, even as he is righteous: John is now ready for a conclusion and a direct application to the problem under discussion. In a (1) world that ridicules the Church, (2) a world rampant with sin of all shapes and sorts, (3) a world that is lawless, and (4) a world that is blind and ignorant of Jesus Christ, look out!

My little children - this is again the use of TEKNIA, the special term of endearment which John has been using.

let no man lead you astray - the KJV and NASB use the term "deceive," but the word literally means to "lead astray" (see 2:26). This is an unusual use of the present tense imperative, for these churches were not at the present time astray. The use of "no man" (MADEIS) in such a construction usually calls for the termination of actions already in progress. Here, however, John is perhaps saying "you continue in not letting any lead you astray." This would satisfy the necessity for continual action in the present tense. Also, this shows the aggressive behavior of the false teachers. If they were not working among the Christians, seeking to turn their minds and hearts, there would be no need for such a warning. Oh, that saints would be as aggressive with the Truth!

Perhaps the major error to which John was pointing was licentiousness. The Gnostics felt they could live any type of immoral life and still be in fellowship with God and the saints. The next statement about righteousness seems to bear this out. And this would then refer back to the warnings begun in chap. 1:8 about claiming fellowship while yet walking in darkness by claiming no accountability for sin. Also included in John's warnings would be the problem of the anti-christs from the previous chapter.

doeth righteousness - This is the plain simple truth, an obvious fact; one who does righteousness is righteous, even as Jesus is righteous. There is no way to avoid the force of this fact. It is true and consistent. The present tense of "doeth" is forceful, for it makes the word portray a practice, a habit, durative actions. This is the family trait, handed down by Him who is perfect in righteousness. One cannot separate conduct and character. Just as faith without works is dead (James 2:26), so character without conduct is impossible. If one claims to have good character without good conduct, the true Christian will show his character by his conduct. Using the definite article with "righteousness," literally "doeth the righteousness," repeats the usage in 2:29 and emphasizes that this righteousness is of a special class. It is the same class of righteousness as that which Christ has.

It should be noted here that the practice of righteousness is not the way one initially becomes righteous or justified. It could have been written that way if such were true. The sense is that because the child is in a family that practices righteousness, the child is expected to practice righteousness. Righteous is used two ways in the New Testament: (1) as one's standing before God, as was so often used by Paul in Romans, actually synonymous to the idea of justification, and (2) as the conduct of a person. In this book, John uses righteous and righteousness in the second sense, one's conduct and behavior. He is not claiming that one can change his standing before God and become justified by right actions. Only the blood of Jesus Christ, upon the condition of the obedience of a sinner to His will, and upon the principle of faith, can change one's standing or permit God to justify him. Once someone is justified before God, has the right standing, then he will subsequently practice righteousness.

as he is righteous - This refers to Christ, not the Father, as He is our example and standard. And Christ is the one under question by the anti-christs, so it is John's claim that Jesus Christ is the "Righteous One" (as did Peter, Acts 3:14). Christians can imitate the righteousness of Christ in doing the same kind of things, but not to the same extent or degree. His was perfect, ours will be frail and faulty.

Verse 8 he that doeth sin is of the devil; for the devil sinneth from the beginning. To this end was the Son of God manifested, that he might destroy the works of the devil.

doeth sin - As in all of John's writing thus far, this refers to continual practice. It is a life dominated by sin and the fleshly appetites, not controlled by the Spirit of God, and not producing the fruit of the Spirit (Galatians 5:22-24). This is ceaseless action, perpetual, recurring, incessant sin. One's life is habitually in such a course. The KJV again uses the translation "committeth sin," and could mislead the reader to think it means committing of one sin. It is to be pointed out here also that verse 8 is set in direct and bold contrast to verse 7 by the definite articles. In verse 7 it is "the righteousness" that is to be done; in verse 8 it is "the sin" that is of the devil. This use of the definite article heightens the contrast. One is **the** righteousness which is characteristic of God, the other is **the** sin which is characteristic of the devil.

is of the devil - shows the origin and source of such a way of life. Those who thus act are kin spiritually to the devil. They are following a family trait. John does not say "born of the devil," and no other New Testament writer uses such terminology. Yet the thought of this kind of relationship is there. Jesus said, "Ye are of your father the devil" (John 8:44); "he is a liar and the father thereof" (John 8:45). Paul spoke of Elymas as "thou son of the devil" (Acts 13:10), Christians had been "children of wrath" (Ephesians 2:3), and the tares were called "sons of the evil one" (Matthew 13:38). Remember that "Satan entered into him" (John 13:27) speaking of Judas; and the "man of sin," the "lawless one" has his work "according to the working of Satan" (2 Thessalonians 2:3, 8-9). So it is not hard to see that the Bible speaks of a spiritual kinship to the devil by those who are not in fellowship with God.

sinneth from the beginning - This is a most difficult passage to explain with any definiteness. There is so little information on the origin of the devil within the scriptures that a study of such always ends with some kind of conjectures. The word certainly means that the devil has engaged in continuous sins since the beginning, as it uses the present tense. Several options are held by scholars about this "beginning": (1) it means from eternity past, prior to the creation, (2) it means from the beginning of his existence, (3) it means from the beginning of sin actions, (4) it means from the beginning of sin in this world. We can hardly believe it means Number 1, from all eternity, for this would involve the belief of "Dualism," the co-existence of good and evil eternally. This interpretation is unthinkable, for it would place God in a position of being unable to defeat the devil, impotent to overthrow Satan. It would also mean the devil has attributes that belong only to Deity, such as eternity, omnipotence, omnipresence, and omniscience. If we take Number 2, we then would have to conclude God created something evil, for the devil would be a creature originating from God. Numbers 3 and 4 are much more palatable to scripture-lovers. Number 3 is the most likely, since sin was present among the angelic hosts prior to creation. To obtain this idea, one has to study some facts about angels: (1) Some angels sinned and were cast down to be reserved to judgment [2 Peter 2:4]; (2) some angels kept not their first estate, left their habitation and are reserved in chains unto judgment of the great day [Jude 6], (3) the devil is a murderer from the beginning [John 8:44], and (4) the devil is the father of lies [John 8:45]. The belief that the devil was originally created as one of the angels, later taking a stance of rebellion, is not without some force.

91

Many connect this with the war mentioned in heaven and say this all happened prior to the creation of man (Revelation 12:7ff.). We will just have to leave this as one of the questions to be answered for us in eternity.

To this end was the Son of God manifested - This is a clear purpose clause. "Manifested" (PHANEROO) is John's choice to show that this person known as Jesus was manifested after a prior existence. If the coming of Jesus to the earth had been His first point of existence, John would have used a term meaning to come into existence (GINOMAI) or begotten (GENNAO).

that he might destroy the works of the devil - Jesus intends to destroy all the devil initiates, all that has to do with lawlessness (v. 4), all that is counter to the immediate subject of the context — righteousness, all works of the flesh (Galatians 5:19-21), all the things one is to put off from the old man (Colossians 3:5-11), and all of that resulting from the reprobate mind (Romans 1:28-31). This is the use of the aorist tense of "destroy" (LUSA), which means to "loose," "dissolve," "break up," "demolish." It is spoken of as a one-time event, though it may cover any length of time. There is a sense in which it was accomplished at the cross, also a sense in which it is still being done in the loosing of our sins, and again a sense in which it is still yet to be completed in judgment. Perhaps one can speak of this destruction as potential, perennial, and perpetual. When it is accomplished, it can be looked back upon as a one-time action done by the Lord.

John's treatment of Jesus' purpose to destroy the works of the devil is not by itself. The devils spoke of a "torment before the time" (Matthew 8:29) and of a time of destroying (Mark 1:24). Elsewhere we read of a prince of the world who is to be judged (John 16:11), deeds of the body that are put to death (Romans 8:13), death swallowed up in victory and the sting of death nullified (1 Corinthians 15:54-56). Jesus led captivity captive when He ascended on high (Ephesians 4:8), Jesus abolished death (2 Timothy 2:10), and Jesus came to bring to nought the power of him who brought death (Hebrews 2:14).

Verse 9 Whosoever is begotten of God doeth no sin, because his seed abideth in him: and he cannot sin,

because he is begotten of God.

whosoever is begotten - Again we have the use of the perfect tense, indicating an action completed in the past with continuing present results. There is a puzzle here, however, in the use of the term "born" in the KJV, NASB, RSV and NIV. The word used (GENNAO) most generally refers to begetting children, not the birth of children. It refers to begettal or generation.[11] It is therefore used chiefly in describing the part the man has in the procreation, not the part of the woman or mother. This is more accurately portrayed in our text, the ASV, than in those mentioned above.

doeth no sin - John continues to be consistent in his use of the present indicative tense, and the meaning necessitates the idea of continuing action (see v. 6). The begotten ones no longer practice sin, do not persist in such a life, and refrain from continuing to do such sinful actions. The KJV translates this phrase "doth not commit sin," and this has led to much misinformation and interpretation. Bluntly stated, "This is a wrong translation, for this English naturally means 'and he cannot commit sin'. . . . The present active infinitive. . .can only mean, 'and he cannot go on sinning.' "[12]

because his seed abideth in him - Something stays continuously (MENEI, present indicative tense) within the begotten one. For examples of John's prior uses of "abideth," see 2:24,27,28. There are several options as to the meaning of this seed. **First,** this seed could be the Word of God, since Jesus used this metaphor in His parable of the soils (Luke 8:11). The word is known to dwell within Christians (Colossians 3:16), and this word has the power to beget one again (1 Peter 1:23). Christians are said to be brought forth by this word (James 1:18). Thus it is a strong argument and a viable option that "seed" could refer to the Word of God abiding in and influencing the heart and life of a Christian. **Second,** seed could refer to the new life which the Christian has as a result of being born anew (2 Corinthians 5:17; Romans 6:3-6). It would then be a metaphor of the Holy Spirit as implanted by the birth of the water and the Spirit (John 3:1-5). We would then see ourselves as dead to sin but alive unto God (Romans 6:11,13), as a new creation (Galatians 6:15), renewed in spiritual life force and a new man (Ephesians 4:23-24; Colossians 3:10). The renewal comes about because one is washed and regenerated by the Holy Spirit (Titus 3:5). In this kind of solution, one would think of this seed, or new life, remaining in us. As a result we would follow the new family characteristics. All one would know about this would have come from the Word of God, but the new life is seen as separate from, a result of, knowing the word. **Third,** another solution is offered by many that the seed refers to the Holy Spirit Himself. It is true that every baptized believer receives Him as a gift (Acts 2:38). The physical bodies of those converted, then, are viewed as temples or habitations of the Spirit (1 Corinthians 6:19-20); and no one can be counted as one of God's unless the Spirit does dwell in him (Romans 8:9). Also, since one is regenerated by the Holy Spirit (Titus 3:5), he then produces the fruit of the Spirit in his life (Galatians 5:22-24). John is going to record later that God gave us "of his Spirit" (4:13), so this might be another possible solution. It should be remembered, however, that the New Testament never refers to the Holy Spirit as "seed."

Other solutions offered include a "germ of piety," God's own nature (RSV), or the offspring of God (RSV footnote). The latter must have the grammar mixed up, for it would then be saying that the offspring of God (seed in that sense) abide in Him (God), staying safely as it were in the arms of God! But most concur that the antecedent of the pronoun "him" is man, not God.

It seems preferable to take the second solution above, that the new life, the life force now found by being a Christian, will so influence one in spirituality that he will live the right kind of life. He will be taught only by the Word; and this interpretation, in effect, would almost be a combination with the first suggested solution. There is little difference, only a technicality between the first and second suggestions, but the second seems to be the more accurate. David said, "Thy word have I hid in my heart that I might not sin against thee" (Psalms 119:11).

he cannot sin, because he is begotten of God - There is an ellipsis here, which, when understood, will help with the sense of this critical and forceful statement. "He cannot

continue to sin" is the force of the argument. This present active infinitive carries that idea, not the idea of any single sin. It does not refer to single individual actions, flaws, weaknesses, or frailties of the human spirit. Such a person cannot live in sinful habits where the inner life from God abides too. One or the other will have to vacate!

Verse 10 In this the children of God are manifest, and the children of the devil: whosoever doeth not righteousness is not of God, neither he that loveth not his brother.

the children of God are manifest - It will be obvious whose children belong to whom! The Divine seed in one child shows the Divine family and parentage; the lawlessness in the other child shows devilish origins. This characteristic is not only a test of character, but also a distinguishing mark. The constant way of life shows one's origins. "Manifest" (PHANERA) again suggests a previous condition now being brought to knowledge. This will be true except to those who are blinded by ignorance, as "darkness hath blinded his eyes" (2:11), and "hath not seen him, neither knoweth him" (3:6). "In this" (EN TOUTO) is a prepositional phrase indicating the means by which such is known; i.e., the actions that can be observed in their lives indicate parentage.

children of the devil - This is the only time such a statement occurs in the New Testament, and it is never said that one is "born of the devil" (see v. 8). The expression means the life these children live is derived from the devil.

whosoever doeth not righteousness is not of God - The present tense is used here, showing habitual performance. "Of God" (EK TOU THEOU) is clearly the same as those "begotten" of Him (2:29). This phrase occurs often in John's writings. In fact, the student will see it six times in the first six verses of the next chapter. Some feel it is a synonym, or a shortened form at least, of "begotten of God."[13]

neither he that loveth not his brother - Now John introduces, at the close of this section of the Christian's response to purity (see Outline), a new thought, the thought of love for a brother. Among writers of inspiration, this style is peculiar to John. He uses a thought at the close of one section that will be expanded and developed in the next section (see Intro. remarks about Style, especially "Duadiplosis"). Lenski has described John's style of writing as "an inverted pyramid or cone. . .spirals in rising, widening circles until all is complete."[14] What he points out here is John's "wider circle," which was begun in 2:9-11.[15] John began a "first circle" of love between brethren in 2:9-11; now he will expand and widen this theme of love in 3:10b-24. Finally, he will complete the theme of brotherly love in 4:7-21. Lenski's unique description of John's style is interesting, and surely we have here one of the ongoing themes that threads throughout the book.

"Loveth not his brother" is stated in the negative, since the affirmative has already been introduced in 2:10: "He that loveth his brother abideth in light." The practice of righteousness is a general test of the sonship of God (variously mentioned already as "walk in the light" [1:7], "keep his commandments" [2:3], "doeth the will of God" [2:17], "doeth righteousness" [2:29]). Now John gives a general example of what he has been propounding — love for brethren. It will not be an isolated incident of brotherly love; it will be a continual trait, a family trait (present tense participle AGAPON). And this test is easy to observe and judge, simple to understand, clear to see. Either we are lovers or we are not. John will expand this even further, but the test is unmistakable.

One writer gives an interesting twist to logic — that the Christian who fails to love his brother actually has no brother! He is an orphan and has no brother. And he is an orphan due to the fact he has failed to love his brethren. This failure to love the brethren has therefore excluded him from God's family.[16]

Verse 11 For this is the message which ye heard from the beginning, that we should love one another:

message which ye heard from the beginning - This is similar to 2:7, "an old commandment which ye heard from the beginning." "Message" (ANGELIA) is here used with the force of a command or an order.[17] It was first used in 1:5 by John, "this is the message which ye have heard from him." John is not claiming to bring something new, never heard of before, as did the Gnostics; he reminds his readers that such messages of truth never change once they are revealed. There is no need for any changes; truth is constant, needs no change or updating, never goes out of style, and its power to save is never going to diminish. John calls on the very highest authority, the message of God.

"From the beginning has several meanings (see 2:7), and this context suggests that the words mean since they first heard the gospel themselves. John said they had "heard," so the expression means within their own personal involvement, the first acquaintance by them of the gospel truths. This may be some years after the Church began and after the gospel in its fullness was preached. It was, however, a much older message than all the new claims of the Gnostics!

that we should love one another - Literally, this is "keep on loving one another" (present subjunctive tense, AGAPAO). It seems obvious the words refer back to the previous instructions and practices, the new commandment to love one another (John 13:34-35). It is the old commandment from the beginning (2:7-11). Christians are to love all men: "abound in love. . .toward all men" (1 Thessalonians 3:12), "fulfill the royal law. . .love thy neighbor" (James 2:8). Yet there is a special family love and consideration for brethren to which this context refers by "one another." This is the same as Paul's teaching about doing good toward all men, "especially toward them that are of the household of faith" (Galatians 6:10). Thus, kinship is shown by the deeds done. The family characteristic of love shines through.

Verse 12 not as Cain was of the evil one, and slew his brother. And wherefore slew he him? Because his works were evil, and his brother's righteous.

not as Cain was of the evil one and slew his brother - The first recorded death in the Bible was a murder (Genesis 4:1-8). And it was over the matter of worship of God! How strange to involve worship, but stranger still to see the ongoing hatred over differences in worship among mankind. This serves as a perfect example of the contrast to "doeth righteousness" and "love one another." Here is the very opposite. Here the kinship to the devil is shown, not the kinship to God. This is one of the most memorable and remarkable cases of a man's failure to love "one another." It is a true demonstration of just what John pleads for Christians to avoid. In doing so, John aims to show the

reason Cain slew Abel, not just to record another statement of the fact of the slaying.

Another ellipsis is used here, and it is easily understood; i.e., "Let us be not like Cain, who was of the evil one and murdered his brother." This is the only specific Old Testament reference in the book by John.

"Of the evil one" is synonymous to "children of devil" (v. 10) and tells us since he showed a family trait of the devil, he was obviously a part of the devil's family.

"Slew" is an interesting term (from SPHAZO or SPHATTO) and is used mainly to refer to animal sacrifice.[18] Normally, such animals were slaughtered by cutting their throats. Some think this shows the way Cain killed Abel, but the Old Testament is not that specific.

The New Testament mentions that Abel was righteous and that he offered his sacrifice by faith (Hebrews 11:4). John uses the same idea of being righteous in the last part of this verse. Doing something by faith, as did Abel, is to do what God commands. Noah did all that God commanded (Genesis 6:22), yet it was said the ark was built by faith (Hebrews 11:7). Also Moses and the children of Israel were said to have done "as Jehovah had commanded Moses and Aaron, so did they" in keeping the original Passover (Exodus 12:28). And again, in the New Testament it was said to have been done by faith (Hebrews 12:28). These two examples serve as easy ways to see just what it is to do something by faith. Doing something by faith is to obey the instructions or commands of God. This is strengthened further when one considers that faith comes from hearing the word of God (Romans 10:17). So it is a simple case of a righteous and faithful man carrying out the Lord's instructions about his worship. Abel did this, while Cain did not.

We are not told what God's instructions to Cain were; whatever they were he did not choose to obey, and God did not accept his offering. Some have concluded that it was acceptable for Cain to offer fruit of the ground, if only he had offered enough. They get this idea from the description of Abel's sacrifice as "more excellent" (Hebrews 11:4 - PLEIONA), which is a comparative degree adjective that usually refers to quantity, not quality. So, as their argument goes, if Cain had only offered more of the fruit of the ground than he did, his worship would have been accepted. The Genesis account does assume that both men knew what they should offer. Abel obeyed but Cain insisted on something according to his own will, not God's, and thus his offering was not accepted. From the acceptance of Abel's offering, we can conclude he offered what God told him to offer, the proper amount, and the proper way. He was righteous in doing so.

Wherefore slew he him? Because his works were evil, and his brother's righteous - This is a question for clarity and emphasis. Literally, the word means "for the sake of what" (KARIN TINOS), and it is not used much in the New Testament. Versions differ, "Why did he" (RSV, NIV), but all the translations mean "for what reason" (NASB). It is a striking way to emphasize the example.

John answers immediately: one was evil and one was righteous. And, as has followed in all generations since, evil persons are disconcerted greatly by righteous persons. Godlessness is always upset by godliness. The actions and lives of the godly serve to judge the lawless and ungodly among whom they live. It has always been that way, and it still works that way. So, the world "hateth you," and it should be no marvel to us (next verse). It first hated Jesus Christ and so will hate His followers (John 15:18). This is a vivid, ever-present contrast between evil and righteousness.

John does not say Cain "hated his brother," but perhaps it is implied by connecting other passages. Hatred in the heart precedes murder (Matthew 5:21-22), and murders come out of the heart (Matthew 15:19). John will also shortly speak to the brother-hater (3:15) as a murderer. Working backwards, John may be thus arguing: (1) Cain's works were evil, (2) we know they were because he murdered his brother Abel, (3) this shows first that he hated him in his heart, (4) this is an example of failure to love a brother, (5) and that in turn is an example of not doing righteousness, (6) which manifestly shows the family to which he belongs — "of the devil," and "children of the devil." The logical progression that John is espousing might be shown in this way.

3. Love and Hate: Life and Death 3:13-24

We now enter the third section of the reminders of the proper relationship to God, under the major thrust of the heading "The Christian and the World: Walking in Love (see Outline). So, after a brief glimpse at the close of the section about purity, John now expands into a fuller discussion ("circle" as per Lenski?) of love and hate, life and death.

13Marvel not, brethren, if the world hateth you. 14We know that we have passed out of death into life, because we love the brethren. He that loveth not abideth in death. 15Whosoever hateth his brother is a murderer: and ye know that no murderer hath eternal life abiding in him. 16Hereby know we love, because he laid down his life for us: and we ought to lay down our lives for the brethren. 17But whoso hath the world's goods, and beholdeth his brother in need, and shutteth up his compassion from him, how doth the love of God abide in him? 18My little children, let us not love in word, neither with the tongue: but in deed and truth. 19Hereby shall we know that we are of the truth, and shall assure our heart before him: 20because if our heart condemn us, God is greater than our heart, and knoweth all things. 21Beloved, if our heart condemn us not, we have boldness toward God; 22and whatsoever we ask we receive of him, because we keep his commandments and do the things that are pleasing in his sight. 23And this is his commandment, that we should believe in the name of his Son Jesus Christ, and love one another, even as he gave us commandment. 24And he that keepeth his commandments abideth in him, and he in him. And hereby we know that he abideth in us, by the Spirit which he gave us.

Verse 13 Marvel not, brethren, if the world hateth you.

Marvel not, brethren, if the world hateth you - There is no reason to marvel, wonder (RSV), be surprised (NIV), astonished, or perplexed about enmity from the world. This "world" (KOSMOS) is the world Jesus was sent to save

(4:14), i.e., the people of the world (see 2:15). There is a parallel within the context, in the mind of John, between Cain and Abel, and the world and Christians. Both pairs are examples of hatred in action. One is history and one is history in the making. The world first hated Christ (John 15:17-19), and it is no marvel it shows this same disposition as did Cain (v. 12). The present imperative of "marvel" (THAUMAZETE) seems to have the force of ceasing to do something that was already in process. Christians should cease being astonished about the world's hatred. This world is the same one to which Cain belonged, the one we are not to love (2:15-17), and the one where anti-christs flourish (2:19ff.). The use of "you" also places an emphasis. John is pointing out the world has hated everyone else all along in its history who has been righteous, and it will also hate "you."

"A foe to God was ne'er true friend to men."[19]

This is the only time John refers to "brethren" in the epistles. Prior to this he has used "little children" and "beloved"; now John places himself on the same level with all the readers to emphasize brotherly love. It is most striking that he would change the address, clearly indicating that he is not at this time coming to them as the aged to the younger.

Verse 14 We know that we have passed out of death into life, because we love the brethren. He that loveth not abideth in death.

We know that we have passed out of death into life "We know," perhaps harking back to a previous reference about light and darkness (2:9-11), that hate and darkness are partners. So also are righteousness and light partners. As the emphasis was on "you" in v. 13, now the emphasis is on "we." There is a redundancy here in the text (HUMEIS OIDAMEN), as the word for "we" is added to the verb. Since the verb already had the first person plural within it, adding the extra "we" increases the emphasis. Thus, "they" are haters in darkness; "we" are to be lovers in light. We have a different stance and relationship. Therefore, why worry, since we occupy a purer climate, a loftier plain? Let them hate and stumble in darkness; let us love, be righteous, and bask in the light.

"Passed" describes a geographical movement. It was used when Jesus was asked to "depart" Galilee for Jerusalem (John 7:3) and when John wrote that Jesus would "depart" out of the world for the Father (John 13:1). It is perfect tense, so the transfer has already occurred. Christians began their new life at conversion (John 5:24); thus something was begun in the past and the effects are continuing into the present. One translation uses "stepped over."[20] This eternal life is already being experienced, and it is a part of and preview of the ultimate eternal life (see 2:25).

The use of the definite articles make this a distinctive verse: "the" death and "the" life. These are two definable spheres. This idea is not foreign to Bible students, since "dead" in sin is a common expression (Ephesians 2:1,5; Colossians 2:13; Luke 15:24,32; Romans 11:15; 1 Timothy 5:6). This concept can be discerned by the intellect but not seen with the physical eye. Death and life can be distinguished by the activities observed in one's life.

because we love the brethren - These actions can be observed, and John will continue to enlarge upon them later within this epistle (4:20-21; 5:14-16). The present tense of love (AGAPAO) means that he is discussing the practice of love or love as a pattern of life. This serves as a proof to ourselves as to the sphere in which we are operating. He is building to a conclusion, somewhat obscure now, about assurance toward God (v. 19ff.), and such a way of life must be known to us if we are to have such assurance. Also, this way of life is proof to others as our actions will be seen by them.

Loving the brethren is not the way to obtain eternal life, and John is not so claiming. "Because we love the brethren" explains **how we know,** not how the passing from death to life took place. John does not say that simply by loving the brethren we can pass from death to life. Rather, this love assures one that he has this new life and is living properly. This love for brethren did not obtain for him this new life. It did not earn the "passing," it only shows that it has happened. If, however, we ever show we have life, it will be by love of the brethren. It will not be proven by showing that we have been baptized, that we have rarely missed eating

102

the Lord's Supper, that we give generously, sing loudly and pray soulfully, or that we have an almost perfect attendance record. Jesus said there is another way to know about our discipleship, to love one another (John 13:34-35).

He that loveth not abideth in death - This again is a present tense in both verbs: he that continues not to love continues to abide in death. As life already exists in the one loving, the state of death already exists in the one not loving (see scriptures cited above). As life is not caused by loving the brethren, neither is death caused by not loving the brethren. Death is caused by previous sin in the non-lover's life, not the absence of love. This absence of love is the sign that one is dead to God. As long as he remains in this death state, he is separated from God. The man who lives only by his earthly and fleshly inclinations is dead in trespasses and sins (Ephesians 2:1-4). And as long as he fails to love the brethren, it is a sign he remains so. This is a simple statement and concept: life has love, death has absence of love, and even yet more — hatred (as is shown next)!

Verse 15 Whosoever hateth his brother is a murderer: and ye know that no murderer hath eternal life abiding in him.

Whosoever hateth his brother is a murderer - This is a rather startling and broad sweeping statement. The absence of love, according to this concept, is much more serious than just a heart where there is a vacuum of love. This heart can be called the heart of a murderer, for its spirit is the same as a murderer. Only outward restraints have restricted the action already contemplated within the heart. This person is a murderer in his heart though he has not committed the act. His disposition is such that his heart is turned to evil thoughts and intents; he is the opposite of what the begotten ones should be. The society or the government in which he lives may restrain him, due to the fact that murder is a crime. But hate is not a crime, so this person engages freely in this hate. This is the Cain-nature, world-nature, devil's child-nature, not the Jesus-nature! "Hate" (MISEO) is present tense, so this is not just a temporary thought in one's heart; but here John discusses a continual hatred and contempt. Vines has a pertinent comment, ". . . in 1 John 3:15, he who hates his brother is called a murderer; for the sin lies in the inward disposition, of which the act is only the outward expression."[21]

Is there any neutral ground between loving and hating? Not with John, there is not. Coupled with verse 14b, "loveth not," the expression "hateth" (both present tense verbs) speaks of the same person. This is a stark reality. It may be startling, but John declares that the one not loving is the one who hates! And these under consideration are brethren, since he speaks of this hate as toward a brother. How many murderers are there walking the earth today who are being restrained only by society? How many murderers are there in the congregations of the saints? This spirit of hate is what splits churches, separates brethren, promotes gossip, prints "yellow journalism" papers and bulletins, and stirs up squabbles.

The introspective saint shudders to evaluate self. Is it possible that when one reads daily accounts of murder that one can say, "There go I but for the grace of God?" How far away are we from such murder, if indeed we are far away in disposition at all?

The words of Jesus need to be recalled as to His warnings about the condition of our hearts. He warned about calling others "Raca" or "fool" (Matthew 5:21-22). He cautioned the Jews about blasphemy and said evil things come out of the heart of man (Matthew 12:34-35). He also warned about the possibility of committing adultery in the heart (Matthew 5:28). It is true the heart can be deceitful above all things and exceedingly corrupt (Jeremiah 17:9), and the Wise Man said because the sentence against evil is not executed speedily, man's heart can be set to do evil (Ecclesiastes 8:11).

"Murderer" (ANTHROPOKTONOS), literally a "man-slayer," is used only twice in the New Testament, here and in reference to the devil (John 8:44). Thus John now extends the application to all the children of the devil, not limiting it to the devil himself. And this makes a double sentence of condemnation upon the children of the devil: they are liars (1:6,10; 2:22), and they are murderers.

ye know that no murderer hath eternal life abiding in him - No one needs to apprise you of this, as you already possess this much spiritual discernment. This is a maxim, a truism; it is axiomatic and ought to be intuitive even to

104

those of spiritual discernment. The possessor of such murderous hatred in his heart does not have this eternal life in the same heart. Light and darkness do not abide together; one pushes the other out. So love and hate cannot co-exist in the heart of a man. Such is the very point of being "unequally yoked together with unbelievers" (2 Corinthians 6:14-7:1). Those who are righteous, walk in light, follow Christ, are believers and are the temple of God have not a chance when yoked unequally with iniquity, darkness, Belial, unbelief, and idols. So it also refers to hate and love; there can be no fellowship within the same heart.

It is of note that the devil has only the power of sin and death, not the power to give life (Romans 5:12, 6:23; 1 Corinthians 15:22; Hebrews 2:14; James 1:15).

"Eternal life" (see 2:25) is that in which the believer already participates, the fruition of which is yet to be consummated. The hater and eternal life are not to be together. This verse has no reference to inability to seek and obtain forgiveness, for such can be done by any man. As presently portrayed, the hater does not have eternal life. Eternal life cannot abide (MENO) or remain in him.

Verse 16 Hereby know we love, because he laid down his life for us: and we ought to lay down our lives for the brethren.

Hereby know we love - Here is the zenith of love; here is the revelation of supreme love. The possession of eternal life was tested by whether one loves (vv. 14-15); now love is tested by whether one will lay down his life for his brethren. Next, the test will be whether one is willing to lay down his possessions for his brethren (v. 17). The perfect tense of "know" (GINOSKO) shows we have already come to know, perhaps at the cross, what God's love is. We continue to value it at the present time.

"Love" (see 2:7-10) seems to refer to both the Father's love and the love of the Son. This is the sacrificial love expressed in the mercy and grace of God (John 3:16; Romans 5:8; 1 John 4:10).

he laid down his life for us - "he" (EIKONOS is literally "that one") is Christ, and this translation of the pronoun is used consistently by John throughout the book (2:6; 3:3,5,7).

105

"Laid down" aorist of TITHEMI that means to "put, place, set, frequently signifies to lay,"[22] or "to place, set, lay. . .to lay down."[23] It also refers particularly to the voluntary death of Jesus. It was His free will and choice; it was intentional, not accidental. The same verb is used when Jesus laid aside His garments (John 13:4) and when Peter claimed he was ready to die for the Lord (John 13:37). Jesus said the good shepherd lays down his life for the sheep (John 10:11), that He was going to lay down His life (John 10:15-17), and that He would do it Himself since He had the power to lay it down and no one had the power to take it away from Him (John 10:18). It is sad to hear men speak of His blood being "spilled" at the cross, as if it were an accident.

There is a beautiful couplet here and in John 3:16. Together they express the essence of love, grace, and mercy.

"For" (HUPER) in this verse is the subject of much dispute as to whether it has the force of "instead of." Other instances of this substitutionary meaning are found when Caiaphas spoke (John 11:50; 18:14) and when Paul stated that Christ "became a curse for us" (Galatians 3:13). In these instances, it means "instead of" and does in this present verse also. "Surely the very object of such death is to save life."[24] Woods also has a useful comment, "The picture in the preposition is of one who sees, for example, another one who has fallen, and who rushes to him, stands over him, fights in his behalf, and enters the fray in his stead."[25]

we ought to lay down our lives for the brethren - This is the example of Christ now applied to the brethren. Man's sense of "oughtness" (only man of all God's creatures has this sense) leads him to this application and conclusion. It is a moral obligation. It is interesting that John used "we ought" (OPHELOMEN, present indicative plural) which means "to owe, to be indebted. . .to incur a bond. . .to be bound or obliged. . .to be due or fitting."[26] He could have used DEO, which would have had the force of a command, making it binding and necessary. Perhaps it was not so done, for Christ did not lay down His life in response to a command either. He laid down His life out of love, and so should we. It would not be Christ-like to lay down one's life

106

in response to a legal command.

The extent of man's love for others is surely challenged here! There is no limit to this love, nothing is too precious to be excluded, even life itself. The expression is an exact parallel in calling for men to lay down their lives, as did Jesus, for it uses the same verb, verb tense, and preposition (aorist of TITHEMI plus HUPER). Thus it is that Peter called for us to "follow His steps," or "follow His tracks,"[27] and He "bare our sins in His body upon the tree" (1 Peter 2:21-24). "Greater love hath no man than this" (John 15:13). Christians in the first century were thus perceived: " 'Behold how they love one another; they are ready to die for one another' (Tertull. Apol. c. 39). So Eusebius (Ecclesiastes His. vii. 22) says of Christians that 'in a time of plague they visited one another, and not only hazarded their lives, but actually lost them in their zeal to preserve the lives of others.' "[28] Barnes goes on to note five instances of duty which the Christian should enjoin upon himself: (1) to love the church as a patriot would love his country, (2) to love Christians in need or in peril, (3) to love the truth rather than deny it, (4) to love the cause of Christ and evangelize even at risk of death, and (5) to love the church and engage in all its work and service.

Parents will have such sacrificial love for their children in many ways of this physical life but are often fearful to tell them of Christ. Elders might show the same inconsistency when they neglect those who are in spiritual danger, unwilling to sacrifice time and effort to go and find the straying sheep. Preachers sometimes are so busy with ethical, community, and counseling problems that they forget to tell the wicked of their wicked ways; and thus blood will be required at their hand (Ezekiel 3:17-21; 33:7-9). Who is it today who will put himself in jeopardy for souls? Paul was willing to be anathema for the sake of his brethren, and this takes it much further than just physical life (Romans 9:3).

The context is now building toward an application: (1) we are children, begotten as a product of God's love [v. 1], (2) we ought to purify ourselves [v. 3], (3) we will no longer practice sin [vv. 6-10], (4) thus we love the brother, not hate as did Cain [vv. 11-12], (5) proper love is limitless as was

Christ's [v. 16], and (6) next will be the application of such brotherly love [vv. 17-18].

Verse 17 But whoso hath the world's goods, and beholdeth his brother in need, and shutteth up his compassion from him, how doth the love of God abide in him?

But whoso hath the world's goods, and beholdeth his brother in need, and shutteth up his compassion from him - "But" (DE) is an adversative conjunction that introduces a negative application and example. John has soared into the sublime realms with the idea of laying down one's life for the brethren, so he now carries us into the mundane world in which we live, and an application that can be all too common. This is the practical test of love, a concrete example to us of whether we pass any test of love at all. The absence of compassion for the needy guarantees that no love like Christ's will ever be seen; there will be no laying down of one's life when there is not even the laying down of one's goods. This is actually an argument from the greater degree to the lesser, much as Paul did when he argued about the gifts of God (Romans 8:32). As Paul argued that God spared not His own Son (greater gift), neither will He spare things needful (lesser gifts) to the Christian life. So, if we have the laying-down-life kind of love (greater degree), surely we will also show compassion for the needy (lesser degree). If we are willing to give up our lives, then we would be ready to make smaller sacrifices also.

Three things are seen in this passage: (1) a brother who has this world's goods, (2) he beholds a brother in need, (3) he shuts up his compassion and does not help. All that is left in the completion of the thought is the rhetorical question, "How doth the love of God abide in him?"

"World's goods" (BIOS) literally means "world's life." BIOS has been used previously by John to refer to material possessions or life style ("pride of life" - 2:17). Also, it is used to refer to what the famous widow gave away, her "living" (Mark 12:44). It is used here similarly to describe the material goods necessary to sustain life. One brother has them, the other does not.

"Beholdeth his brother in need" includes the continued knowledge of the need of the brother by continued beholding. Two present subjunctives and one aorist subjunctive are used here ("has" - ECHEI, "beholdeth" - THEOREI, "shutteth up" - KLEISEI), for the thought is conditional: **if** we see this brother. But the brother's description is neither theoretical nor conditional; it is actual ("having" - ECHONTA, present participle). The brother who has goods sees the need fully, there is no mistake. "Need" is sometimes translated "necessity" (Acts 20:34; Romans 12:13).

"Shutteth up compassion" is the switch from two present subjunctive verbs to an aorist subjunctive. John has said some things are continuing: (1) a brother having goods, (2) that brother beholding another brother in need, (3) the second brother continuing to have needs. Now John switches to an aorist: we shut up compassion. We close off the situation by one pin-point action. We might say "we slammed the door" of opportunity once and for all. "Compassion" (SPLANCHNON), translated somewhat unhappily as "bowels" (KJV), does literally denote intestinal organs, the viscera. This word was usually regarded figuratively by the Greeks as the seat of more violent passions, and by the Hebrews as the seat of tender affections.[29] "Heart" (RSV, NASB) is fitting for this idea, for the brother turns away in nonchalance and disinterest. Here again, the meaning is expressed as if it were just a vacuum of interest and feeling; but it is far worse than just emptiness. If there is no help, there is no love. And if there is no love, there is hate (vv. 14-15)!

How can the love of God abide in him? - This is a rhetorical question and needs no answer given by John. It is clear that this is the way that John declares no love abides in such a man. The love under description in this verse is man's love, not God's. The man who thus acts has not the God-like love within himself; for if he did, he would be motivated to better actions. Man cannot separate theory and practice. To try to avoid help to a needy brother is just empty words (James 2:15-16). John may also have in mind here those traveling preachers he will mention shortly (2 John 10-11; 3 John 10-11) as being needy to continue their work. Paul urged his readers to "set them forward on their journey" (Titus 3:13). It is true that if there is no love for the "earthlings," there is also no love for the "heavenlies." Love cannot be seen, much less defined. Paul personified it and came as close as any to a definition (1 Corinthians 13:4-7). One can see the evidence only when love passes by.

Verse 18 My little children, let us not love in word, neither with the tongue; but in deed and in truth.

My little children - This is again the tender appeal to John's children in the faith, and the present subjunctive of "love" (AGAPOMEN) is hortatory. It is an admonishment of tender address.

not love in word, neither with the tongue - There is an ellipsis here, for John is not calling for saints never to speak words of love. Rather, the passage would read, "not love in word **only**, neither with the tongue **only**." Words and the tongue are good to use in telling of love, but using them alone without any actions is not what would please the Lord. One translator, usually more a paraphraser, stated it well, "My dear children, let us put our love not into words or into talk, but into deeds and make it real" (Moffett).

John thus draws a general statement of conclusion, or a brief summation about love properly expressed. If love is expressed only verbally, is it then too weak for John?

but in deed and truth - John's contrast for emphasis now calls for action, and an action that is of the proper spirit. It must be not hypocritical but authentic. It must be genuine, sincere, real. Love ought to be demonstrated, particularly in this case, for there is known to be a brother in need. Without a demonstration, without action, there is simply no love.

Verse 19 Hereby shall we know that we are of the truth, and shall assure our heart before him:

There begins here a sub-section in which the grammatical construction is unusually difficult, and several textual questions arise. Questions center on: (1) whether "and" (KAI) should be in the text as in the KJV at the beginning of v. 19, (2) the meaning and use of two occurrences of HOTI in v. 20, usually meaning "that. . .for that, for, because . . .seeing that,"[30] (3) the meaning of PEITHO in v. 19, which usually means "to persuade. . .endeavor to convince,"[31] and (4) whether proper punctuation is used in the KJV and NIV to make two sentences of vv. 19-20, or just one as in ASV, NASB, and RSV. For the avid student, it would be well to read Burdick,[32] as he details ten different ways to understand these verses in question.

In this context John tells us now that confidence gained by brotherly love assures us that we are in the truth and that we can approach God properly in prayer and in judgment. John has already established a test of genuine love, a deep sacrificial love of brothers (vv. 16-18). Now he proposes some wondrous results (vv. 19-24). They will include: (1) we can know we are of the truth, (2) we can assure our own troubled consciences when they prick us for our mistakes, (3) we can rely on God to know us even better than we know ourselves, (4) in spite of not measuring up to the perfect standard of God in our actions, we can yet approach God properly in prayer, (5) our prayers, offered within bounds of scriptural and spiritual propriety, will be answered affirmatively if we continue to please Him, (6) we will continue to believe in the name of His Son and obey His commandments, and (7) He will continue to abide in us, as proven by the indwelling Holy Spirit that He gave us. This is the threading together of John's arguments and proposals in this section.

Hereby shall we know that we are of the truth - The love of one's brother gives evidence one is of the truth. "Shall we know" (GNOSOMETHA) is future tense, though the KJV and NIV both translate it as if it were present tense. This future tense shows that one looks forward to fulfilling this requirement of knowledge: when one loves the brethren properly, has the continuing love of brethren in life and heart (deed and truth), then one can know one is "of the truth." This shows source and can be equated with saying "of God," one of John's favorite expressions. The one loving his brother in the proper way is truly "of God," "of truth." This brotherly love is vital; being "of the truth" is vital, for without these two, what follows in John's teaching could never be.

and shall assure our heart before him - This assurance, so necessary to sensitive, soft-hearted, seeking, searching saints, can come only to one who has his source in the truth. He has his source in the truth if he loves his brother in deed and in truth. How sad it is to see a few brethren fighting, carping, criticizing, dividing, church-splitting, proudly puffed up with self-esteem and self-will in their arrogant, prideful, boastful claims to be the great "saviors of the brotherhood" and "defenders of the faith." It seems every generation unfortunately has its share.

"Shall assure" (PEISOMEN, future active of PEITHO) uses a verb tense parallel to the previous "shall know." The ASV has a footnote to Matthew 28:14, where it is translated "persuade." The NASB uses the translation "win him over." It seems the meaning can be a persuasion to set one at ease, pacify and assure, and "to appease, render tranquil, to quiet, 1 John 3:19. . ."[33] It seems here John assumes we have a heart that lacks assurance, since we know our frailties, mistakes, and sins. We know how tragically we are out of step with the Lord. The heart (conscience) that is of the truth and full of brotherly love, as is the heart under discussion now by John, is also one of great tenderness, sensitivity, and troubled questioning. It is the heart that wonders constantly whether it has lived up to God's expectations and wishes for the faithful. The heinous evil-doer, the deceitful hypocrite, the pride-blinded need take no comfort from these words. The rebel to righteousness, the desecrator of decency, the castigator of the church, and the persistent perpetrator of sin cannot have this assurance. This context assumes the assured man is the one who is demonstrating his love for God and his sacrificial love for the brethren (vv. 16-18).

"Before him" portrays a legal drama. We appear before God wondering what the verdict will be. Our own pre-trial judge (our conscience) had condemned us as guilty. There is no other way for us to plead than guilty when we are asked by the Judge. Yet the Judge of all eternity can say, "I declare you innocent," knowing full well we are nothing but guilty. Wonder of all wonders! He can declare us, who are so sinful and guilty, to be innocent on the **merit of the blood** of His Son, by the **principle of faith,** and upon the **condition of obedience.** This is Biblical justification (or God's "righteousness") as argued by Paul (Romans 3:21-28; 5:1-3). There is no merit of any kind on man's part. He can only trust and obey, fulfilling the condition and principle upon which God can still be "just and the justifier of him that hath faith in Jesus" (Romans 3:26).

How marvelous it will be for the saints to appear before Him, the God of all grace (1 Peter 5:10)!

Verse 20 because if our heart condemn us, God is greater than our heart, and knoweth all things.

because if our heart condemn us - The RSV states, "whenever our hearts condemn us," and another thought could be, "in whatever our hearts condemn us." John is not leaving any question, for our hearts will condemn us. We will have no peace unless our conscience is seared (1 Timothy 4:2), something every Christian must avoid. All children of God who have proper perspective and balance will have this same troubling of mind, heart, and conscience. In fact, we would be in trouble if our heart did not so work! Note that John includes himself in this with the use of the first person plural.

God is greater. . .and knoweth all things - Is there another ellipsis here? Most likely there is; and if considered such, it will offer the least difficulty. Thus it would read, ". . .and shall assure our heart before him: because if our heart condemn us, **it is evident that** God is greater than our hearts. . . ." Or, it could read "**we know that** God is greater than our hearts." Either way it suffices to help John's thrust: (1) love in deed and truth, i.e., love of the brothers, is proof we have passed from death to life [vv. 13-18], (2) still we are judged continually by our conscience that we do not follow perfectly God's law [vv. 19-20], (3) we can have assurance due to our life of brotherly love, in spite of uneasy and troubled consciences [v. 20], (4) because God knows all things, both the mistakes and sins which our own consciences condemn, but also the quality of our faith and trust in His Son [v. 20].

"Knoweth all things" does not block off the findings of our own conscience. We still are self-condemned, self-acknowledged sinners. John does not say God overlooks or pays no attention to these sins or that our sins do not matter; rather, John affirms that God knows all things. God knows how much we trust, how much we try, how much we regret and repent. Mercy and grace must enter in, and how marvelous it is that God knoweth all things! This theme of the omniscience of God needs to be on the mind and heart

113

of all Christians, for there is an "all-seeing eye watching you." He beholds all the sons of man (Psalms 33:13), knows the secrets of the heart (Psalms 44:21), has all the ways of man laid out before Him (Psalms 119:168), searches and knows men (Psalms 139:1), which knowledge is too wonderful for man (Psalms 139:1-16, especially v. 6), and knows the heart of men (Acts 1:24).

The wonder of God's love is shown all the more: He knows us, all of our warts and blemishes, all of the secrets of our hearts and minds, **and still loves us!**

Verse 21 Beloved, if our heart condemn us not, we have boldness toward God:

Beloved, if our heart - Again John uses "beloved" (AGAPTOI), one of six times in this epistle (2:7; 3:2,21; 4:1,7,11). Four of these six occurrences involve love of the brethren. The "heart" is the same as v. 19, the inner man, the conscience.

condemn us not - Happy is the man who hides no secret sins, but is following faithfully the known wishes of God! This is now stated in the negative, back to back with the affirmative, a grammatical tool often used by John. Some say this uncondemned class of folk is only theoretical, does not actually exist.[34] Contrary to such evasion, John is speaking of individuals who have "followed after sanctification" (Hebrews 12:14), grown in the "grace and knowledge of our Lord and Savior Jesus Christ" (2 Peter 3:18), "escaped the corruption that is in the world" (2 Peter 1:4), and who "are guarded though faith unto a salvation ready to be revealed in the last time" (1 Peter 1:5). Such a person is not (1) one who is confident in personal merit of life to save, i.e., the "good moral man," (2) one who is ignorant of God's ways and teachings, and thereby not troubled by an ignorant conscience, (3) one who is satisfied he is heaven-bound just because he has been baptized but then makes no effort to grow spiritually, (4) one with perverted, convoluted trust in man's knowledge, but who is also base, vulgar, and worldly.

we have boldness toward God - There are four major truths that now "we know" from John's teachings: (1) We have passed out of death into life [v. 14], (2) no murderer hath eternal life [v. 15], (3) we know love due to Christ's example (v. 16), and (4) we are of the truth (v. 19). Additionally, we have two approvals: (1) of God [v. 20], and (2) our own heart [v. 21]. The approval of our own heart is not infallible, nor is it based on faulty concepts. Rather, it is based on teachings such as these by John that God is gracious to sinful men who have a quality of trust and a quantity of trying. Therefore we can approach the Throne with "boldness" (PARRHESIA). This PARRHESIA originally meant "freedom of speech."[35] If a person's conscience does not condemn him, he can pray with more "confidence," (NASB) assurance, and boldness. This boldness was previously connected by John to one's attitude in the coming again of the Lord (2:28). This avenue of approach is open (1) by the new and living way of the blood of Christ [Hebrews 10:19-20], (2) because of the new High Priest, the Son of God [Hebrews 4:14-16], (3) as a way by which we can hold fast unto the end [Hebrews 3:6]; and (4) as a source of great reward [Hebrews 10:35]. Our prayers **will be heard and answered;** God has so promised, we trust, and results will come. We can be "face to face" (PROS, "toward" in the ASV, has been called the "face-to-face" preposition) toward God in prayers and in judgment.[36] Our boldness is not in self, but in God's grace, mercy, and love, plus our total trust in Him.

Verse 22 and whatsoever we ask we receive of him, because we keep his commandments and do the things that are pleasing in his sight.

and whatsoever we ask we receive of him - This assurance of answered petitions is not without limitations. Known scriptures about prayer are not here ignored; John assumes all such prayers are within proper bounds and conditions. Never would this be an encouragement of demands of God, commands for selfish things, or pleadings for things inconsistent to the will and nature of God. Man would do well to remember some limitations and bounds placed upon prayer: Man cannot regard iniquity in his heart (Psalms 66:18), God will not hear the cries of the ungodly (Job 27:8-9), God will refuse to answer those who do not regard Him and set at naught His counsel (Proverbs 1:28), the prayers of one who turns his ear away from God's law will be an abomination (Proverbs 28:9), one whose hands are full of blood will get no answer (Isaiah 1:15), iniquities will cause God to refuse to hear (Isaiah 59:1-2), and a desire to spend blessings in selfish pleasures will cause God to refuse them (James 4:3). On the other hand, one can be encouraged about praying, for as Augustine said, "He who gave us love cannot close his ears against the groans and prayers of love."[37]

"We ask" (AITOMEN) and "we receive" (LAMBANOMEN) are both present tense and are durative here in the sense that we will keep on receiving as long as we keep on asking. This is a truism accepted by all believers.

because we keep his commandments and do the things that are pleasing in his sight - There is a casual conjunctioni HOTI ("because"), and it refers only to the **condition** upon which prayers will be heard, not the **merit** thereof. Again, the two verbs "keep" (TEIROUMEN) and "do" (POIOUMEN) are present tense, matching the previous two verbs. Therefore, we understand this to say that "we continue asking and we continue receiving because we continue keeping His commands and continue doing things which please Him."

Here is evidence that can assure our hearts. God does not need all this to know about us; He is the Knower of hearts already and has always been (1 Samuel 6:7; 1 Chronicles 28:9). This statement gives us assurance, not proof that we should be heard. We are the ones who need ease and comfort. The tender conscience of the dedicated saint always feels its own inadequacies. Yet there is an assurance of salvation (to be expanded upon later in 5:13-15) that gives the saint the "peace of God which passeth all understanding," and that "guards" our "hearts and thoughts" in the life Jesus wants us to live (Philippians 4:7). This peace comes only in our trust in God's mercy and grace, for certainly our own hearts tell us we deserve only punishment and death. John is emphasizing that we will not get what we, as sinners, deserve; rather, we will get what sons can inherit. This evidence and assurance can come only to those who please Him and keep His commandments.

Verse 23 And this is the commandment, that we should believe in the name of his Son Jesus Christ, and love one another, even as he gave us commandment.

And this is the commandment. . . - To speak now of a single command (ENTOLE) seems paradoxical since the previous verse speaks of "keep his commandments" (ENTOLAS). Also in this verse, John will call for two things — belief and love. How can John command two things yet call it a single command? Lenski says, "they coalesce into just one. . . .These are not two commandments: to believe and to love. These two are one. You cannot believe without loving nor love without believing."[38] Such could be considered only if this loving and believing were of the highest spiritual sort, remembering that "demons also believe" in some inferior sense (James 2:19). John does sum up the essence of the saintly life in this statement: belief and practice, faith and works, trust and duty. The Gnostics tried to separate these (see Intro.), but John denies that such separation could ever happen and be pleasing to God. When Gnostics failed in their faith toward the Son of God, could they even have a serious relationship with God? Could they be begotten again and have the new life without the proper belief in Jesus as the Christ? Could they expect to be heard in their prayers? Could they have their consciences assured accurately and properly? Could it be said that any acts of compassion they did toward fellow men were done in respect and obedience to the Christ? Hardly can there be an affirmative answer to any of these questions. John is presently to show the terrible danger of false trust due to inaccuracy of doctrine.

believe in the name of his Son Jesus Christ - To believe in His name is to do more than just accept the Divine Personhood of Jesus; it is to believe in all for which such a name stands. It includes belief in Him as God, Deity (1:1-3), as incarnated (1:1-3; 4:2), as one who brought the new birth (2:29-3:3; 5:1), and as one who gives eternal life (5:10-12). This is the way John develops accuracy of doctrine about Jesus Christ throughout this book, and it serves to show the width of such meaning of faith. He is the Eternal One, the Anointed One, the Resurrected One, the Revealing One, and the Returning One. Some claim it matters not what one believes as long as one's life is upright and moral. How utterly false this is in view of John's statement here! Accuracy of doctrine is vital and is later a matter of much further discussion, some of which is most pointed (4:1-3; 2 John 7-11).

The "name" was very important in New Testament days. It was a common way of speaking about what is called "Christianity" today. There was to be life in this name (John 20:31), one was baptized in this name (Acts 2:38; 10:48), salvation was in this name (Acts 4:12), they rejoiced in suffering for this name (Acts 5:41), men would go forth in this name (3 John 7), men could glorify God in this name (1 Peter 4:16), and it was the name above all others, one that will be confessed finally by all men in judgment (Philippians 2:9-11). Let none degrade this name, let none think it unimportant.

and love one another, even as he gave us commandment - We must be real in life as well as accurate in doctrine. John's conclusion to this line of thought is here stated: Proper relationship to God requires proper beliefs and proper actions.

The verb "love" (AGAPAO) is in the present tense as was also "believe" (PISTEUO) in reference to the "name." Some commentators argue that "believe" is aorist and that there was a change by a copyist in the text.[39] Whether "believe" is present tense ("continue to believe") or aorist tense ("once for all belief") matters little to the sense of John's statements. There must be a genuine faith in the Son of God, coupled with a life of loving the brethren if one is to please the God of Heaven.

This command to brotherly love is given by the Lord and is the same one given by Him during His personal ministry (John 13:34-35; 15:12,17).

Verse 24 And he that keepeth his commandments abideth in him, and he in him. And hereby we know that he abideth in us, by the Spirit which he gave us.

And he that keepeth his commandments abideth in him, and he in him - Going back to v. 22, the keeping of His commandments, John returns to the prior thought and now claims a mutual abiding. This mutual abiding was promised by the Lord (John 14:20) but upon the condition of submission (John 14:23-24). It is simply a condition of fellowship with God, union with God. Jesus added both He and the Father would abide in the believer (v. 23). Christians are in a sphere of a special relationship spiritually with God. Bede said, "Let God be a home to thee, and be thou a home to God."[40]

And hereby we know that he abideth in us, by the Spirit which he gave us - Mention of the Holy Spirit at the close of this section of thought produces another duadiplosis (see Intro. under topic of "Style"). It introduces the next subject and is peculiar to John's style of writing. The indwelling Holy Spirit gives certain and sure evidence that one abides in God and has fellowship with God. Our keeping the commands of God proves our mutual abiding (v. 23), and additional evidence and assurance comes by the fact the Holy Spirit is given to us and dwells within us. Literally, John says about the Spirit: "He continues to dwell in us" (MENEI, present tense of MENO). The verb "dwell" is used often to refer to such durative remaining (2 Corinthians 3:11; John 5:38; 14:10; 15:4; 1 John 5:14). On the other hand, "which he gave us" (ENDOKEN) is aorist, indicating the gift of the Holy Spirit to us is a one-time giving, completed as an action on the spot. The expression is not durative in tense; the Holy Spirit is not something which God continually gives to man. The KJV "hath given" and the NASB and RSV "has given" might hint at the perfect tense; "gave us" (ASV, NIV) portrays a better sense of the tense.

This verse makes no claim that the Holy Spirit speaks directly to the heart, or that He reveals anything new, or that He gives special knowledge or understanding when one reads the Bible. In fact, it makes no mention of any communication between the Christian and the Holy Spirit dwelling in him! It does establish the fact that the Holy Spirit, a person, is given in some spiritual way to each Christian. It does establish the fact the Holy Spirit indwells each individual Christian. The only way one knows about this indwelling is the same way one knows he is saved at baptism from his past sins or that he is born again: God's word says so. We take Him at His word though we may not understand it very well.

There are legitimate things the Spirit does in the course of one's life with Christ. John does not address them here; he only announces the fact that the Spirit does dwell in the

Christian. How this dwelling is accomplished is not described here either. This is the first mention of the Spirit in the book, though allusion had already been made when John wrote of the "anointing" (2:20,27), a declaration perhaps of His work.

Though this verse has been the object of much false teaching and abuse, there are several major things to know about the Holy Spirit. His relations and work among men can be divided into three categories: (1) His work among the apostles [John 14:26; 15:26; Acts 1:8; 2:1-4; 1 Corinthians 2:13], (2) His work among the teachers and prophets in the churches, those upon whom the hands of the apostles were laid and who thus received miraculous gifts enabling young churches and Christians to grow and mature [Acts 8:17-18; 19:6; 1 Corinthians 12:4-11; 1 Peter 4:11], and (3) His work among all Christians as the Indweller [Acts 2:38; 5:32; Galatians 4:6; Romans 5:5, 8:26; Ephesians 1:13-14; 2 Corinthians 1:22; 2 Timothy 1:14].

Much fanaticism and false doctrine has been fostered about the work of the Holy Spirit, both in New Testament times and in modern times. John will deal shortly with some errors of his day (4:1-4). These have been multiplied greatly in today's bloat of pentecostalism, spiritualism, and mysticism.

---

[1]R. C. H. Lenski, *The Interpretation of the Epistles of St. Peter, St. John and St. Jude*, (Augsburg Publishing House, Minneapolis, Minnesota, 1963), p. 449.

[2]Lenski, *Interpretation*, p. 450.

[3]Lenski, *Interpretation*, pp. 451-452.

[4]Alexander Ross, *The New International Commentary on the New Testament, the Epistles of James and John*, (Wm. B. Eerdmans Publishing Co., Grand Rapids, Michigan, 1954), p. 180.

[5]Colin Brown, as quoted by Donald W. Burdick, *The Letters of John the Apostle*, (Moody Press, Chicago, Illinois, 1985), p. 235.

[6]A. T. Robertson, *Word Pictures in the New Testament*, (Broadman Press, Nashville, Tennessee, 1933), Vol. VI, *The General Epistles and the Revelation of John*, p. 221.

[7]Marvin R. Vincent, *Word Studies in the New Testament*, (Charles Scribner's Sons, New York, 1911), Vol. II, *The Writings of John*, p. 346.

[8]Samuel Bagster, *Analytical Greek Lexicon*, (Samuel Bagster & Sons, London, England, 1852, Revised Edition by Harold K. Moulton, Zondervan

Publishing Co., Grand Rapids, Michigan, 1978), p. 9.

[9]C. N. Dodd and I. Howard Marshall, as quoted by Burdick, *Letters*, p. 246.

[10]Albert Barnes, *Notes on the New Testament, James, Peter, John and Jude*, (Baker Book House, Grand Rapids, Michigan, 1949), p. 317.

[11]Bagster, *Analytical Lexicon*, p. 79.

[12]Robertson, *Word Pictures*, p. 223.

[13]C. H. Dodd, as quoted by Burdick, *Letters*, p. 249.

[14]Lenski, *Interpretation*, p. 366-367.

[15]Lenski, *Interpretation*, p. 464.

[16]Guy N. Woods, *A Commentary on the New Testament Epistles of Peter, John and Jude*, (Gospel Advocate Co., Nashville, Tennessee, 1954), p. 274.

[17]W. E. Vine, *An Expository Dictionary of New Testament Words*, (Riverside Book and Bible House, Iowa Falls, Iowa, 1952), p. 736.

[18]Bagster, *Analytical Lexicon*, p. 394; see also Vine, *Dictionary*, p. 1053.

[19]Adam Clarke, *A Commentary and Critical Notes*, (Abingdon-Cokesbury Press, New York and Nashville), Vol. II, *Romans to Revelation*, p. 916.

[20]Lenski, *Interpretation*, p. 468.

[21]Vine, *Dictionary*, p. 528.

[22]Vine, *Dictionary*, p. 648.

[23]Bagster, *Lexicon*, p. 404.

[24]Robertson, *Minister and His Greek New Testament*, as quoted by Lenski, *Interpretation*, p. 471.

[25]Woods, *Commentary*, p. 281.

[26]Bagster, *Lexicon*, p. 296.

[27]Lenski, *Interpretation*, p. 118.

[28]Barnes, *Notes*, p. 322.

[29]Vine, *Dictionary*, p. 28.

[30]Bagster, *Lexicon*, p. 294.

[31]Bagster, *Lexicon*, p. 314.

[32]Burdick, *Letters*, pp. 271-275.

[33]Bagster, *Lexicon*, p. 314.

[34]Lenski, *Interpretation*, p. 477.

[35]Bagster, *Lexicon*, p. 310; see also Vine, *Dictionary*, p. 130.

[36]J. W. Roberts, *The Living Word Commentary, The Letters of John*, (R. B. Sweet Co., Austin, Texas, 1968), p. 98.

[37]Ross, *NIC*, p. 193.

[38]Lenski, *Interpretation*, p. 479.

[39]Burdick, *Letters*, p. 279; also Lenski, *Interpretation*, p. 480.

[40]Ross, *NIC*, p. 194.

4. Truth and Error 4:1-6

The fourth reminder of proper relationship to God is the difference between truth and error. The first was God's example of love (3:1-2), the second was the response to purity (3:2-12), the third was the treatment of love and hate: life and death (3:13-24). Now comes the fourth, the challenge to differentiate between truth and error.

¹Beloved, believe not every spirit, but prove the spirits, whether they are of God; because many false prophets are gone out into the world. ²Hereby know ye the Spirit of God: every spirit that confesseth that Jesus Christ is come in the flesh is of God: ³and every spirit the confesseth not Jesus is not of God: and this is the spirit of the anti-christ, whereof ye have heard that it cometh; and now it is in the world already. ⁴Ye are of God, my little children, and have overcome them: because greater is he that is in you than he that is in the world. ⁵They are of the world: therefore speak they as of the world, and the world heareth them. ⁶We are of God: he that knoweth God heareth us; he who is not of God heareth us not. By this we know the spirit of truth, and the spirit of error.

Verse 1 Beloved, believe not every spirit, but prove the spirits, whether they are of God: because many false prophets are gone out into the world.

Beloved, believe not every spirit - Having spoken in the vein of love and life (3:13-24), John continues in his address as "beloved" (AGAPTOI), showing continual concern in tenderness. "Beloved" is used three times in this chapter, vv. 1, 7, 11. The use of the present imperative (PISTEUETE) may suggest they had a weakness toward gullibility, since it states literally "stop believing" every spirit. This idea of belief does not refer to believing in the strongest sense of full acceptance of false teachings but carries more the idea of giving credence to false claims. It is a fact there were true and false teachers in John's time. Careful distinctions were to be made by brethren. Simply because some came into a congregation claiming to be true teachers did not qualify them as such. All claims must be put to a test, and teachers were not to be trusted until they passed the test.

"Spirit" is a synecdoche referring to the false teacher; and even more, perhaps, it is a reference to the spirit that led him. Ghost-like apparitions, visions, or spirit-world phenomena are not what John has in mind. Simply put, he is warning brethren that men will come among them with false teachings. He uses "spirit" to refer to these men, linking them with the source of their false ideas. And it is possible that these men are being led by supernatural spirits, since such was not totally absent in New Testament days. Anti-christs would surely be included here (2:18ff.), but there were also other false teachers. The criterion of this test centers on the concept of the incarnation of the Son of God.

but prove the spirits, whether they are of God - Christians are to prove, test, try (DOKIMAZETE, present imperative) these spirits. The history of this word includes testing metals,[1] proof of gold,[2] and the testing of calves for sacrifices and of public officials for public offices.[3] The reason for such testing will be evident from the next phrase, but the necessity of such testing is stated here.

Some things are notable about this testing called for by John. (1) All Christians are called upon to do this testing. It is not just the business of presbyters, evangelists, etc.; it is the business of all "little children" [v. 4]. Significant will be the fact that any idea of a pope as the standard bearer of testing is excluded totally. (2) In order to do such testing, there must be some objective standard by which to test. This standard will be stated later in vv. 2-3 and will be summed up in the idea of the "spirit of truth" in v. 6. Contemplation of a standard will also remind the student that such a standard is that which was "heard from the beginning" [2:24]. (3) Such testing requires methodology. In the first century men could be tested by one who had the gift of "discernings of spirits" [1 Corinthians 12:10] or by comparison with the "apostles, teaching" [Acts 2:42; Galatians 1:6-9]. In present times, one can be tested by comparison with the written word [Jude 3; 2 Timothy 3:16-17; Romans 10:17; 1 Corinthians 14:37-38]. (4) The testing that John called for was nothing new to God's people. "But the prophet, that shall speak a word presumptuously in my name, which I have not commanded him to speak, or that shall speak in the name of other gods, that same prophet shall die. And if thou say in thine heart, How shall we know the word which Jehovah hath not spoken? when a prophet speaketh in the name of Jehovah, if the thing follow not, nor come to pass, that is the thing which Jehovah hath not spoken: the prophet hath spoken it presumptuously, thou shalt not be afraid of him" [Deuteronomy 18:20-22]. Also note, "The prophet that prophesieth of peace, when the word of the prophet shall come to pass, then shall the prophet be known, that Jehovah hath truly sent him" [Jeremiah 28:9]. One might remember the false prophet Hananiah who broke the yoke off the neck of Jeremiah. He said the yoke of Nebuchadnezzar would vanish from off the necks of the Israelites in two years. Only two months later Hananiah died and Nebuchadnezzar continued his dominance over Judah, thus showing Hananiah to be a false prophet and Jeremiah to be the true prophet Jeremiah 28:12-17 . See also Deuteronomy 13:1-5; Jeremiah 23:13-22. God's children have always been called upon to test the word of their teachers, so John did not introduce anything new.

because many false prophets are gone out into the world - A prophet (PROPHETEUO) is one who speaks for another. In the case of Jehovah, it would be someone who speaks in behalf of, or for, Him. It is not necessary to the meaning of the word, or necessary to the major work of prophets, to include predictive powers. Their major work was not prediction; it was speaking for God. However, some of their work included predictions; and, perhaps because their predictions are so outstanding in history, they are often thought of more as predictors than spokesmen. False prophets (PSEUDOPROHETES) were those not in accord with the truth. They were not God's spokesmen. They might be speaking on their own initiative, or there is the possibility they were speaking under the leading of the devil. Of the former, speaking on their own initiative, Jesus said, "Many false prophets shall arise, and shall lead many astray" (Matthew 24:11). He added, "For there shall arise false Christs, and false prophets, and shall show great signs and wonders; so as to lead astray, if possible, even the elect"

(Matthew 24:24). Paul warned the overseers at Ephesus about false teachers from within and without the congregation (Acts 20:29-30; see also 2 Peter 2:1-2).

As to the latter, false teachers led by the devil, it is possible the devil could have been leading teachers in supernatural ways in the spirit realm. As long as the powers to control and cast out these demons was present, it is possible the demons and their work were present. When apostolic powers ceased, upon the death of the apostles and all those upon whom they had laid their hands and imparted any miraculous gifts, diabolical powers also ceased. John spoke of the devil being bound (Revelations 20:2), that is, in some way now limited in his powers and work. Paul applied a similar thought to Jesus, "he led captivity captive" (Ephesians 4:8) when He ascended on high. That which had man in captivity (sin, death, powers of the devil) was led away, captured by the victorious Jesus Christ. Jesus is also said to have brought to naught the power of the devil (Hebrews 2:14) and to have despoiled principalities and powers (Colossians 2:15). And regarding the possibility of demon-inspired teachers, Paul once referred to "one of themselves, a prophet of their own. . . ," whose testimony happened to be true (Titus 1:12-13). Paul could have been referring to a "prophet" under the guidance of the devil. If teachers were being led in some supernatural way by the devil, it all would have ceased at the close of the first century, at the same time God's miracles ceased.

Verse 2 Hereby know ye the Spirit of God: every spirit that confesseth that Jesus Christ is come in the flesh is of God:

Hereby know ye the Spirit of God - In connection with this problem, there is an accuracy test for teachers: how one accepts Jesus of Nazareth. If they accept Him and teach Him to be the Son of God, they can be trusted. If they do not accept Him as the Son of God, they are false teachers. Man can know (GINOSKETE, either present indicative active or present imperative active) in the sense of observation, deduction, and conclusion. Just as Peter confessed, "Thou art the Christ, the Son of the living God" (Matthew 16:16), there is a sure and infallible test of teachers.

125

every spirit that confesseth that Jesus Christ is come in the flesh is of God - "Every spirit" means every teacher or prophet among them. "Confesseth" (HOMOLOGEI, present indicative) refers not only to a formal one-time acknowledgement, a solemn statement of faith in Jesus as the Christ, but also an on-going agreement. This may tie in more closely with the confession spoken of by Jesus when He sent out the twelve on the limited commission (Matthew 10:32-33) than with the confession made prior to baptism (Romans 10:9-10). See under 1:9.

The real test as stated by John was this: Was there a true enfleshment of God? Was there a union of natures, Divine and human, into one person known as Jesus of Nazareth? Was there an indissoluble union of two natures, human and Divine? In regard to this, there are several things of note.

1. John did not say Jesus came **into** the flesh. This would have been what Cerinthus claimed: God descended, said Cerinthus, into a person already existent and left this person prior to His death. This would mean there was a physical child born to Joseph and Mary into whom God came, a total denial of the virgin birth.

2. John avoids any idea that Jesus only appeared to have a fleshly body, as the Docetics taught. They said this man Jesus was only some sort of apparition, some type of phantasmal being. This would negate any pain, suffering, humiliation, death, shedding of blood, and resurrection. And without these things, there is no meritorious cause for any man's redemption. All saving efficacy would thus vanish, if such were true.

3. The confession that was true would be something expressed like this: Jesus-Christ-come-in-flesh. True incarnation was the enfleshment of God the Son (Hebrews 2:14; John 1:14). It was the actual assumption of human nature in permanent union with Divine. Lenski writes, "Like the seamless garment of Christ, Jesus Christ is one. He who clips off or alters any part never deals with what is immaterial although he may think so!"[4]

4. The use of two names is significant: Jesus is the human name (Matthew 1:21; Luke 1:31; 2:21), and Christ is the title expressing what He became, was made (Acts 2:36; Luke 2:11). He became the "anointed" One, Messiah (Old

Testament), Christ (New Testament). Jesus and the Christ are one and same person; no distinction can be made. He is the Anointed Ruler and King.

5. This union of Divine and human natures was still existent in the days of John. "Is come" is in the perfect tense and shows action done in the past with continuing present results. The union existed in the days of John; the Son of God was still the God-man. This was after the ascension, so John could not have been referring to anything in flesh and blood form, since such could not inherit the kingdom of God (1 Corinthians 15:50). Obviously, one would say, Jesus Christ, at the right hand of God exalted (Acts 2:33), could not have been in any fleshly form. But that He was still both God and man cannot be denied either. This use of the perfect tense does not guarantee anything in the way of permanency, only that it was done in the past and the results remain even now, that is, when John wrote. It was true in John's day: There was a body resurrection, an ascension, plus a return promised (Acts 1:9-11). Jesus was in some form. Either He was still the God-man, both human and divine, or else His humanity ceased to exist somewhere along the line. What could have happened to the human being born of Mary, with human soul? Was it annihilated? Did it just disappear? Or could this be a permanent union? Further study might include Acts 17:31 where we are told our judge will be a **man**; 1 Timothy 2:5, which mentions that the mediator between God and man is **Himself man, Christ Jesus**; and Philippians 3:21, which teaches that our physical bodies in heaven will be conformed to the **body of His glory.**

"Is come" is the more accurate translation in this verse, though NASB, NIV, and RSV all use "has come." This seems to present a weakness in John's argument, making his statement merely a proposition with which to agree. It is not just a proposition, it is a "persona" whom we are to know and love. Jesus Christ is not one who merely "has come"; He is one who "is come."

"In flesh" (EN SARKI) is accurate, as there is the use of the anarthous construction here. It is not "into the flesh," or "in the flesh"; it is simply "in flesh." John gives consistent emphasis to this idea when he specifies that the blood and water came from the body of Jesus (John 19:34-35), as John himself witnessed, and furnished the details of the incident with Thomas (John 20:24-29). In addition, later in this epistle he will mention the water and the blood (1 John 5:6).

"Is of God" - this shows the origin and source of the teachings that any teacher might bring to them. The expression repeats the use in the previous verse.

Verse 3 and every spirit that confesseth not Jesus is not of God: and this the spirit of the anti-christ, whereof ye have heard that it cometh; and now it is in the world already.

and every spirit that confesseth not Jesus is not of God - The same test is now stated in the negative, but there is added some vital information: this problem now involved the spirit of the anti-christ. "Every spirit" (PAN PNEUMA) leaves no room for any exceptions. Those led by the Holy Spirit confessed Jesus; those led by the spirit of the anti-christ did not.

confesseth not Jesus - Literally, this is "not confesses the Jesus," as the definite article ("the") lends emphasis as to which Jesus it is to whom John refers. It is the same Jesus to whom John referred previously (v. 2). Lenski calls this the article of previous reference.[5] That being the case, "the Jesus" is the one previously mentioned in vs. 2 in the fullest sense: "Jesus Christ is come in the flesh." Numerous variant readings are found here in the early manuscripts,[6] but the reading used in the ASV, NASB, and KJV is rated the most accurate.

If God the Son did not assume actual humanity and clothe Himself with flesh and blood, then every action in His life was only a sham. The temptations were not real; He was only acting out a deception. Hunger, sleep, rest, weeping, and all human activities were only the genius of the world's greatest actor. There was no suffering, no pain, no grief, no humiliation. It was all an appearance, a fantasy, a sham. There was no shedding blood, no death, no resurrection; in short, it is the world's worst deception. And we who believe in this Resurrected One are of all men most pitiable (1 Corinthians 15:14-19). This is the crux, the center of all controversy. Either the Son of God became incarnate, died, and rose again, or else all faith is vain.

There is a curious variant reading here that several scholars point out, one that is included in the Latin Vulgate. It would read "who dissolves or divides Jesus," with the use of the verb LUEI, rather than HOMOLOGEI. Such a variant would mean these false teachers divide or separate this person Jesus Christ into two persons — one who appeared, and one who was the reality. The evidence does not support this reading, though it is interesting to study, as it is so close to the thrust of what John is claiming about false teachers and their presentations of Jesus Christ.[7]

and this is the spirit of the anti-christ, whereof ye have heard that it cometh - This spirit who denies proper deity of Jesus is not the Spirit of God as identified in verse 2, but it is another spirit, the spirit of the anti-christ. John seems not to refer to one individual only, but to an entire class of individuals led by the false spirit (see 2:18ff.). Previously, John mentioned they had heard about this anti-christ; now he points out this opposition is come and is working in the world. This denial of Jesus as God is a sample of the false doctrine propagated by this spirit. Previously, John has spoken of "anti-christ" and "the anti-christ"; now he speaks of "the spirit of the anti-christ."

in the world already - "World" is used in the spatial sense, the region where this spirit can run rampant, rule in the lives of sinners, and cause havoc in the lives of saints. His coming to wreak havoc is not something to be experienced only by later generations; it is also now present in John's time. Urgency is the implication. This spirit is here now: be on guard!

Verse 4 Ye are of God, my little children, and have overcome them: because greater is he that is in you than he that is in the world.

Ye are of God, my little children - In an emphatic contrast with "many false prophets" (v. 1), "ye" are "from God" (NASB, NIV) and "ye" are not like "them." Those referred to as "them," next stated in this verse, are the ones the true children of God have overcome. They have overcome the false prophets. John's emphasis is thus given even greater force as he reminds them they are "children," children of God. As children of God they are not among

129

those who imbibe of the spirit of the anti-christ. They are not swayed in their convictions by any of these false teachers. They belong to God, as children of God; false teachers belong to somebody else.

and have overcome them - "them" (AUTOUS) is masculine in gender and refers back to v. 1, the false prophets. If one wished to apply this to the anti-christ spirit (PNEUMA), one would need to notice PNEUMA is neuter in gender, and disagreement in gender will not work in proper interpretation. So the antecedent would go back to the false prophets. "Overcome" (perfect indicative from NIKAO) also carries the meaning of "vanquish, subdue. . .conquer, prevail."[8] Being in the perfect tense, it carries the idea that these believers had gained the victory previously and were still victorious as John presently writes to them. It guarantees nothing in the future but gives hope due to the past and present prevailing. How had they overcome? Physical violence is not suggested; they had only refused the false teachings. They were holding firm to the truth. John mentions an overcoming (also from NIKAO) later and gives three reasons for it: (1) because of the blood of the Lamb, (2) because of the word of their testimony, and (3) because they loved not their lives even unto death [Revelation 12:11].

because greater is he that is in you than he that is in the world - "because" tells why these children were overcomers. The victory is because God is in them ("he that is in you"), as has been claimed previously (3:24). Since God can prevail over the devil and all his teachers, so can God's children, since God dwells in His children. The children must use this power supplied by God; they cannot prevail without God. The conflict is between God and Satan; the Christian has only to choose one of the two. If the choice is God, there is victory.

"He that is in the world" concurs with other references to the spiritual enemy of God, the devil. He is the "prince of this world" (John 14:30; 16:11), "prince of the powers of the air" (Ephesians 2:2), "spirit that now worketh in the sons of disobedience" (Ephesians 2:2), "world rulers of this darkness' (Ephesians 6:12), "spiritual hosts of wickedness in the heavenly places" (Ephesians 6:12), "the god of this world" (2 Corinthians 4:4), and "the evil one" (1 John 5:19). The place of his work is "in the world," using "world" in both a spatial sense and moral sense.

The way one makes a choice, the way one can overcome the devil is by letting God's word abide within (2:14). This is one of the works of the Holy Spirit, who dwells within Christians, the work of helping them overcome. Paul refers to this as being "led by the Spirit" (Romans 8:11). John uses this language: "the word of God abideth in you" (2:14), or conversely "his word is not in us" (1:10), "ye have not his word abiding in you" (John 5:38), or "my word hath not free course in you" (John 8:37). This is the way the "fruit of the Spirit" is produced within the life of a Christian (Galatians 5:22).

Some apply "he that is in you" to God as Triune Deity or to the Second Person, the Son of God. The context suggests that the above reference applies to the Holy Spirit, however, since He was introduced in 3:24, and 4:6 contrasts two spirits. Later, the study of the Holy Spirit will be amplified as the witness-bearer and the truth (5:7-8).

Verse 5 They are of the world: therefore speak they as of the world, and the world heareth them.

They are of the world: therefore speak they as of the world - Again for emphatic contrast, John uses the pronoun "they," standing in apposition to "ye" (v. 4). Perhaps it is also contrasted strongly with "we" (v. 6), which will include even John himself. Thus these false teachers are drawn in sharp contrast with teachers of the truth, "we" (v. 6), as well as those who accept the teachings of truth: "ye" (v. 4). Another special contrast is that of source, or origin. One source is God (vv. 4,6), the other source is the world. "World" is used in the same sense as that when John cautioned them about loving the world (2:15).

Since their source is the world, their speech is also of the world. It is designed to appeal to their worldly senses, their fleshly and carnal appetites. They reflect philosophies, attitudes, and encouragements that debilitate the spiritual nature of man, drawing him down to baser beliefs and ways of life. These false teachers produce what the world in its wisdom can devise; and such is, in reality, foolish in the halls of eternity (1 Corinthians 1:18-25; Colossians 2:8-10).

131

It is not hard to distinguish between teachers who depend upon the Word of God and those teachers who fill their lessons and sermons with worldly wisdom! Unless one is dazzled by human expertise and professional showmanship, it ought to be easy to see whether a man is teaching the Word or sophistry. When a teacher's heart and head are full of worldly wisdom and philosophy, the teacher's mouth will so proclaim (Matthew 12:34; Luke 6:45). It is dangerous to begin to enjoy the messenger more than we enjoy the message! It should be noted also that this message about which John speaks here is a continual speaking, as he uses the customary present terms (LALOUSIN).

and the world heareth them - John pinpoints one of the ways to identify false teachers — the audiences with whom they are popular. The masses would rather hear falsehoods than truth; the masses want someone who will pander to their fleshly appetites, bolster their egos, flatter their pride, and encourage their selfish indulgences. After all, the way to destruction is broad and easy and "many are they that enter in thereby," while at the narrow gate and the strait way, "few are they that find it" (Matthew 7:13-14). Jesus said, "If ye were of the world, the world would love its own" (John 15:19). Jesus also gave the other side of the picture, "And ye shall be hated of all men for my name's sake" (Matthew 10:22), as He sent out the disciples. Paul adds, ". . .not many wise after the flesh, not many mighty, not many noble, are called" (1 Corinthians 1:26). Paul showed consistent concern about this problem, reminding the congregation in Corinth how carefully he came among them initially. ". . .that your faith should not stand in the wisdom of men, but in the power of God" (1 Corinthians 2:5).

It is sad but true: Throngs are too often with the lustful, the itching ears, the ones turning aside from the truth, the fable seekers (2 Timothy 4:1-4). It is not often that the masses are excited about teachings of sacrifice, selfless-ness, service, and the strait way. Woe to the generation of Christians flocking to those who encourage their beds of ease (Amos 6:1).

But what is true about teachers also applies to every Christian. Who are the close friends, who are the closest companions and confidants of Christians? Just who are these that are drawn to us to be our main associates? If they be men and women of worldly pursuits and secular interests, and if this be the continuing thrust of our fellowship, with but few persons and infrequent times of spiritual association, what does that say about us? Is there much cultivation of higher things, spiritual appetites, and appreciation of spiritual values?

Verse 6 We are of God: he that knoweth God beareth us; he who is not of God heareth us not. By this we know the spirit of truth, and the spirit of error.

We are of God: he that knoweth God heareth us; he who is not of God heareth us not - "We" is again noticed to be an emphatic contrast to "they" (v. 5), the false teachers who are of the world. John's use of the first person plural here seems to include John himself as one of the teachers from God. John then proceeds to an indisputable truth: The reception of truth depends upon one's knowledge and one's origin. Whether one receives the truth does not depend upon the skill of the messenger or the arrangements and usages of methods. The reception of truth depends upon the hearer — whether the hearer knows God and whether the hearer is of God. This is similar in thought to Jesus' story of the four soils in which seed was sown (Luke 8:4-8). In His explanation asked for by the disciples, Jesus emphasized that the difference in the harvest depended upon the nature of the soils — not the sower and not the seed (Luke 8:9-15).

The knowledge of God (GINOSKO) is that which is gained by experience and is used in contrast with the falsely claimed knowledge of the Gnostics. Paul also taught that the Gentiles had once known God but rejected Him, ". . .knowing God, they glorified him not as God. . ." (Romans 1:21). Later, Paul mentioned a false philosopher who was "dwelling in the things he hath seen, vainly puffed up by his fleshly mind" (Colossians 2:18), language used to refer to false teachers who claimed special knowledge by visions and revelations, which, in reality, they had not experienced. One of the major differences between the partial knowledge of the Law of Moses and the fuller revelation known in the Law of Christ was that "all shall know me, from the least to the greatest of them" (Hebrews 8:11). The knowledge of God is crucial in one's life;

ignorance leads only to danger and destruction.

Being "of God" is perhaps the shortened form of "begotten of God," referring to those who belong to Him in the family as a child (v. 4).

"Heareth" (AKOUEI) includes listening, giving heed to, understanding, plus a sense of compliance (Matthew 18:15; Acts 4:19). Jesus so stated the same principle, "He that is of God heareth the words of God: for this cause ye hear them not, because ye are not of God" (John 8:47). Is it any wonder some are bored with gospel preaching? Is it possible that those uninterested in the Lord and His church while they live on earth will be interested even in heaven? How could they find heaven exciting and interesting when they have not cultivated any appreciation for heavenly things during their lifetimes? Pretensions of piety will be stripped away in that day, and true interests will be made manifest of those whose actions in life showed a refusal to hear the pleadings of the Lord.

John states the principle both affirmatively and negatively: To know God is to hear His teachers; to be not of God is to refuse to hear His teachers. The change from using "knoweth God" to using "of God" shows that the two ideas are interchangeable. To know God in the biblical sense is to be of Him; and to be of Him is to know Him.

by this we know the spirit of truth, and the spirit of error - The practical summary of this easy identification is how one reacts to the teaching of God's word. A sympathetic, interested, compliant listener is altogether different from the bored, distracted, aloof person, present perhaps in body but not in heart and mind. In the immediate context and problem, John refers to the truth about Jesus Christ who came in the flesh. Gnostics and Docetics were skeptical, aloof, and unreceptive about these verities. The reason they reacted this way was obvious to John: (1) They did not know God in any real, spiritual understanding, and (2) their dispositions and attitudes were emanating from the devil, not prompted by or originating with God.

"Spirit of truth" does not refer to the Holy Spirit, though He is called this in other writings (John 14:17; 15:26; 16:13). It refers more accurately to the spirits that were to be tested and tried (4:1). Surely no one would say the Holy

Spirit ought to be tested for the sake of veracity, and certainly He should not to be tested by Christians. So this use of "spirit of truth" refers more acceptably to the testing of men coming among them in the first century as teachers and the spirit that prompted them. The attitudes, dispositions, and doctrines that characterized them came from a source other than God. Some teachers were characterized by truth, some were characterized by error. The sources were either truth or error, the inner natures of the teachers were prompted by either truth or error. They must be tested, lest false doctrine enter and destroy the faith of some of God's children. "He who hears the apostles shows thereby that the spirit of truth is in him; he who, on the contrary, does not hear them, shows that the spirit of error is in him; it is in his relation to the apostolic teaching that any one shows of what spirit he is the child. But according to the train of thought in this section, it is not the spirit of the hearers, but that of the teachers, that is the subject. . . . That the spirit of error prevails in the false prophets, may be known by this, that the world hears them; that in us, on the contrary, the spirit of truth dwells, may be perceived by this, that those who know God, i.e., the children of God, hear us."[9]

The same test is applicable today. Men who teach accurate doctrine are from God and know God. Men who are careless and ignorant of accurate doctrine, saving truth, are not from God and do not know God. Neither are they doing the work of God, in spite of their public acceptance, popularity, acclaim, and personal expertise. This is why it is so dangerous to be wrapped up in the lovableness and warmth of a teacher's personality; he just might not be from God and might not be teaching the things of God. Following him will damn one's soul, regardless of how much he is admired and loved.

B. Response To Love 4:7-21

1. Accepting God's Love 4:7-11

7Beloved, let us love another: for love is of God; and every one that loveth is begotten of God, and knoweth God. 8He that loveth not knoweth not God; for God is love. 9Herein was the love of God manifested in us, that God hath sent his only begotten Son into the world that we might live through him. 10Herein is love, not that we loved God, but that he loved us, and sent his Son to be the propitiation for our sins. 11Beloved, if God so loved us, we also ought to love one another.

We now enter into the second major division of the subject of the Christian and the world — the response to love (see Outline). We first studied John's reminders of the proper relationship to God; now John proceeds with the response to love. He will speak about accepting God's love, confessing God's love, abiding in God's love, and practicing God's love in these remaining verses in Chapter 4.

John changes topic here, and some say the change is abrupt. It is difficult to see the flow from the previous topic to the present one here, though many profess to see the connection. If so, it is difficult to see. John has been reminding readers of the proper relationship to God (3:1-4:6) and now turns to God's love. This seems to be John's favorite subject, as he dwells on it more than any other. He has introduced love as the basis of treatment of brethren (2:7-11) and then added that love is related to eternal life (3:1-11). One scholar said John's writings about love are the only ones that equal Paul's classic chapter, 1 Corinthians 13. A. T. Robertson said, "Paul's chapter is a perfect prose poem, while John's is like a diamond turned round and round for different angles of light to flash on it."[10]

Verse 7 Beloved, let us love one another: for love is of God; and every one that loveth is begotten of God, and knoweth God.

Beloved, let us love one another - Literally, the expression can be translated "Beloved, we love," if it be translated as a present indicative. It is usually translated as a present subjunctive, therefore the exhortation "let us love." "Beloved" (AGAPATOI), one of six occurrences in the epistle (2:7; 3:2,21; 4:1,7, 11), is now in the context of an exhortation about love itself. The beloved ones are lovers. The present tense means that the beloved ones are continually to love one another.

for love is of God - The origin of true love is God, and this is not just any love. It is "the love" (HA AGAPA), with the use of the definite article. Curiously, this is omitted in most translations (KJV, ASV, NASB, RSV, NIV), but Lenski picks it up in his translation.[11] This is not in general, it is only that love that originates in God. John already had cautioned about love for the world (2:15), so one can love without experiencing this true kind of love. Surely no one would argue that a man's love for the world originated with God! Neither could such a world-lover be begotten of God, as John will teach in this context also. Many men are able to show great love for families and friends, but these men are not God's children; they are not begotten of God, and they do not know God. God is the source of all true love. God has boundless benevolence and an unquenchable good will toward all men. As we learn to imitate this love, we become more godly, like Him.

and every one that loveth is begotten of God, and knoweth God - John used the present participle "loveth," which brings to bear the continual action that matches the continual action of the beginning exhortation. "Is begotten" is the usual perfect tense, as it is an action completed in the past with continuing present results. Having been begotten previously, the child of God now loves and knows.

This is not a description of how one is begotten; it is a description simply of what the begotten ones practice — love. Love is the proof, the sign, the identifier of the ones who belong to God by the new birth. Such is one of the favorite themes of John.

And this love is not just any and every kind of love. Many love families, friends, etc., but they are not among the begotten. This love is a knowing-God love. This love is practiced by a Christian, a true disciple, a follower, a child of God. He "knoweth God" (present indicative active GINISKEI), carrying the force of "he continues to know God." In the shadow of myriad claims of the Gnostics to superior knowledge, John will show that true love and true knowledge are hand in hand. One who loves truly does so out of genuine knowledge. One who is in ignorance of God cannot walk properly in this love. He may practice something similar, but it is not the same love.

Verse 8 He that loveth not knoweth not God; for God is love.

He that loveth not knoweth not God - John's use of both affirmative and negative statements is seen here again. One who loves is begotten of and knows God, and the one not loving does not know God. The continual practice, pattern of life, is suggested again by the use of the present tense participle (AGAPOWN). Next, a purposeful change in verb tense is seen with the use of the aorist "not knoweth God" (EGNO). When describing the Christian, begotten of God, in v. 7, John used two present indicative tenses, "loveth" and "knoweth." Now, in describing the non-Christian, John uses the present indicative tense of "loveth," then changes to the aorist indicative tense for "knoweth." He is saying the non-Christian has not ever come to know God. He presently does not know God and never has known God at any time in the past.

This is a most forceful denial of the Gnostics' claims of knowing God. Exhibiting neither the love of God nor obedience to Him, they do not know Him and **have never known Him!** Let them boast all they please, let them make all the claims they wish; they are not knowledgeable of God. Cerinthus and his crowd may have known much **about** God, but they did not know **Him.** Paul spoke of knowing "him and the power of his resurrection, the fellowship of his sufferings, being conformed unto his death" (Philippians 3:10). Paul enlarged on this, "They profess they know God, but by their works they deny him, being abominable, and disobedient, and unto every good work reprobate" (Titus 1:16). Gnostics were prideful, arrogant, trusting in their own wisdom, education, and knowledge. Showing contempt for other brethren who did not share their educational attainments, they proved their lack of true knowledge by their lack of brotherly love.

for God is love - Literally, this is stated "the God love is." John's use of the definite article leaves no doubt as to the subject and predicate. The language cannot be translated "love is God." The anarthous use of the noun "love" also emphasizes quality, not identity. God is love in the sense that love is the essential quality of His being. No love would equal no God; without love, He could not be God. It is what men style as an attribute, an essential element of deity, without which He cannot be God. Other attributes are listed as eternity, power, knowledge, presence, goodness, mercy, justice, etc. God is infinite, and each of these attributes is infinite in degree within itself. We stagger, we stumble in striving to plumb the depths of His infiniteness. He is, He will ever be this infinite nature. We accept such by faith.

Note some things about the fact that God is love. **First,** when John makes this statement that God is love, he is not intending to give a comprehensive definition of the nature of God. He is only giving a statement of fact that God's nature is characterized by love, permeated by love, and evinces love at every turn. "Love is not so much a quality which God has, as rather the all-embracing total of what he is."[12]

Second, God is said to be spirit (John 4:24) and light (1 John 1:5). Neither of these is intended to be comprehensive in definition. It is just one way John helps man who is striving to understand the Infinite One. Man is thereby able to view from different aspects this one who is God.

Third, everything God does is done in love. He rules out of love for man, He chastens because He loves man, He forgives out of love, He gives gifts unto men because of love, He created the earth and mankind by love, He commands instructions for the good of man because He loves man, and He will judge us all some day in love. Nothing God does or has ever done was prompted in the absence of love. God is love and everything He does is done in love.

Fourth, love (understood accurately) is always in harmony with God's law. It is in harmony with His commands, His chastening, and His judgments. Love is always holy, pure, righteous and just. Man may not see at

139

present how the perfect love of God destroyed Sodom (Genesis 19; Luke 17:28-32), but the destruction took place out of love, for God is love.

Fifth, twisted and inaccurate views of love are those that say that God cannot punish good moral people, damn any souls to hell, or demand a blood sacrifice of His Son. This is to limit God to what man can see. It is to say God's concept of love is no higher than man's. Our own concepts do not make our God! He is, has ever been, will ever be; we see so imperfectly and struggle so ineffectively to understand. We can stretch our finite minds only so far; even at these limits we can only grasp an infinitesimal fraction of His being and nature. "O the depth of the riches both of the wisdom and the knowledge of God! how unsearchable are his judgments, and his ways past tracing out. For who hath known the mind of the Lord? or who hath been his counsellor? or who hath first given to him and it shall be recompensed unto him again? For of him, and through him, and unto him, are all things. To him be the glory for ever. Amen." (Romans 11:33-36)

God is not "full of love"; He is love. He is not simply the "most benevolent of all beings"; He is love. He did not simply "show love to His creatures"; He is love. He does not "manifest love to man"; He is love. These false concepts, and many like them, are man's mistaken musings. John says God is love. Love originates with God and is the indivisible essence of His very being.

John has now given four reasons for us to be loving persons as His children: (1) love is of God [v. 7], (2) everyone that loveth is begotten of God [v. 7], (3) he that loveth knoweth God [v. 7], (4) God is love [v. 8].

Verse 9 Herein was the love of God manifested in us, that God hath sent his only begotten Son into the world that we might live through him.

Herein was the love of God manifested in us - John now moves away from the abstract idea that God is love and declares the practical proof of such love: He sent His Son. The incarnation is the best proof of God's love. This is the supreme act of love; no other comes close in comparison. Paul spoke of the love in terms of "breadth and length and height and depth" (Ephesians 3:18). Job spoke of the futility of man's seeking to know God in similar terms, as God is "high as heaven. . .deeper than Sheol. . .longer than the earth, and broader than the sea" (Job 11:8-9).

The use of the aorist "was manifested" (EPHANAROTHA) shows completed punctiliar action and perhaps suggests a former statement found in John 3:16. The use of "manifested" means God's love had previously existed, then was later shown to man. This is consistent with John's claim that the very nature of God is love. Since God existed previously, love must also have been in existence. Since God is love, His love is as timeless as He is; it is essential to His nature, and without it He is not God. This love could not be man's love for God, since this love prompted God to send His Son (John 3:16). Man's love for God did not cause the sending of Jesus, for man's love was not that which was first present in the relationship of man and God. God's love was first present, and God's love is that which prompted Him to send His Son. It was while we were "yet sinners" and "enemies" that "God commendeth his own love toward us" (Romans 5:8-10).

"In us" has an interesting footnote in the ASV, "in our case." And another footnote in the NIV and RSV has "among us." The KJV translates this phrase "toward us." This phrase simply refers to a historical event that took place among mankind.

that God hath sent his only begotten Son into the world - The word order of this explanatory clause is significant. When something is placed first in the grammatical construction, it is emphasized as more important. Literally, the text reads "because the Son of him the only begotten has sent the God." The emphasis is therefore on this "only begotten Son."

"Hath sent" (APESTALKEN, perfect indicative active) is a verb that is related closely to the noun "apostle" (APOSTOLOS). It is used of one sent on a mission, speaking in behalf of another, a messenger. Thus, the Son was sent on a mission and is a messenger with a message.

his only begotten Son - This word "only begotten" is a subject of much controversy, as there are important textual problems here. "Only begotten" is not used in the RSV, the NIV, or most of the more recent translations. Rather they use "only Son" (RSV), "one and only Son" (NIV, while the footnote has "Or, his only begotten Son"). The term used (MONOGENES) comes from two words: MONOS "only," and GENOS "kind." MONOS is defined as "singly existent, sole, only. . .alone," while GENOS is defined as "kind, sort, species. . .offspring, progeny. . .family, kindred, lineage . . .race, nation, people."[13] MONOGENES is defined in John's writings as "only begotten in respect of peculiar generation."[14]

John is speaking of a unique son, a single one of its kind, the only one, one-of-a-kind, a solitary one. There is no other son like him. John mainly uses TEKNA and TEKNIA (children and little children) for himself and other Christians, while using HUIOS (son) mostly to refer to Jesus Christ. Some make a hard and fast distinction and claim that John does not use HUIOS for believers, that he reserves that term only for Jesus Christ. This presents a problem in at least two passages: (1) "While ye have the light, believe on the light, that ye may become sons of light;" [John 12:36] and (2) "He that overcometh shall inherit these things; and I will be his God, and he shall be my son" [Revelation 21:7]. In both of these passages, HUIOS is used and must refer to believers, Christians. A peculiar twist is given at this point, as those same claimants say these are the sayings of Jesus and not John, as John is only quoting Jesus and would not have used the word himself! Yet the very fact John is quoting Jesus shows the Lord used HUIOS to refer to believers. Do the claimants want to say John disagreed with the Lord? Jesus did not make this artificial distinction between HUIOS and TEKNA, as if HUIOS can be used only to refer physical begettal and to the Only Begotten Son, for He even used it to refer to James and John as "Sons of thunder" (Mark 3:17)!

Further, Paul often used HUIOS to refer to believers (at least ten times, perhaps seven more times if he be the author of Hebrews; see Romans 8:14; 9:26; 2 Corinthians 6:18; Galatians 3:26; 4:6, etc.). Will the claimants say there is a difference in the theology about Jesus between Paul and John? Did Paul not believe as John? If this be the claim, the very heart of inspiration is attacked.

Since Jesus and Paul did not make this distinction in their use of HUIOS, and since John included the use of HUIOS twice within his writings to refer to believers, it is unwise to make such distinction a point of too much controversy.

This unique relationship does not imply or entail that Jesus ever began to be the Son of God; rather, it suggests an eternal relationship. He was the Son of God before His enfleshment. The birth by Mary was not the beginning of His existence or even His existence as the Son of God. All she bore was the human baby. And the baby's father was the Holy Spirit (Matthew 1:20; Luke 1:35). The begettal of the baby was the action of the Spirit, not the Father. If this word refers to the physical birth of Jesus by Mary, then Jesus would have been the Only Begotten Son of the Spirit! It is not enough to say the Father generated this baby by the agency of the Spirit and thus is still the Father. The Father sent the Son to die for sins, but it is never said the Father died for sins. Separations cannot be made within the Godhead, but distinctions of their work and function can be seen and ought to be respected. Thus this word MONOGENES cannot refer to the birth by the virgin. Jesus was surely born of a virgin named Mary in Bethlehem, but this word is not what proves that. This word is not used by John to refer to Jesus' physical birth at all.

MONOGENES is used nine times in the New Testament, five times by John in reference to Christ (John 1:14,18; 3:16,18; 1 John 4:9). It is used elsewhere in reference to the son of the widow of Nain (Luke 7:12), the daughter of Jairus (Luke 8:42), the son in whom a demon dwelled (Luke 9:38), and Isaac (Hebrews 11:17). In the case of the widow's son, MONOGENES could not mean she begat an only son, for a woman gives birth, she does not beget. In the case of Isaac, the Bible tells of others sons of Abram: Ishmael, Zimran, Jokshan, Medan, Midian, Ishbak and Shuah (Genesis 16:15; 25:1-2). So in neither one of these cases could MONOGENES be taken literally. It must mean a son in some figurative, not literal sense, a unique son, a one-of-a-kind son. Isaac was such to Abram in the sense that he was the only son by promise.

In the LXX, MONOGENES is used to translate the Hebrew YACHID, which means "only" and "only beloved." So the translators of that time did not take MONOGENES to refer to physical begettal or generation, but to that which was the only one of its kind.

If John had intended to refer to the begettal of Jesus when He was born of Mary, he would have used another word; and it would have had to be in the passive, not active verb tense. He would have used GENNAO, not GENOS. He would have thus used the word MONOGENNETOS, not MONOGENES. Even when the verb GENNAO is used and translated "begotten" (Acts 13:33; Hebrews 1:5; 5:5), it is not used in reference to the birth of Jesus Christ. It is used of His resurrection and coronation (Acts 13:33) and of the eternal preexistent relation the Son had with the Father in eternity past (Hebrews 1:5; 5:5). One must remember this Second Person of the Godhead never began to be; He is eternal. Incarnation began at the birth from Mary.

"In 1 John 4:9 the statement 'God hath sent His Only Begotten Son into the world' does not mean that God sent out in the world one who at His birth in Bethlehem had become His Son. Cp. the parallel statement, 'God sent forth the Spirit of His Son,' (Galatians 4:6, R.V.), which could not mean that God send forth One who became His Spirit when He sent Him."[15]

It seems the idea of earthly sonship, begettal in Mary, and the use of "only begotten Son" can be attributed to Jerome when he revised the Old Latin Bible. In the Latin, Jerome added the idea of "son," and it has been retained by the translators of the KJV, ASV, NASB, etc.[16]

"Only begotten Son" in this passage is much like other words and phrases with which we are familiar in our English Bibles. If we know what "church," "baptism," "Holy Ghost," and "bishop" mean in our English Bibles, there is no problem. "Bishop" is a poor translation of EPISKOPOS used in the KJV four times (Philippians 1:1; 1 Timothy 3:2; Titus 1:7; 1 Peter 2:25). Two other times a variation is used (Acts 1:20; 1 Timothy 3:1). The word is translated more correctly as "overseers" (ASV, NASB). When modern readers, who realize the correct meaning of the word, use the KJV and come across "bishop," they will understand it to mean "overseer." The words "church" and "baptism" often are accorded the same mental discernment. Sometimes "church" refers to a local congregation (Acts 14:23), sometimes it refers to the entire called out body of people who belong to the Lord (Matthew 16:18), and it can refer to a secular assembly of people in any given town (Acts 19:32,41). "Baptism" can refer to the religious experience of the new birth (Romans 6:2-5, 16-17), it can refer to ceremonial ablutions of the Jews (Mark 7:4; Luke 11:38), and it can refer to an immersion that was invalid, out of date (Acts 19:3). And "Holy Ghost" is not even used consistently by the KJV, the only modern version which still translates PNEUMA as "ghost" rather than "spirit," for there are numerous times the KJV translates the word as "spirit." (See Luke 11:13; Ephesians 1:13; 4:30; 1 Thessalonians 4:8; Isaiah 63:10-11). So, being accustomed to such differences in meanings, informed readers will make proper distinctions. The use of "only begotten Son" will remain that way to discerning readers and students. That it does not refer to the enfleshment of Jesus through Mary is something that needs to be remembered.

into the world - Again John uses the word in a spatial sense. It is where the people live who needed the Son.

that we might live through him - This clause expresses purpose — life with God. Jesus claimed to be the "life" (John 14:6), for "in him was life" (John 1:4), and He is "the resurrection and the life" (John 11:25), He has life in Himself (John 5:26), and those who follow Him have "passed from death into life" (John 5:24). It is as John will later say, "He that hath the Son hath life" (1 John 5:12).

Verse 10 Herein is love, not that we loved God, but that he loved us, and sent His Son to be the propitiation for our sins.

Herein is love, not that we loved God - Explaining that of which love consists, John will give the example in the latter part of this verse. This great gift is the highest expression ever of love. It is not our love for God that can demonstrate the true nature of love, for mankind is imperfect. This love is found in perfection only in the nature of God. This love does not originate with man and is not that demonstrated very well by man. It is a love that is ultimately for the benefit of man, but it cannot be said to be attributable to man.

145

but that he loved us and sent his Son to be the propitiation for our sins - John uses a strong adversative conjunction "but" (ALLA) to draw a sharp contrast between any love man can muster and the highest of all love, that of God. Again John uses the aorist tense "loved" and "sent" to indicate the point of time of the incarnation. His love was not only verbal, it was active. He expressed His nature by action taken; He sent His Son as the propitiation. God's love therefore provided the holy and righteous basis on which man can be forgiven of his sins. Otherwise, God could not be just and righteous in justifying men from their sins (Romans 3:26). God's law is violated by sin; God must not be unjust or partial in any way. God's love enacted a way to save man: God provided God Himself, in the person of the Son, to satisfy His own holy demand of death for sins. (On the study of "propitiation" in full, see 2:2).

Notice the statements leading up to this in the context:

- v. 8 God is love
- v. 8 Anyone who knows God must also love.
- v. 9 God's love was manifested among us.
- v. 9 God's love was manifested among us by His Son.
- v. 9 God's love brings life to man.
- v. 10 True love is not from man.
- v. 10 True love is from God.
- v. 11 True love is shown by sending His Son.

John's gradual unfolding of this topic of love has led students up to the practical consequences of such love. This will be a challenge to the "oughtness" found in every Christian.

Verse 11 Beloved, if God so loved us, we also ought to love one another.

Beloved, if God so loved us - Here is the final place "beloved" (AGAPATOI) is used by John. Perhaps, in the use of "if" (EI), there is an unhappy translation. There is no doubt that God loves us, and any translation that opens the way to suggesting such a false idea is, to say the least, an unhappy translation. EI used with the indicative states what is rhetorical and obvious. Perhaps it would make better sense to translate it "since God so loved us," or even "if thus God did love us."[17] He surely and certainly did love us, as just stated in sending His Son to be the propitiation for our sins.

The adverb "so" (HOUTOS) can refer to manner or extent. It is best understood here as an adverb of extent, as it shows how far God is willing to go for the benefit of mankind. These exact words are also found in John 3:16.

we also ought to love one another - "Ought" (OPHEILOMEN, present tense of OPHEILO) refers to an ongoing obligation; it continues. It is used three times in this epistle: (1) ought to walk [2:6]; (2) ought to lay down our lives [3:16]; and (3) ought to love one another [4:11].

Is it strange that the conclusion is to love one another, rather than to love God? John has just spoken of God's love to man, thus giving the reason for man to love someone in return. Why does John not say that man, loved so wonderfully by God, ought to love God in return? Why speak of the obligation to love man in return for God's loving us? It is because John has already taught the mark of identity of those who belong to God is the love of their fellowman (2:7-11; 3:14,23; 4:7). Gnostics could ignore brethren yet claim to love God. John says such is not the case if it be proper love. God's love was directed to others in need (all men are sinners), so "also" (KAI) we ought to direct our love to others in need, our fellowman (3:17-18 "brother in need").

2. Confessing God's love 4:12-15

¹²No man hath beheld God at any time: if we love one another, God abideth in us; and his love is perfected in us: ¹³hereby we know that we abide in him and he in us, because he hath given us of his Spirit. ¹⁴And we have beheld and bear witness that the Father hath sent the Son to be the saviour of the world. ¹⁵Whosoever shall confess that Jesus is the Son of God, God abideth in him, and he in God.

In dealing with the Christian and the world, John has remarked to us of the proper relationship to God (3:1-4:6), and now the study has proceeded to the response to love (4:7-21). John has covered the area of accepting God's love (4:7-11), so now we advance to confessing God's love (4:12-15). It is most important for the Christian to declare the truth about the Son of God, as churches were infiltrated with many who were incorrect in their concepts of Jesus.

Verse 12 No man hath beheld God at any time: if we love one another, God abideth in us, and his love is perfected in us:

No man hath beheld God at any time - Again John uses word order in the sentence for emphasis, placing the direct object of the verb first in the sentence. He writes (literal translation), "God no man ever has beheld." The thought seems to be that even though God cannot and has not been seen by man, His influence on man can be seen when brethren evince love toward one another. This love provides proof that God abides in men. Many may claim visions and special knowledge, but in actuality, no man has ever seen God. The proof that God abides in one is seen if that one is a lover of his brothers. All verbal protestations could be voiced; but if his conduct is to the contrary, he does not have much relationship with God.

"Beheld" (perfect tense of THEAOMAI) refers to careful scrutiny and examination. No man has ever, "at any time," been able to thus scrutinize the character and person of God. God is "spirit" (John 4:24), and all references to men seeing God are temporary theophanies, anthropomorphic in nature. No man hath seen God at any time (John 1:18), He is the invisible God (Colossians 1:15), He is eternal, immortal, invisible (1 Timothy 1:17), He is the One whom no man hath seen or can see (1 Timothy 6:16), and He is the one who is unseen (Hebrews 11:27). Even Moses' remarkable experience of seeing His "back" but not His face (Exodus 33:17-23) did not allow Moses to see the very nature of God, for such is impossible to be seen by the fleshly eyes of man. Moses was given an extraordinary experience, but one must realize the impossibility that the finite can see the infinite.

if we love one another, God abides in us - The proof of God abiding in us is not whether we have seen God, it is whether we love one another. When we love the brethren, we can know God remains in us. Our acquaintance with God is not by mortal sight; it is by perfecting love in our lives. Our assurance of His presence depends not on beholding Him in some special vision or manifestation; our assurance

148

is from our practice of the same kind of love He first showed toward us.

It should be remembered John is not teaching the **means** of God's coming to abide with us. He is emphasizing that loving one another is the **evidence** of such a relationship. Merely practicing love for fellow man does not make one a Christian. It is not the way to establish the relationship; it does not cause one to be born anew. A Christian, however, has evidence in his life that he is truly born again if he shows love for the brethren. If he is a hater, if he enjoys hurting others, if he takes delight in gossip, slander, busybodying and tearing down others, he is missing the presence of God in his life.

his love is perfected in us - Lenski translates this: "his love has been brought to its goal in us."[18] This helps one understand that God's kind of love is what is shown when brethren love one another. It is godly love. "Is perfected in us" is said by many to be periphrastic, an additional way of saying God's love is in us. When we love the brethren, God's love has reached its intended goal in our lives. It is not a claim of perfect or flawless love in our lives. It only proves that God's influence in our lives is not demonstrated well until we learn to love our brethren. If our life is characterized by continual conflict and anger toward brethren, we are not among those who evidence God's instructions.

John has thus picked up a theme previously introduced — the perfecting of love in the life of a Christian. It is one of the major themes interwoven throughout the book: love.

2:5 — "whoso keepeth his word, in him verily hath the love of God been perfected."

3:1 — "Behold, what manner of love the Father hath bestowed on us"

3:16 — "Hereby know we love, because he laid down his life for us"

4:8 — "God is love"

4:9 — "Herein was the love of God manifested in us"

In this way, John builds on and on to a crescendo climax. God's love is the source of our love, the expressions of our love are to be reflections of His love, we are the recipients of God's love and, in turn, others should receive our love.

So, a practical test is coming, announced later in this context: Do we love or hate our brethren (4:20-21)?

Verse 13 hereby we know that we abide in him and he in us, because he hath given us of his Spirit.

hereby we know that we abide in him and he in us - By this the writer means that we can have assurance of God's fellowship. This is almost a restatement of 3:24, "And he that keepeth his commandments abideth in him, and he in him." This means is described subsequently as the gift of His Spirit. And this is not at all surprising, since the fruit of the Spirit begins with the principle of love (Galatians 5:22-23). "Love perfected in us" (v. 12) and God's abiding "in us" are interlocked by John's statement. If love is perfected in us, God is in us; if love is not perfected in us, God is not in us. John will now give three indicators that we have such a relationship with God: (1) by the indwelling Spirit, (2) by the witness of the apostles, and (3) by the confession Christians are called upon to make, verses 14-15.

because he hath given us of his Spirit - This is one way a man knows he is abiding in God: is God (the Spirit) abiding in him? "He has given" (DEDOKEN) is perfect tense, showing completed action in the past but with present results continuing. In similar language, "by the Spirit which he gave us" (3:24), John used EDOKEN, an aorist tense which showed completed past action. There John speaks of a simple fact: God gave us His Spirit. Here John adds the idea of continuing possession by the change in verb tenses. It is true He has given us of His Spirit. Additionally, we can understand that the results of such a gift continue into the present relationship.

There is some disagreement and puzzlement in this verse, however, by John's use of EK when God gave us "of (EK) his Spirit." Lenski claims the preposition shows source and is not partitive at all. He translates it, "he has given to us from his Spirit."[19] His question about all this is intriguing: "Since when is the Holy Spirit divided into parts?" This is a most appropriate question since obviously the Holy Spirit cannot be divided into parts (which would it be: pints, quarts, and gallons or ephahs, hins and homers?). A person is not divided into parts, and the Holy Spirit is truly a person, not a power to be rationed out in parts. (Now let's

150

see, did each of the apostles have one-twelfth of the Holy Spirit? Was the quantity thinned down even more when the apostles laid their hands on other men and imparted spiritual gifts? When Paul received the Holy Spirit, was it now only one-fourteenth, counting Matthias? When Paul imparted this to twelve other men in Ephesus [Acts 19:6], did they have one-twelfth of one-twelfth, or one-one hundred and forty-fourth? Such is so ridiculous to all; why even consider such a concept!) When one remembers the Holy Spirit either dwells or does not dwell, then the oft-made mistakes of saying a man has "more of the Holy Spirit in him than another" will not be made. The Holy Spirit is a person and just cannot be conceived as being given out in parts and pieces to men. He can abide in all believers, even as he could abide in all the apostles, plus all of those upon whom the apostles laid their hands. This could be done without a ridiculous idea of parts and measures on the one hand, or the equally ridiculous idea of pantheism on the other hand.

There is a major difference in the abiding of the Holy Spirit in the first century and His abiding in the succeeding centuries. Then it was for the purpose of working miracles; now it is not for the working of miracles. The Person dwelling is the same; the empowering is not the same. The Spirit came upon the apostles at Pentecost (Acts 2:1-4) to empower them to perform their work as apostles (Luke 24:49; Acts 1:8). The Spirit came also upon the house of Cornelius (Acts 10:44-46), empowering them to perform **only on and for that occasion.** They were not empowered to perform as apostles; their speaking in tongues and magnifying God confirmed to Peter and the six accompanying brethren that God wanted the gospel preached to the Gentiles. Such coming of the Spirit was "even as on us at the beginning" (Acts 11:15) and was called the "like gift" (Acts 11:17). The gift given was the same: the Holy Spirit Himself. The empowerment differed. The Holy Spirit was given to the apostles to do the work of an apostle. The Holy Spirit was given to Cornelius to do a work of approving Peter's announcement of the gospel to Gentiles. The Holy Spirit is given to each Christian today to effect fellowship and sanctification. Thus one should not conceive of the Holy Spirit as being given out in parts. Cornelius had no less of the Spirit than did an apostle; the apostles had no more than Cornelius. They both simply had Him. He did with them what the will of God required in both cases.

How does one know today of the indwelling? God's indwelling Spirit cannot be known in any physical way today. He cannot be felt, heard, seen, or sensed in any empirical way. In New Testament days, men could perform observable miracles; today men cannot. Yet, there are some deeper insights which one might study.

1. How does one know he is saved? It is known only because God's word says so (Mark 16:16; Acts 2:38; 22:16). So also does the Christian know the Holy Spirit dwells in him: God's word says so.

2. Is one producing the fruit of the Spirit in daily life: "love, joy, peace, longsuffering, kindness, goodness, faithfulness, meekness, self-control" (Galatians 5:22-23)?

3. Has one crucified the flesh (Galatians 5:24), the world (Galatians 6:14)?

4. Has one obeyed God (Acts 5:32)?

5. Is one a son of God (Galatians 4:6; 3:26-27)?

6. Does one believe the witness of the Spirit (Romans 8:16)?

7. Has one heard the gospel, believed it, and been sealed (Ephesians 1:13-14; 2 Corinthians 1:22)?

8. Is one putting to death the deeds of the body (Romans 8:13)?

9. Does one love God and one another (1 John 4:12)?

All of these things will show to the child of God that God's Holy Spirit is dwelling in him. There will be no communication directly to the Christian by such indwelling Spirit; the only method of communication available from heaven to earth is the only one that will ever be used, the written Word! One either believes in such promises and relationships or one does not. The Word is very plain about these things, and Christians can understand them, trust in the promises, and wait patiently on the Lord as such sanctifying effects are produced in the growing and maturing Christian (2 Peter 3:18).

Verse 14 And we have beheld and bear witness that the Father hath sent the Son to be the Saviour of the

world.

And we have beheld and bear witness - Who is the "we"? It could be understood in several interpretations: (1) an "editorial we," common among writers of all ages; (2) the apostles as eyewitnesses; (3) the author and his readers; or (4) the first century church. Since the apostles were commissioned to "bear witness" (Acts 1:8; Luke 24:48; John 15:27), since the successor of Judas has to be a witness (Acts 1:22), and since John emphasized this so greatly in his introduction to this epistle (1:1-4), it seems best to apply this only to the apostles. Christians have never been told to "witness" in this sense, and the denominational concepts and practices are unwarranted.

"Have beheld" (TETHEAMETHA) is perfect tense and reminds us of the apostles, including John, who saw, heard, beheld, and handled the resurrected Jesus. This was a subjective witnessing of historical fact. It happened. John and the other apostles saw and experienced it. Now they are ready as witnesses to attest to the facts of the matter. "Bear witness" (MARTUROUMEN) is present tense and attests to continous testimony from John and the other apostles.

that the Father hath sent the Son to be the Saviour of the world - Interestingly, this is literally "has sent the Son Saviour of the world." The KJV, ASV, NASB show accuracy by putting "to be" in italics, since they are words added by the translators. RSV says, "sent his Son as Saviour," while the NIV uses "to be" without italicizing. Jesus is the "Son-Saviour" whom God "hath sent" (APESTALKEN, perfect tense), emphasizing abiding results of past action by God. This is similar to John 3:16 in that this Person was already a Son when given or sent (Galatians 4:4). Jesus was the unique "Son-Saviour" before being sent. Now sent, He is to accomplish something for the benefit of the entire human race ("the world").

"Saviour" (SOTER) is used only twenty-four times in the New Testament, only two times by John (here and in John 4:42). It means "saviour, deliverer, preserver."[20] John already introduced this concept when he spoke of Jesus as the propitiation for the entire world (2:2).

Verse 15 Whosoever shall confess that Jesus is the Son of God, God abideth in him, and he in God.

153

Whosoever shall confess that Jesus is the Son of God
This "whosoever" is consistent with "the world" of the previous sentence. Anyone who can come to belief is acceptable. No sense of limited atonement is found here. "Shall confess" (see 4:2 and 1:9 for full discussion of N. T. confessions) is an aorist tense (HOMOLOGESE) and shows the one-time confession made at the beginning of one's relationship to Christ. It is the same as that mentioned in Romans 10:9-10, exemplified by Timothy's statement in the "sight of many witnesses" (1 Timothy 6:12). Such confession excluded all Gnostics, as they would not confess "Jesus Christ in the flesh" (4:2). Any inspired teacher could be identified easily, for men thus led by the Holy Spirit confessed this truth (1 Corinthians 12:3). Gnostics would not and could not so confess; therefore, they were not inspired by the Spirit. As far as the matter goes, they were not even true Christians. When one remembers that the Docetics taught the Son of God only appeared to have a physical body and that Cerinthus taught the physical body of Jesus was inhabited only for a short period of time by God (from the baptism to the arrest and trial), then one can see neither party could be genuine in any confession that Jesus Christ (Anointed Messiah) was come in the flesh. Neither theory would allow for the body and blood of the Lord to be given in the stead of sinners.

God abideth in him, and he in God - This is stated in the reverse order of v. 13, but the meaning is the same. There is mutual spiritual indwelling, a reciprocal abiding, the closest fellowship and communion possible. "Abideth" (MENEI) is present tense, with the force of continuous action, i.e., now abides and continues to abide.

John now progresses in his interweaving of great themes to God's love and the practicing of God's love, which will take up the rest of the chapter.

3. Abiding in God's love 4:16-18

[16]And we know and have believed the love which God hath in us. God is love; and he that abideth in love abideth in God, and God abideth in him. [17]Herein is love made perfect with us, that we may

have boldness in the day of judgment; because as he is, even so are we in this world. [18]There is no fear in love: but perfect love casteth out fear, because fear hath punishment; and he that feareth is not made perfect in love.

Verse 16 And we know and have believed the love which God had in us. God is love: and he that abideth in love abideth in God, and God abideth in him.

And we know and have believed the love which God hath in us - John changes the use of "we" from v. 14 where it referred to the apostles. Now he uses "we" to refer to himself and all his readers. One reason for this might be that "in us" is where God's love is manifested, and such love is manifested more broadly than just in the apostles, as stated back in v. 9. **Second,** the apostles beheld (TETHEAMETHA, that is, carefully observed) and bore witness (MARTUROUMEN), v. 14. **Third,** the verbal ideas change to "come to know" (EGNOKAMEN, perfect indicative of GINOSKO) and "have believed" (PEPISTEUKAMEN, perfect indicative of PISTEUO). John's readers are the ones coming to know and believing, not the apostles. His readers are also continuing in the results of this knowledge and belief since these verbs, as cited above, are in the perfect tense.

The word order of these two verbs, know and believe, is interesting. Knowing (GINOSKO) is generally thought of as preceding belief (PISTEUO), as it is used here. GINOSKO generally speaks of "to know. . .to perceive. . .to ascertain by examination."[21] Vine adds, "to be taking in knowledge, to come to know, recognize, understand, or to understand completely."[22] Such knowledge precedes belief, as used here by John. It is necessary to know some facts about Jesus Christ before one can have proper faith in him as God's Son (John 20:30-31). Faith does not come out of ignorance, but rather from knowing the facts in the Word of God (Romans 10:17). However, John also used the reverse order "and we have believed and know that thou art the Holy One of God" (John 6:69). He used the same two verbs in the perfect tense (PEPISTEUKAMEN and EGNOKAMEN). So, in some spiritual matters of maturity, it can be said properly that because one believes, one will accept God at His word and know some difficult things within the gospel. A man knows, not by his own perceptions and examination of facts, but by accepting God's account of the matter. Thus the Christian can know God created the world, or that a judgment day is coming, etc. Such knowledge follows our faith, proceeds out from it.

This "love which God hath in us" includes the entire scope of the incarnation. One cannot have proper belief if one does not include the epitome of God's love: "For God so loved the world that he gave his only begotten Son. . ." (John 3:16). How could Cerinthus understand properly the love God has in us if he believed the physical body born of Mary was inhabited only temporarily by the Son of God? He missed the scope and breadth of God's love. By faulty knowledge, his belief had to be faulty also. If he and the Docetics could have come to know that God's unique love succeeded in making the vital connection with man in the incarnation, he could have had proper faith. Without such knowledge, his faith could never be right, his life could never be right.

This love "in us" refers to more than just the love that God has "for us." Most versions use "in us" (ASV, NASB, NIV, RSV) and a footnote in the ASV says "Or, **in our case.**" This love "in us" may refer to the fact that as Christians love one another, this is God's love "in us" at work. Perhaps the same thought is given as "because the love of God hath been shed abroad in our hearts through the Holy Spirit which was given to us" (Romans 5:5). When the Christian can rejoice in tribulation (Romans 5:3), Paul claims God's love is at work in our hearts as we love others. So John declares Christians are the ones loved by God in a way that, in effect, causes this same godly love to flow through them to the brethren and all men.

God is love; and he that abideth in love abideth in God, and God abideth in him - "God is love" looks back to v. 8, "for God is love." It is common for John to repeat for emphasis. When Christians love properly, they are that much godly; i.e., they are developing traits and characteristics in their lives that are similar to God. God in His essence is love (AGAPE), His actions are out of love, and He is the source of love. Therefore, one dwelling in God will practice love. Or, it can be said, one dwelling in love dwells in God.

This love is not simply an object of righteous chatter and glib talk. John had predicated love about which he speaks on several things: (1) the confessing of Jesus Christ in the flesh, v. 2; (2) proper knowledge of God versus the spirit of error, v. 6; (3) being begotten of God, v. 7; (4) the acceptance of His unspeakable gift of His Son, vv. 10-14. So this love is not shallow, simpering sentiment or affection; it is knowledgeable, active, obedient, and such as will bow before its Maker. The Gnostics could claim all the fellowship with God they wished by citing their abilities to be loving. Their true stance as heretics would show when their claimed love did not include the proper knowledge, beliefs, and allegiances to and about Jesus, along with proper actions toward the brethren.

This statement by John, "God is love," is the essence of good news to mankind. God's very nature, essence, is expressed by sending His Son for our sins. What better news can come to sinful man? Paul argued that such salvation, provided by a loving God, brought rejoicing in man's heart (Romans 5:6-11). And this same knowledge of God's willingness to justify man by faith, rather than by perfect obedience of lawkeeping, would produce faith in the hearts of searching men (Romans 1:17). This "righteousness' spoken of by paul refers to justification, not to the righteousness that is the attribute of God's holy nature. This is the righteousness-of-God-by-faith, and it will be "unto faith"; i.e., it will produce faith in the yearning hearts of men. Who can give full gratitude to such a staggering concept? When a world, justly condemned by its own wretchedness and sinfulness, is given the gospel out of the overflowing heart of our loving God, who can describe that gift adequately? It is incredible, indescribable, and certainly beyond the knowledge and acceptance of the first century Gnostics. "Thanks be to God for his unspeakable gift" (2 Corinthians 9:15).

A key word expressing this glorious relation with God is "abide" (MENEI), which appears three times in the latter part of v. 16. It is the present tense all three times and multiplies the idea of duration. In effect, we have "the one who continues to dwell in love, continues to dwell in God, and God continues to dwell in him." Ross stated the thought aptly as he said, "John thus repeats the great words **God is love,** but in the words that follow he does not merely repeat himself, for, instead of writing 'he that loveth,' he writes, 'he that has his home in the blessed domain of love has his home in God and God has his home in him.' "[23]

The fact this mutual abiding is similarly stated in v. 15 is interesting. There the mutual dwelling and remaining is conditioned on confessing the truth of Jesus as the Son of God. Here, the dwelling and remaining is conditioned on whether one loves as God loves. It is altogether proper therefore to say one who does not confess Jesus as the Son of God and the Christ does not love as God loves. Or, the one who does not love as God loves is the one who refuses to confess Jesus to be the Son of God. Let the Docetic and Gnostic heretics claim all the love they wish; their lack of true confession about Jesus as God Incarnate shows their lack of proper love. This lack of proper love indicates also a lack of proper fellowship with God.

Verse 17 Herein is love made perfect with us, that we may have boldness in the day of judgment; because as he is, even so are we in this world.

Herein is love made perfect with us - Other versions have "In this" (RSV) and "By this" (NASB), but John now shows the application of this love, or a result of this love. This mutual-dwelling, like-loving, home-abiding relationship with God will produce a fruitful result in our lives. True maturity of love will result. This "love" has the definite article (HA AGAPE), showing a previous reference to the love of v. 16, God's love in us. "Made perfect" (TETELEIOTAI, perfect tense of TELOO) refers to maturity, completion, development, and not to love without any flaw. Love in us has come to maturity when we can love others as God has loved us. Lenski states it well in his translation, "love has been brought to its goal."[24] Love will be what it should be, what God intended all along for it to be in us.

"With us" (METH HAMON) is somewhat peculiar in this verse and minor textual questions are raised about it.[25] Previously, John had used "in us" (EN HAMON) in vv. 12 and 16. Varied phrases are suggested to illuminate John's intent: "in our case," "sojourning with us," or "in company with us." In any case, the language refers to what love reaches in its development in our lives.

that we may have boldness in the day of judgement - John speaks of having boldness (PARRHESIA), a freedom of speech expression. As John uses it, the expression means the fearless trust with which a faithful soul may meet God in judgment (see more fully in 2:28). The believer's works will be coming to light (John 3:21) and will bring no condemnation to the faithful (John 3:18). It is an assurance and a confidence in two senses: (1) confidence that one has been born again in obedience to Jesus' wish and that he has been given the new life in Jesus; and (2) assurance most of all in the merit of the blood of Christ and the promises of forgiveness predicated on that sacrifice. John's context gives additional confidence when a Christian practices love as God would have him do. This assures the Christian that the work of God in his life is producing properly. John has already spoken of boldness at His coming (2:28) and assurance of the heart (3:19) in spite of condemning fear within self (3:21). So "abiding in him" and "keeping his commandments" are used previously by John as reasons to have boldness. He now adds a third reason to have boldness: loving as God loves.

Jesus called for a life of love and service and even pictured the judgment based on such service. "Then shall the King say unto them on his right hand, Come, ye blessed of my Father, inherit the kingdom prepared for you from the foundation of the world: for I was hungry, and ye gave me to eat; I was thirsty, and ye gave me drink: I was a stranger, and ye took me in; naked and ye clothed me; I was sick, and ye visited me; I was in prison, and ye came unto me. Then shall the righteous answer him, saying, Lord, when saw we thee hungry, and fed thee? or athirst, and gave thee drink? And when saw we thee a stranger, and took thee in? or naked and clothed thee? And the King shall answer and say unto them, Verily I say unto you, Inasmuch as ye did it unto one of these my brethren, even these least, ye did it unto me" (Matthew 25:34-40). It is significant that no charges of immorality, idolatry, or rebellion are brought against those who are rejected on this day. It is only that the love of God has not grown in their hearts and thus the correct practices of life have not developed. "Then shall he say also to them on his left hand, Depart from me, ye cursed, into the eternal fire which is prepared for the devil and his angels: for I was hungry, and ye did not give me to eat; I was thirsty, and ye gave me no drink; I was a stranger, and ye took me not in; naked, and ye clothed me not, sick, and in prison, and ye visited me not. Then shall they also answer, saying, Lord, when saw we thee hungry, or athirst, or a stranger, or naked, or sick, or in prison, and did not minister unto thee? Then shall he answer them, saying, Verily I say unto you, Inasmuch as ye did not unto one of these least, ye did it not unto me. And these shall go away into eternal punishment: but the righteous into eternal life" (Matthew 25:41-46).

A caution must be shown here, for John is not claiming that a loving, serving life merits salvation. It is not the **cause** or **grounds** for salvation; it is **evidence** of God's work in our lives. It gives us assurance to look forward to judgment, not a dread, servile fear. One must be careful of presumption, for our lives are never without flaw. But we grow in the grace and knowledge of the Lord (2 Peter 3:18), we grow more like Him every day as we are transformed into the same image from glory to glory (2 Corinthians 3:18), and our love abounds more and more in knowledge and discernment (Philippians 1:9). This is solid evidence we can come to judgment as having striven to do our best. This kind of life will not bring one to a judgment of condemnation (John 5:24), but rather to the resurrection of life (John 5:29).

This "judgment" (KRISEOS) matches perfectly with "his coming" (PAROUSIA) in 2:28. In spite of the claims of modern religions of several comings of the Lord separate from the Judgment Day ("rapture," etc.), John, along with all the New Testament writers, talks of the coming of the Lord and the Judgment Day as being together, happening at the same time. "Day of judgment" is often used (Matthew 10:15; 11:20,24; 12:36; 2 Peter 2:9; 3:7), and only one resurrection day is ever mentioned (John 5:28-29; 6:39,44,54; 11:24; Acts 24:15). This resurrection is spoken of as a general physical resurrection of all men, both righteous and unrighteous. It will be accomplished on the "last day," with the sounding of the "last trump" (1 Corinthians 15:52), for the judgment and the last day are synonymous (John 12:48).

because as he is, even so are we in this world - if we have become godly, "god-like" (2 Timothy 3:12), and have practiced godliness (1 Timothy 4:7; 6:11; 2 Peter 1:6-7; 3:11), then we will resemble Christ, having walked in His steps (1 Peter 2:21), and will not be alarmed at His coming. We will look forward to being "manifested with him in glory" (Colossians 3:4). Such will be producing love in the lives of Christians, even as Christ loved and continues to love. One difference is that He is at the right hand of the Majesty on high (Hebrews 1:3), while we remain "in the world."

Verse 18 There is no fear in love: but perfect love casteth out fear, because fear hath punishment; and he that feareth is not made perfect in love.

There is no fear in love: but perfect love casteth out fear - When love is allowed its full and proper course in our lives, it will eliminate fearful apprehension. John uses fear (PHOBOS) as the opposite of boldness (PARRHESIA). Neither word expresses its absolute sense; the concept can be expressed in varying degrees. This fear is the faithless dread or terror — quaking, tormenting, slavish shrinking from appearing before God in the last day. It is servile and cringing, rather than trusting, confident, and bold.

There is a proper fear to have for God. "The fear of Jehovah is clean, enduring forever" (Psalm 19:9). "The fear of Jehovah is the beginning of wisdom" (Psalms 111:10). "I am a companion of all them that fear thee, and of them that observe thy precepts" (Psalms 119:63). "My flesh trembleth for fear of thee; and I am afraid of thy judgments" (Psalms 119:120). "Fear God and keep his commandments; for this is the whole duty of man" (Ecclesiastes 12:13). ". . .[H]e that feareth him, and worketh righteousness, is accepted with him" (Acts 10:35). "Be not highminded, but fear. . ." (Romans 11:20). ". . .Work out your own salvation with fear and trembling" (Philippians 2:12). "Fear God and give him glory" (Revelation 14:7). So some kind of fear is proper in the life of the believer.

This fear about which John is now writing is exclusive of the love he mentions. Fear and love do not, indeed they cannot, abide together. They are contrary one to the other, even as are flesh and spirit (Galatians 5:17). They are produced by the flesh and the spirit. A life after the flesh brings fear; the Spirit-led life (Romans 8:14) will bring love into our lives. As this love is "shed abroad in our hearts through the Holy Spirit which was given to us" (Romans 5:5), it will crowd out, cast out (EXO BALLEI) fear. Love, properly ensconced in our lives, throws out servile fear. This present tense (BALLEI) is used gnomically, for such truism can always be depended upon. It does not mean love continues to cast our fear; rather, it means under the proper development, love will cast out fear. This will always be true, thus the gnomic use of the present tense. John shows that fear, self-centeredness, is unable ever to abide alongside godly love, other-centeredness.

Clarke makes some vital suggestions about this relationship of fear and love. He suggests some types of fear are necessary to our well-being, such as filial fear, fear for the preservation of life, and the fear of sudden alarm. Further, he points out that love destroys the fear of want, the fear of death, and the fear of judgment. All these latter fears "bring torment and are inconsistent with perfect love."[26]

This "perfect love" (TELEIA AGAPE) is not flawless, for only God has such love. Rather "perfect" is used again in the sense of mature, complete, fully developed, cycled sufficiently, amply and satisfactorily. This love will give a calm and dignified acceptance and assurance in the "meeting in the sky."

because fear hath punishment; he that feareth is not made perfect in love - This wrong kind of fear is connected to punishment and the dread thereof. "Punishment" (KOLASIN) is translated "torment" in the KJV, but the KJV also translates this same word as "punishment" in Matthew 25:46. Some say this dread is all there is to the punishment. Some say this dread constitutes one kind of punishment prior to judgment, with eternal punishment to follow the judgment. Since John used the present tense of "hath" (ECHEI), the word seems more likely to refer to the latter sense. Fear now in this life is the beginning of the sinner's mental anguish, the completion of which will come after he appears in judgment.

"He that feareth" (PHOBOUMENOS, present participle) shows continuous terror and fear. Such strangles the completion of the goal of love in one's life. When an individual's life is full of impurities and sins, he will be unable to develop God's love very well in his life. He knows his utter incompatibility with God, dreads facing God in the resurrection, and cannot rid himself of this terror. So he does not succeed in living as love would lead him to live.

To be made perfect in love allows one to understand that God's love and grace has covered his sins, forgiven his trespasses, and washed him clean in the blood of the Lamb. He can have a heart still lurking ready with self-condemnation (3:19-20), but he will have assurance and boldness upon the account of God's love (3:21-22). A proper perception of God's love and promises, plus the maturing and developing of love in one's life, will bring this much sought after assurance and confidence. A believer simply puts his trust in God and not self.

4. Practicing God's Love 4:19-21

19We love because he first loved us. 20If a man say, I love God, and hateth his brother, he is a liar: for he that loveth not his brother whom he hath seen, cannot love God whom he hath not seen. 21And this commandment have we from him, that he who loveth God love his brother also.

John continues in the response to love, as the Christian in his relationship to the world is called upon the walk in love (see Outline). The Christian accepts God's love, confesses God's love, abides in God's love, and now we learn that he will practice God's love in his life.

Verse 19 We love because he first loved us - John has already affirmed in v. 10 that God's love was first in being active. He loved us first, whether or not we ever return that love. This statement serves as the reason for our love: God first loved us. The verb action of man's loving is present indicative tense (AGAPOMEN), showing a continuing way of life. Some claim this verb is present subjunctive rather than indicative tense, being thus, "Let us love." Whether it is indicative or subjunctive, the use of the present tense is

163

still forceful. This love will continue. The verb action of God's love is aorist (HAGAPASIN), showing a point in history when His love was manifested supremely, the crucifixion. He loved us when we were shameful sinners (Romans 5:8) and utterly unlovable in our sinfulness (Titus 3:3-7). God's love was prior to man's love, but it provides the stimuli for man's love. This is shown **first** in being a great example to follow; **second,** in providing the new life in which to develop godly love; **third,** in providing the power to develop this love in this new life; and **fourth,** in giving the motive of gratitude for His goodness, since such goodness leads to repentance (Romans 2:4). Only ingrates would refuse to return His love.

"Him" in the KJV, ("We love him") is unwarranted as there is no corresponding word in the later and best Greek manuscripts for "him." Thus the Received Text is not corroborated, and such an idea provides inaccurate limitations. Not having God as the only object of our love in this verse gives a much wider sense of our love. It would refer to the utmost capacity of man to love all men in all ways. It would include love for God, fellow man, enemies, the brotherhood, etc. All kinds of love are enjoined by John in this text.

Verse 20 If a man say, I love God, and hateth his brother, he is a liar: for he that loveth not his brother whom he hath seen, cannot love God whom he hath not seen.

If a man say, I love God, and hateth his brother, he is a liar: - This is John's fourth use of a very strong word: liar (PSEUSTES). He has used it (1) for the one who claims no sin [1:10]; (2) for one who claims to know God but does not keep His commands [2:4]; (3) and for the one who denies that Jesus is the Christ [2:22]. Now John adds (4) the one who claims to love God but hates his brother. This use of the **liar** by John covers all functions and relations of man: moral (1:10), functional (2:4), doctrinal (2:22) and social (4:20). One other use of this word PSEUSTES by John will be noted in a statement of incredulity, for the infidel, in effect, would make God a liar if the infidel were correct (5:10).

John uses a hypothetical case to show an impossibility, the utter foolishness, of the actions of sinful men. The professions and claims of Gnostics to love God are shown to be baseless by their disregard of their brethren. The highest term for "love" is used here (AGAPAO, not a lesser word, PHILEO), and it is used in the present tense. This means a claim of continous, uninterrupted devotion and love to God. The corresponding verb for "hate" (MISEO) of the brother is also present tense. So it also depicts continuing action. Both actions run side by side, one as strong and continuous as the other. John emphasized the latter action of hatred for brethren by the word order. It is literally, ". . .a man say I love God and the brother of him hates." Putting "brother" before the verb produces a striking emphasis. This hatred is not necessarily actions of harm and destruction, for it could be only lack of love. John has already used the failure to love and care for a brother as synonymous with hatred (3:14-18).

This is a general statement to all Christians as John uses TIS, more generally translated "anyone" (RSV, NIV), or "some one" (NASB). The use of "a man" (KJV, ASV) is not quite as strong and shows the general application of this statement.

John shows the utter foolishness of man's imaginary gods. Perhaps he is alluding to the self-made god of the Gnostics. What kind of god would allow brother to hate brother? What kind of god would allow a brother to hate a brother who is made in the image of God? What kind of god would allow a brother to hate a brother, made in the image of God, and in whom God dwells? This use of a hypothetical case is vivid and forceful?

for he that loveth not his brother whom he hath seen, cannot love God whom he hath not seen - John now explains the previous strong statement. It is impossible to love God while hating a brother. It is much easier to love what one can see and be near than it is to love what is unseen, abstract, and, in the physical sense, far away. That God is invisible to man's physical senses is amply known already (see 3:2). The emphasis here is on two objects of man's love: brothers who are **visible,** and God who is **invisible.** Which is the easier and more likely? No doubt it ought to be easier to love a brother who is near and seen. This argument is from the easier to the harder. This kind

165

of comparative/contrastive argument is not unknown in scriptures, as Paul used it often. One case is outstanding, "He that spared not his own Son, but delivered him up for us all, how shall he not also with him freely give us all things?" (Romans 8:32). The argument is from the greater to the lesser. Our God, who has already given the greatest gift possible, will not fail in lesser gifts needed by man. So, here in this text, John says if we cannot love the easier object, it is sure we cannot accomplish proper love to the more difficult (loving the Unseeable).

Since both verbs for "seen" (EORAKEN) are perfect tense, John is describing action completed in the past with the results continuing up to the time of his writing. A man has seen his brother in past time and the impression lingers on until the present. This argues forcefully for an implication that the situation might be continuing with no hint of cessation. The speaker who claims to love God while hating his brother has had many opportunities in the past to observe and love his brother, **and has not done so.** It is as one writes, "The perfect indicates the permanent state. . . ."[27]

The insertion of "how" in the KJV seems unwarranted and lessens the force of the statement. Most manuscripts omit this and concur that John categorically denies any possibility, rather than simply asks an incredulous question.

Verse 21 And this commandment have we from him, that he who loveth God love his brother also.

And this commandment have we from him - Here is an obligation, a command. It is just as binding as the command to love God. If one is true and should be obeyed, so should the other. There is no convincing evidence of one without the other. John used logic in v. 20 to convince a man in error he was a liar; now he states a specific instruction, a command from God. This "commandment" (ENTOLE) probably refers back to former statements of Jesus (John 13:34-35; 15:13; see also comments 1 John 2:7-11; 3:13-18). "Him" has caused some discussion whether it is the Father or the Son who gave the command. It is certain this command has come from Deity, and John seems to switch back and forth indiscriminately, with no

166

particular desire to separate between God the Father and God the Son, when authority of heaven is called upon. It is no less a command if John attributes it to either.

Many other commands are known to have been given by God about love for men: love for neighbor, one another, enemies, and brethren. Whether it is love for **neighbor** (Leviticus 19:18; Matthew 19:19; 22:39; Galatians 5:14), **one another** (John 13:34-35; 15:12,17; 1 John 3:11; 4:7,11,21), **enemies** (Matthew 5:43-48; Luke 6:27-29), or **brethren** (Romans 12:10; 1 Thessalonians 4:9; Hebrews 13:1; 1 Peter 1:22; 2 Peter 1:7; 2:17; 3:8), it must be included in the personality and makeup of a Christian. Technical differences among these four objects of love can be made, but each of them is necessary to be incorporated into the life and practice of a true follower of the Lord. In this context, John seems to center on the brethren and one another, which he uses interchangeably.

that he that loveth God love his brother also - John cannot be misunderstood, as the instruction is clear: Lovers of God in truth will be lovers of fellowman. The conjunction "that" (HINA) usually carries the force of "in order that." This shows the object clause: "this is the commandment"; i.e., (in order that) "he that loveth God love his brother also."

Jesus stated, "On these two commandments the whole law hangeth, and the prophets" (Matthew 22:40). The two commandments were love of God and love of neighbor (Matthew 22:37-39). Jesus thus briefly summarized all the duties of man as stated in Moses' Law. If such were done truly and consistently by any man, he would have fulfilled all the duties of man in all relationships as a human being before God. John here reiterates the same two duties, one vertical (to God) and one horizontal (to fellow man). What other relationships would be neglected if these two were done?

It may be easy to claim, yea, even pretend to love God. One might even fool one's own self, genuine in belief, but blind to the reality of an empty, loveless heart. John gives a proving ground that will change the false beliefs and clear away blindness. As one holds ill will, grudges, and revenge in one's heart toward other men, so lacks that one the proper corresponding love toward God! Therefore, very important indeed, is brotherly love. It will prove to disciples whether they are becoming godly. It will serve as an accurate gauge of one's ability to imitate one's Lord Jesus Christ. If someone dares to take his own spiritual temperature, he can simply review honestly his relations with the brethren. Constant poor relations with other brethren ought to tell disciples that something very dangerous is happening in their hearts. Warm, open, active, and stedfast love connections with other brethren ought to assure disciples that they are growing in this grace.

[1]Samuel Bagster, *Analytical Greek Lexicon,* (Samuel Bagster & Sons, London, England, 1852, Revised Edition by Harold K. Moulton, Zondervan Publishing Co., Grand Rapids, Michigan, 1978), p. 105.

[2]William F. Arndt, and F. Wilbur Gingrich, *A Greek-English Lexicon of the New Testament,* (University of Chicago Press, Chicago, Illinois, 1957), p. 201.

[3]James Hope Moulton and George Milligan, *The Vocabulary of the Greek New Testament,* (Wm. B. Eerdmans Publishing Co., Grand Rapids, Michigan, 1960), p. 167.

[4]R. C. H. Lenski, *The Interpretation of the Epistles of St. Peter, St. John, and St. Jude* (Augsburg Publishing House, Minneapolis, Minnesota, 1963), p. 488.

[5]Lenski, *Interpretation,* p. 488.

[6]Donald W. Burdick, *The Letters of John the Apostle,* (Moody Press, Chicago, Illinois, 1985), pp. 297-298.

[7]For fuller discussion, see Albert Barnes, *Notes on the New Testament, James, Peter, John and Jude,* (Baker Book House, Grand Rapids, Michigan, 1949), p. 328; and J. W. Roberts, *The Living Word Commentary, The Letters of John,* (R. B. Sweet Co., Inc., Austin, Texas, 1968), pp. 107-108.

[8]Bagster, *Lexicon,* p. 277.

[9]Joh. Ed. Huther, *Meyer's Commentary on the New Testament, Critical and Exegetical Handbook to the General Epistles of James, Peter, John and Jude,* (Funk & Wagnalls, Publishers, New York, 1887), p. 583.

[10]A. T. Robertson, as quoted by Alexander Ross, *The New International Commentary on the New Testament, the Epistles of James and John,* (Wm. B. Eerdmans Publishing Co., Grand Rapids, Michigan, 1954), p. 201.

[11]Lenski, *Interpretation,* p. 495.

[12]Joh. Ed. Huther, *Critical and Exegetical,* p. 584.

[13]Bagster, *Lexicon,* pp. 272, 79.

[14]Bagster, *Lexicon,* p. 272.

[15]W. E. Vine, *An Expository Dictionary of New Testament Words,* (Riverside Book and Bible House, Iowa Falls, Iowa, 1952), p. 813.

[16]For a fuller study of this term and its textual problems, see R. C. H. Lenski, *The Interpretation of St. John's Gospel*, (Augsburg Publishing House, Minneapolis, Minnesota, 1963), pp. 77-81, 95-102, and Roberts, *Letters*, pp. 113-115.

[17]Lenski, *Interpretation*, p. 503.

[18]Lenski, *Interpretation*, p. 504.

[19]Lenski, *Interpretation*, p. 506-507.

[20]Vine, *Dictionary*, p. 994.

[21]Bagster, *Lexicon*, p. 80.

[22]Vine, *Dictionary*, p. 627.

[23]Ross, *NIC*, p. 205.

[24]Lenski, *Interpretation*, p. 510.

[25]Burdick, *Letters*, p. 334.

[26]Adam Clarke, *A Commentary and Critical Notes*, (Abingdon-Cokesbury Press, New York and Nashville), Vol. II, *Romans to Revelation*, p. 921.

[27]Joh. Ed. Huther, *Critical and Exegetical*, p. 595.

C. Tests of Love 5:1-12

1. Overcoming the World 5:1-4

¹**Whosoever believeth that Jesus is the Christ is begotten of God: and whosoever loveth him that begat loveth him also that is begotten of him. ²Hereby we know that we love the children of God, when we love God and do his commandments. ³For this is the love of God, that we keep his commandments: and his commandments are not grievous. ⁴For whatsoever is begotten of God overcometh the world: and this is the victory that hath overcome the world, even our faith.**

This is now the third section of the Christian and the World: Walking in Love (see Outline). Previous discussions of this section (Number II in Outline) showed reminders of proper relationship to God, and the proper response to God's love. John now moves into a new section, which will give tests of proper love in the life of a Christian. These are two in number: overcoming the world (5:1-4) and faith in the witnesses God gives (5:5-12).

Verse 1 Whosoever believeth that Jesus is the Christ is begotten of God: and whosoever loveth him that begat loveth him also that is begotten of him.

Whosoever believeth that Jesus is the Christ is begotten of God - Some commit a destructive error in teaching on this verse and isolate it as if it were a proof for teaching God's way, or method, of salvation. Such isolation ignores the context and the flow of John's argument.

John has shown in the previous chapter that one accepts God's love (vv. 7-11), confesses God's love (vv. 12-15), abides in God's love (vv. 16-18), and practices God's love (vv. 19-21, see Outline). Now that same person has tests of his love (5:1-12). In the context John has called for practicing God's love by showing love toward the brethren

Now, who are these brethren that are to be loved? John offers the immediate answer: the ones who are begotten of God. And these begotten ones are the believers in Jesus as the Son of God. So John is not teaching the way to establish the relationship of being a child of God; rather, he is identifying the brethren whom the believer will love. John is not limiting the plan of salvation to belief alone, he is simply showing who it is the believer will love. "Whosoever believeth" is then to be understood as a synecdoche for all the other requirements of God which are necessary prior to one's becoming a child of God.

There are three reasons why a believer ought to love the brethren. **First,** it is a logical necessity (4:20). If the Christian can love the unseen God, he will surely be able to love the seeable brother. **Second,** it is a command of God (4:21). John is still within this context, though the chapter number has advanced. **Third,** it is right that family members love other family members (5:1).

Two syllogisms are actually presented by John in his argumentation:

> Every believer is begotten of God;
> All begotten ones will love the Begetter;
> therefore: Every believer will love the Begetter.

> Every believer loves the Begetter;
> All who love the Begetter also love the begotten ones;
> therefore: Every believer loves the begotten ones.

John continues to interweave the main great themes of his book: belief, love, obedience, righteousness, begettal, etc. Coming down to near the close of this first epistle, he combines all the more these major themes.

In order to do justice to this verse, one author claims that "a full exegesis of our verse would include the exegesis of all that precedes."[1] And truly, these main themes are richly interwoven and lead to stedfast conclusions.

"Believeth" literally means "continue to believe" since it is present tense (PAS HO PISTEUON). John has more in mind than mere acceptance of intellectual and factual arguments. In 3:23-24, John coupled belief in Jesus with love for one another and with keeping His commandments. And in 4:16 the believer of God's love is the one who abides in love. And this one abiding in love is also the one who confesses Jesus as the Christ (4:15). Thus John interweaves believing, abiding and living faithfully, loving, and confessing. A true believer is the practitioner of God's will.

To declare that Jesus is the Christ (HO CHRISTOS) is to believe He is the central focus of all revelation from God. CHRISTOS is the same as the Old Testament "Messiah," both meaning "anointed." One is Greek, the other is Hebrew. This Jesus, the carpenter of Nazareth, is the anointed king of God's kingdom, the one who arose from the dead, the one who began His reign when He was coronated upon David's throne, as Peter declared openly (Acts 2:30-33). This is the faith confessed by one's abiding in God (4:15).

The use of the human appellation "Jesus" gives emphasis to the man, the human person, of Nazareth. John wants to show that the counterclaims of the Gnostics about this man called Jesus are false. It was this very one, the carpenter from Galilee, who was "made. . .Christ" (Acts 2:36). God and man were united in this incarnation, puzzling as it may be to human understanding (Philippians 2:6-8; Hebrews 2:14-18). One must remember that the Gnostics held that Jesus was only a human being, while Christ was the Divine Person who came upon Jesus at His baptism and left Him prior to His death on the cross.

is begotten of God - John uses the perfect tense (GEGENNETAI), the same tense usage as in 2:29 and 3:9. This perfect tense indicates completed action in the past, with results continuing in the present. The believer has been begotten by God in the past, and the results continue even now. By this begettal, i.e., and subsequent birth, John shows that the true believer is the child of God. "Begotten" is another synecdoche, for it stands for the entire process of regeneration. Now, as a child of God, this one is a brother to all believers. So the test can now be made: Does this begotten one love both God and the brethren? This continues the argument advanced in the previous chapter (4:20-21) that the believer should love his brethren.

and whosoever loveth him that begat loveth him also that is begotten of him - If anyone loves God, that same one will love all these begotten ones of God. Perhaps John is writing proverbially here, stating a truism of family life. One has said, "Love me, love my family." Both verbs for "love" are present tense in this verse, indicating a pattern of continuous love. It is unthinkable that one child of God, blessed by a begettal that he did not deserve, would fail to love another sinner so blessed.

Verse 2 Hereby we know that we love the children of God, when we love God and do his commandments.

Hereby we know that we love the children of God - Other translations are useful here: "By this we know" (KJV, NASB), "This is how we know" (NIV), portraying this clause as the means of ascertainment. There is a way to know (GINOSKO), "come to know," which is an inchoative use of the word, as faith is thus helping form the proper love within the child of God. Since it is the natural state of filial relations to love, one can come to know one is loving properly when that one keeps God's commandments and loves the family members. One of God's commandments, after all, is to love the brethren! John argues both ways: Proof of keeping God's commands is to love one's brother (4:20-21); yet proof of loving one's brother is keeping God's commands (5:2). Inexplicably bound together are proper love and proper obedience to God's commandments.

Lenski describes it thus: "There are three boxes. The outer one is doing what God wants. Open that, and in it is loving God, the Father of all children. Open that, and in it is loving his children."[2]

when we love God and do his commandments - Whenever one loves God and performs proper obedience, that one will love fellow children of the heavenly Father. He will "open the third box," as it were, perform in actuality God's commandments.

"Keep his commandments," as used in the KJV, does not show an emphasis John intends. The word is actually "do his commandments" (POIOMEN, first person, plural, present subjunctive active of POIEO). This is the only time in the New Testament this phrase is used. Five times in 1 John, when it is recorded "keep his commandments" (TEREO), a different verb is used (2:3,4; 3:22,24; 5:3, plus 2:5 where it is stated "keepeth his word"). This is the more common expression of John.

The use of "do" (POIEO) perhaps will stress actual performance. Other translations vary from the most literal of the ASV: "carrying out his commands" (NIV), "obey his commandments" (RSV), and "observe his commandments"

(NASB).

"Commandments" is plural here (ENTOLAS) as contrasted with the previous use of the singular "command" (2:7-8; 3:23; 4:21). In the previous references, it may refer to loving one's brother in particular, while here it refers to keeping all God's commandments in general. John is leading into what v. 3 will say in additional emphasis.

Verse 3 For this is the love of God, that we keep his commandments: and his commandments are not grievous.

For this is the love of God, that we keep his commandments - The evidence of true love is the keeping of God's commands. In using "for" (GAR), John shows he is explaining the preceding verse, last clause. One cannot separate obedience and love in regard to God. To do one is to do the other. They are equal to each other. Therefore, no one can do either one properly without the other.

This keeping of the commandments of God is the essence of one's love toward God (see John 14:15,21,23; 15:10). It is a viable demonstration, it is the proof, it is the passing of the test. One never has to wonder about the measure of one's love for God: Simply check to see how well one's obedience is performing.

In 1:6, the claim that one is in God's fellowship can be tested by whether that one walks in the light. Similarly, the claim that one loves God can be tested by whether that one keeps on keeping God's commandments. This is so characteristic of John's writings in this epistle. Note some tests he suggests about knowing whether certain relationships exist:

1:6	Is one in fellowship? — Does one walk in the light?
2:3	Does one know God? — Does one keep His commandments?
2:5-6	Is one in Him? — Does that one walk as He walked?
2:9-11	Is one in the light? — Does one love his brother?
2:23	Does one have the Father? — Has one confessed the Son?

3:14	Has one passed from death to life? — Does one love the brethren?
4:2	How can one know the Spirit of God? — Does one confess Jesus in the flesh as God?
4:7	Is one begotten of God? — Does one love properly?
4:8	Does one know God? — Does one love properly?

Patently obvious it is that the phrase "love of God" (AGAPE TOU THEOU) must be taken as an objective genitive, i.e., "love **for** God." The context demands this to be the love man has for God. To make this a subjective genitive ("God's love" or "love **from** God") would make no sense in this context whatever.

John returns to the more frequent wording "keep his commandments" (TEROMEN, present tense of TEREO), rather than the unusual "do" as in v. 2. The use of the present tense shows that one continues, makes it a pattern of life, to obey God's laws.

and his commandments are not grievous - Other translations say "not burdensome" (NASB, RSV, NIV). The word for "grievous" (BAREIAI, from BARUS) means "heavy; met. burdensome, oppressive, or difficult of observance."[3] Another adds, "burdensome, difficult to fulfill,"[4] while Vine claims the word is always used methaphorically in the New Testament and explains this as "causing a burden on him who fulfills them."[5] In Galatians 6:2 the same word refers to an oppressive load that should be shared by other Christians. A different burden (PHOTION) is used in Galatians 6:5, as this burden is the normal one carried by all Christians. Since it is not oppressive or burdensome, each is able to carry it. Thus, keeping God's commandments is not an unbearable weight, claims John; such is truly not "grievous."

If obedience to God's commandments were too burdensome to accomplish, what would be the point in calling for such? The fact that John says such obedience is the proper test of love is proof that the ordinary believer can obey God's commandments acceptably.

Jesus promised an easy yoke and a light burden to His

disciples (Matthew 11:30), versus those too heavy to bear under the Law of Moses (Acts 15:10). Disobedience to God entangles one in slavery to sin (Romans 6:16), where there is no justification from sins (Romans 6:20), and which brings regretful shame with no good fruit (Romans 6:21). The end result of such a life is death (Romans 6:21). Conversely, the service of God is freedom (John 8:32; Galatians 5:1), life (John 5:24; 1 Timothy 6:19), and joy (Matthew 25:21; Galatians 5:22). What is burdensome, grievous, about these things: freedom from sins, joy, and eternal life?

Verse 4 For whatsoever is begotten of God overcometh the world: and this is the victory that hath overcome the world, even our faith.

For whatsoever is begotten of God overcometh the world - Again John explains a previous statement in a subsequent verse. Keeping God's commandments is not burdensome, "for" (HOTI) the begotten one gains victory in Jesus. The use of the neuter gender "whatsoever" (PAN TO GEGENNAMENON) might be thought unusual here, but it seems to emphasize the state of the begotten, rather than the person who is begotten. Victory thus comes because of the birth, not because of the person or anything the person might do on his own. The person cannot do anything to merit the birth or the victory. The meritorious cause can only be Jesus Christ, His life, His love, His blood. John uses the masculine "whoever" in verses 1 and 18 of this chapter, but here he intends to emphasize the state of regeneration, the gaining of the victory, a gift from God. Man does not gain the victory himself; the new life in him, given by God, gains the victory through Jesus Christ.

overcometh the world - This is a present tense verb (NIKA, from NIKAO) and simply expresses a maxim: This one overcomes now and continues to overcome in the struggles with sin. It is always true that victory over the world can be accomplished by the one with the new life. Without this begettal, there is no hope for victory. The "world" is viewed as the opposing force of evil, the enemy (see more fully on 2:15-17).

and this is the victory that hath overcome the world, even our faith - John reverses the word order for emphasis, letting the sentence build to the climax, "our faith." He could have said "Our faith is the victory," but that would not have been with quite the same emphasis. "Faith" is another synecdoche of all that faith will accomplish in one's life: obedience, love, walking in the light, laying down one's life for the brethren, compassion for a needy brother, confessing Jesus is God in the flesh, etc. These are all great themes already discussed by John and included here in "our faith."

This is the only time the word "faith" (PISTIS) occurs in John's writings, even of all five books. He often uses the verb form, "to believe" (PISTEUO), but he never uses the noun form but this once. This faith is the root of all victories, the means of overcoming, the source of power to win. Faith is that which conquers, as another inspired writer heralded, "And what shall I more say? for the time will fail me if I tell of Gideon, Barak, Samson, Jephtath, of David and Samuel and the prophets: who through faith subdued kingdoms, wrought righteousness, obtained promises, stopped the mouths of lions, quenched the power of fire, escaped the edge of the sword, from weakness were made strong, waxed mightily in war, turned to flight armies of aliens. Women received their dead by a resurrection: and others were tortured, not accepting their deliverance; that they might obtain a better resurrection: and others had trial of mockings and scourgings, yea, moreover of bonds and imprisonment: they were stoned, they were sawn asunder, they were tempted, they were slain with the sword: they went about in sheepskins, in goatskins; being destitute, afflicted, ill-treated (of whom the world was not worthy), wandering in deserts and mountains and caves, and the holes of the earth. And these all, having had witness borne to them through their faith, received not the promise, God having provided some better thing concerning us, that apart from us they should not be made perfect" (Hebrews 11:32-40). Faith conquers all. How glorious is true faith!

John also is distinctive in using the word "victory" (NIKE), as it is used only this once in all the New Testament. It is similar to another word (NIKOS), thought to be a later form of John's word, this latter word being used by Jesus (Matthew 12:20) and Paul (1 Corinthians 15:54,55,57).

"Hath overcome" (NIKESASA, aorist participle) demands a victory at some previous time. Suggestions of when this victory occurred include (1) the victory of Christ when He died on the cross, (2) the victory accomplished when Jesus was raised from the dead, (3) the victory as truth prevailed over error in the preaching of the gospel, i.e., when men began to obey the gospel message in the first century, (4) the victory accomplished in the new birth and life in the conversion of a believer. It should be obvious, since it is "our faith," that the answer cannot be either of the first two suggestions, as believers had no part in them. Neither is John limiting the victory only to the teaching of truth. So the expression must refer to conversion, and this will fit well into John's context. The Christian is doing the commandments of God, not just teaching them. When he does these commandments initially, God causes the believer to be regenerated, thus giving the believing sinner the victory of salvation and new life.

2. Faith in the Witness God Gives 5:5-12

5And who is he that overcometh the world, but he that believeth that Jesus is the Son of God? 6This is he that came by water and blood, even Jesus Christ; not with the water only, but with the water and with the blood. 7And it is the Spirit that beareth witness, because the Spirit is the truth. 8For there are three who bear witness, the Spirit, and the water and the blood: and the three agree in one. 9If we receive the witness of men, the witness of God is greater: for the witness of God is this, that he hath borne witness concerning his Son. 10He that believeth on the Son of God hath the witness in him: he that believeth not God hath made him a liar; because he hath not believed in the witness that God hath borne concerning his Son. 11And the witness is this, that God gave unto us eternal life, and this life is in his Son. 12He that hath the Son hath the life; he that hath not the Son of God hath not the life.

John now moves to a Christological test: Is one willing to believe the witnesses God had provided? John refers to the

Holy Spirit, the water, the blood, and eternal life given to Christians. He calls for three (v. 8), then mentions yet another (vv. 10-11).

This section has one of the most perplexing passages in all the New Testament, "This is he that came by water and blood." Several explanations will be noted and the choice will be made for the one with the preponderate evidence.

Also this section has a textual problem in v. 7, as the King James Version of 1611 includes an additional statement to our text, "For there are three that bear record in heaven, the Father, the word, and the Holy Ghost." This is so obvious a spurious passage that not only is it not included in other major translations (NASB, RSV, NIV, ASV), it is not even afforded a footnote in the ASV, as are other problematical passages (Acts 8:37; John 5:4; John 7:53-8:11, etc.) See further in "Additional Note" under v. 7.

Verse 5 And who is he that overcometh the world, but he that believeth that Jesus is the Son of God?

And who is he that overcometh the world - John now returns to the personal pronoun "who" (TIS) from the previous neuter "whatsoever" (PAN) in v. 4. There, the use of the neuter emphasized the state of victory rather than the person and his own power to obey. Here, John returns to the personal pronoun to emphasize that the person who does the overcoming is the person who believes that Jesus is the Son of God.

"Overcometh" (present participle from NIKAO) will have the force of continued struggles and progress. The fight is still raging, battles are yet to be fought. The life of the Christian is the life of continual temptations, battles, and victories.

John continues his use of "world" (KOSMOS) to refer to the evil order of the world and all that which is controlled by Satan (see 2:15-17).

but he that believeth that Jesus is the Son of God - Everything depends on what one believes! It does make a difference, a vast difference, what one holds as true and trustworthy. Believing error, legend, myth, hearsay, or a lie will bring defeat, not victory. It does make a difference what one believes, the difference between victory and defeat. Accuracy of doctrine is basic. Cerinthus and his devotees never gained a victory in Christ. Disciples who believed accurately and acted on these fundamental beliefs were victorious (note the victory of Stephen, Acts 6-7).

"Believeth" (present participle from PISTEUO) is in harmony with "overcometh," also a present participle. Continual believing brings continual overcoming. If one ceases to believe properly, then that same one will cease to gain victories in Jesus.

Verse 6 This is he that came by water and blood, even Jesus Christ; not with the water only, but with the water and with the blood.

This is he that came by water and blood, even Jesus Christ - Admittedly, this is one of the more difficult passages in the New Testament. There are numerous explanations offered, and perhaps four are of major consideration.

1. The ordinances of baptism (water) and the Lord's Supper (blood).

2. The water and blood which flowed from the side of Jesus at His crucifixion (John 19:34).

3. Purification from sins (water) and redemption (blood), in only a figurative and symbolic usage.

4. Jesus' baptism (water) and death (blood).

John had some forceful purpose in making this part of his argument about Jesus as the Son of God. It is the most forceful if it be also the most obvious. The more obscure is the truth, the less forceful it would be. So, in this context, what is John striving to present with this passage? What is the most obvious?

First, what, in this passage and argument, would deal most forcefully with the Docetism the first century believers faced? These followers of Cerinthus accepted the fact Jesus was baptized and that by that time the person of the Christ was upon Him. What they denied was that Jesus died for the sins of the world, that He shed His blood on the cross for all mankind, and that it was the Incarnate Son of God who thus died. They affirmed that the person of Deity, the Christ, left Jesus prior to His crucifixion; thus, it was merely a man who died. It was not the Son of God, the person of dual nature, the God-man who died. Thus, two ordinances of God, baptism and the Lord's Supper, would have little meaning to these Docetics as an argument. The blood and water which flowed from His side at His death would have little bearing on their thinking, for they did not deny a man died. They only denied that man was the Son of God at that point of time. Neither would purification and redemption, mere figures of speech, do anything with these heretics.

Second, can this passage be taken literally? Were there literal events of history in the life of this man that would make real differences in the faith of those who knew about them? It is an axiom encountered in all serious study of the Scripture that it is best to take passages and words literally when it can be done and when it does no violence to the context and the truth presented. Yes, there were literal events in His life that were momentous in proof of His Sonship and that would correspond to water and blood: His baptism and His death. At His baptism, the voice of the Father acknowledged His Sonship (Luke 3:22); and the shedding of His blood at the crucifixion offered ongoing proofs and arguments of inspired writers (Acts 20:28; Romans 3:25; Ephesians 1:7; Hebrews 9:22-28; 1 Peter 1:19). So, accepting His baptism and His death and understanding these as literal events in the life of Jesus would do no violence to the context.

Third, what "coming" is involved ("This is he that came. . .")? The "He that came," literally, "the one coming" (HO ELTHOWN, aorist subjunctive of ERCHOMAI), has to refer to Jesus, of course. But what coming? Since the aorist tense is used (completed action in some past time), it cannot refer to the second coming of Christ, for that is still in the future. This aorist is called the "historical aorist," due to its use in stating a known historical fact. Whatever water and blood may mean, they must be points of history at the time of John's writing. This would seem to leave out the attempt to understand these words in some figurative way, such as suggestions Numbers 1 and 3 (see above). If one suggests it could at this point mean the water and blood that flowed from His side on the cross, it would then be proper to ask, "How does this interpretation have anything to do with His coming?" Such historical facts of water and blood flowing from His dead body refer to the time of His death, not His coming. And it does not fit well to say this would be a euphemistic use of the terms either. If, on the other hand, the student takes this water and blood to be the baptism and death of the Lord, it would refer to the whole span of His ministry, from beginning to end. John would then be arguing that His entire ministry as Saviour of the world, from baptism to death, would be a proof of His deity.

Fourth, why will John emphasize in this verse "not with water only," unless someone needs to be taught something further about His blood and His death? If these two words refer only to His crucifixion (as in suggestion Number 2 above), what possible purpose could John have? John is giving the greater emphasis to the blood, but blood is always present in one's death and none dispute that. Yet John is seeing the need to emphasize blood, as if someone is willing to accept the water, but not willing to accept the blood. The Docetics would make this very argument and would need this exact kind of emphasis. Thus, if the water and the blood referred to His baptism and His death, it would make sense in refuting the current denials of the Docetics. If other explanations were applied, John's arguments would make little or no sense in the context. Further, it might be noted as an afterthought, if water and blood refer only to His crucifixion, why would John reverse the order in which he wrote these words previously (John 19:34)? Such would have been unusual.

The best explanation, the one with the prevailing weight of evidence, seems to be that water and blood refer to His baptism and His death. It is interesting that Iranaeus places both John and Cerinthus in Ephesus at the same time (see Introduction). It is interesting also that the expression "water and blood" in that day "was kind of a verbal shorthand" to recall Jesus' baptism and death![6]

not with the water only, but with the water and with the blood - Here is the emphatic answer to the denials of the heretic Docetics. It was not water only (historical fact of His baptism by John), it includes also the fact that He gave His blood on the cross for the sins of all mankind. Understanding the denials of the Gnostics, that the Divine Christ was no longer a part of the man Jesus at His death, makes the context fit this suggested interpretation

182

precisely. No other of the major interpretations can fit with such precision. John is destroying the feeble efforts of the Gnostics to defame the Son of God.

John insists Jesus the Christ experienced death as well as baptism. He uses "even Jesus Christ" for emphasis of the exact person about whom he wrote. It is this very Jesus who died on the cross, shed His blood for the sins of the world, and is the True Incarnate One.

Verse 7 And it is the Spirit that beareth witness, because the Spirit is the truth.

And it is the Spirit that beareth witness - "Witness" is more prominent in this section, as both noun (MARTUS) and verb (MARTUREO) forms will be used ten times in vv. 6-11. John is saying there is a reputable person to be used as a witness to the events concerning Jesus Christ, and that reputable witness is the Holy Spirit.

The Holy Spirit was present at the baptism of Jesus, descending upon Jesus in bodily form, as a dove (Luke 3:21-22). In regard to His death, the Holy Spirit was the one who empowered the resurrection of Jesus (Romans 8:11), the one sent by Jesus to empower the apostles in response to a promise (Acts 2:33), the one by whom the apostles could witness the good news (Acts 1:8), and the one who inspired the writers to leave the infallible story for succeeding generations (1 Corinthians 2:13; 1 Thessalonians 2:13; 2 Peter 1:21). Thus, the Holy Spirit was truly involved and able to be a reputable witness of these events.

"beareth witness" (TO MARTOUROUN, present participle of MARTUREO) refers to continual witnessing. The Holy Spirit continues to witness through the apostles and the prophets, whose writings even in the Old Testament continued then (2 Peter 1:19-21) and also today. To be brought to saving faith in Jesus Christ, all one needs to do is heed the message of proofs left available to all men (John 20:30-31).

because the Spirit is the truth - John now goes deeper, far beyond the idea that all the Spirit did was witness and teach. This statement involves the Person of the Holy Spirit Himself. The Holy Spirit and truth are one and the same. Truth is embodied in the Holy Spirit. Just as Jesus, in His person of deity, embodied "the way, the truth and the life"

(John 14:6), so the Holy Spirit, as a person of deity, also embodies "the truth." He not only is the source of truth, He **is** the truth and can speak only truth. As God is called "love" (1 John 4:8), the Holy Spirit is called "truth." He is repeatedly given the title of "Spirit of truth" (John 14:17; 15:26; 1 John 4:6). As such, the Holy Spirit is certainly qualified to be a witness of Jesus Christ.

Additional Note About 1 John 5:7-8

In the King James Version of 1611, the verse order and content are somewhat different from that of our text (ASV). There is an additional statement included in v. 7: "For there are three that bear record in heaven, the Father, the Word and the Holy Ghost: and these three are one." The statement, "And it is the Spirit that beareth witness, because the Spirit is truth," is put in the latter part of v. 6, while our text (ASV) has this statement as v. 7.

The additional statement is not included in the ASV, RSV, NASB, NIV, or any other major work of translation in later times. Footnotes about this additional verse are included in the NASB and the NIV.

That such additional statement should be considered an interpolation is acknowledged almost universally by scholars in the twentieth century. This statement could never have appeared in the King James Version except for the poor judgment of Erasmus in 1516, as he was willing to insert the verse if it could be found in any one manuscript. One of the more succinct and concise statements about it says this: "The addition is spurious without any question. It was added to the quotation in 1 John by a Spanish heretic Priscillian (died A.D. 385) in a Latin sermon. For his work the verse was added to a Latin manuscript of Pseudo-Virgilius and came gradually to work its way into late Latin texts. From these it was copied in Greek translation into only two late Greek manuscripts: 162 (15th. century); 34 (16th. century) and in the margin of 88. Erasmus did not include it in his first edition of his Greek testament (1516) because it did not occur in any of the manuscripts which he collated for his text. It was added to a later edition when a friend asked why he had omitted it. He told the man that he would add it if he was shown it in a manuscript; and so from manuscript 34 it became a part of the Received Text in his third edition. Thus it came into the King James Version, which was translated from a later edition of this text. There is no possibility that this verse could have been a part of the original text."[7] Another put it in much blunter language, but that which cannot be misunderstood, when he said, "Erasmus. . .rashly offered to insert it. . .so it got into the Vulgate and finally in the Textus Receptus by the stupidity of Erasmus."[8]

T. H. Horne, one who could not be faulted as a modern "liberal" by any astute person, gave copious attention to this problem in a famous introductory work published in 1839. Essentially, his argumentation followed these lines:

1. The passage is not found in a single, genuine, unaltered Greek manuscript prior to the 16th. Century.

2. The passage is not in the earliest and best critical editions of the Greek New Testament.

3. The passage is not in any ancient version save the Latin.

4. Not all manuscripts of the Latin version contain the clause.

5. It is not quoted by the Greek fathers, or early ecclesiastical writers.

6. It is not quoted by the "Latin fathers."

7. The Protestant Reformers rejected it or marked it as doubtful.[9]

Another scholar of earlier years adds some thoughts about the disputed passage in regard to the internal evidence of using the clause.

1. The connection does not demand it, since John is writing of witnesses to Jesus, and this statement would be a break in thought.

2. The language is not such as John would use, for when he used "Father," he normally used "Son," not the term "Word." It would be highly unusual, to say the least.

3. Without this passage, the sense of the argument John is making is clear and appropriate.[10]

So, this disputed statement, found only in the King James Version today, contains a statement of truth no doubt, but its claim to authenticity as inspired scripture has no basis. Truth stated does not need spurious, doubtful help. The truth of the "Trinity" is well taught in scripture (Matthew 3:16-17; 28:19; John 14:26; 15:26; 2 Corinthians 13:14; Ephesians 4:4-6; 1 Peter 1:2). The word "trinity" does not occur in scripture, but it is not merely a human concept; the truth of the triune Deity is plenteous. One need not grasp at this disputed passage to see the truth about God taught accurately.

Verse 8 For there are three who bear witness, the Spirit, and the water, and the blood: and the three agree in one.

For there are three who bear witness, the Spirit and the water, and the blood - Further verifying of why the true believer is an overcomer of the world (v. 5), and having emphasized the witness of the water and the blood (v. 6), John now adds the witness of the Spirit (v. 7). John thus portrays three witnesses and their absolute agreement.

The significance of three witnesses would not be lost on a Jew familiar with the Law (Deuteronomy 17:6; 19:15; Numbers 35:30). Since Jewish jurisprudence required multiple witnesses (preferably three), John was within the most acceptable rules of argumentation in citing three witnesses.

The use of the plural present participle (HOI MARTUROUNTES) shows that the work of three witnesses continues even to the present time of John's writing. The Spirit, the water, and the blood are continually bearing witness. Just as Abel's blood continued to speak to the generations long after he died (Hebrews 11:4), it is proper to conclude that the events in the life and death of Jesus, recorded accurately under the guidance of the Holy Spirit, can continue to "speak," or witness, to readers today. These events continue to speak volumes today to inquiring and honest hearts.

The historical events in the ministry of Jesus, water (baptism) and blood (death), show themselves even more credible as a proper interpretation when one accepts the continuing force of John's argument. These two events can continue to speak volumes to generations yet unborn, when they hear the message of His glorious life. Other suggested interpretations can have some significance, perhaps figurative, but these have significance as literal witnesses.

The witness borne at the baptism was unquestioned when John the Immerser gave it (John 1:32-34). And witness was surely borne at the crucifixion to a Roman centurion (Matthew 27:54). This time of remarkable circumstances, able to be seen by all, never has been superseded by anything: the rending of the veil of the temple, the earthquake, the rending of the rocks, and the opening of the tombs (Matthew 27:51-53). Only the end of time and the second coming of the Lord will ever equal it.

and the three agree in one - John states unequivocably that these three witnesses agree. This agreement is to the truth that Jesus was the Son of God. He was of two-fold nature, both human and divine. He was God's offering in love for the sins of the world (John 3:16).

For emphasis, John used an unusual grammatical construction. Literally, it is "the three unto the one are" (HOI TREIS EIS TO EN EISIN). They cooperate to establish the truth about Jesus. The verdict is unanimous. There can be no usefulness to any further argument about it; it is settled. The witnesses are three, they are credible, they all agree.

Verse 9 If we receive the witness of men, the witness of God is greater: for the witness of God is this, that he hath borne witness concerning his Son.

If we receive the witness of men, the witness of God is greater: - John notes it is normal practice to accept credible testimony from men; thus, it is even more sensible to accept Divine testimony. John argues from the lesser to the greater. Men are credible, certainly. God is even more credible, and anyone accepting men must surely accept God.

Interestingly, John used the present indicative tense "receive" (LAMBANOMEN) to express a conditional statement, with the traditional "if" (EI). The usual mode John might have considered would have been subjunctive, rather than indicative. John's use of the indicative is thought to be the gnomic present tense, showing that the truth of the condition is already accepted. This would be using EI as an interrogative particle of a "condition determined as fulfilled."[11] So, though stated conditionally, John emphasizes the well-known fact that men normally accept the testimony of other men. One can realize, however, that the witness of man can be limited, partial, and even from deceptive evidence. Yet, if two or three agree, it is accepted by men.

Next, John claims a far greater witness: God. His witness is absolute in trustworthiness. Now, who knows the Son of God any better than God? Jesus had taught, ". . .no one knoweth the Son, save the Father;" (Matthew 11:27), and also, ". . .the Father that sent me beareth witness of me" (John 8:18). Who was present at His baptism (Matthew 3:17) and His death on the cross (Luke 23:46)? Who is an unquestionable witness?

for the witness of God is this, that he hath borne witness concerning his Son - No more credible witness of the Son could be found than the Father. John concludes a two-part argument about acceptable testimony and witnesses: (1) this witnessing about Jesus is true for it comes from the most credible witness possible, God Himself; (2) this testimony is credible since it is from a father about his own son.

Thus John weaves the three witnesses mentioned in v. 8 into the fabric of God, since this is the way God testifies to man about His Son. The Holy Spirit is God (Acts 5:3-4), and the water and the blood are recorded by the Spirit to be used in all subsequent generations of mankind for the basis of faith. Thus Deity, the Father, has furnished these three witnesses, and what they say is what God said.

This is not an inner "better-felt-than-told" testimony; rather, it is the ever-present testimony of God's holy scriptures. They continue to tell the story of love, grace, mercy, salvation, eternal life, providence, and hope in Jesus Christ. The Spirit leads men, witnesses to men this way, through the use of the scriptures (Romans 8:14,16). It is surely personal, very personal, but it is not subjective.

Verse 10 He that believeth on the Son of God hath the witness in him: he that believeth not God hath made him a liar; because he hath not believed in the witness that God hath borne concerning his Son.

He that believeth on the Son of God hath the witness in him - Ongoing, continuous belief on the Son of God shows the continuing witness and confidence the Christian has within himself. By accepting the witnesses of God (spirit, water, blood) the Christian can maintain his faithful pattern of life.

"Believeth" (PISTEUOWN) is present tense as is "hath" (ECHEI). These two verbs depict the life of continual faith, continual acceptance, and continual demonstration. One of John's oft-used expressions, "believe in" (PISTEUO EIS), used thirty-seven times by him in his writings, emphasizes a faith of personal trust and commitment. It is "in," "on," or "unto" Jesus. It moves on beyond acceptance of mere facts taught about Him and rests on the object Himself, the very person of the Son of God. It is a strong expression, encompassing all there is in trustful obedience to the Lord.

he that believeth not God hath made him a liar; because he hath not believed in the witness that God hath borne concerning his Son - The person who refuses God's three witnesses has, in effect, said God's witnesses are not true. If God has presented false witnesses, that makes God a liar, at least in the mind of the unbeliever. If God's claims are false, then God, is propagating lies (see further in 1:10).

"Hath made" (PEPOIEKEN, perfect indicative of POIEO) shows the greatest force to the fact that the unbeliever "hath made" God a liar in his own mind. The perfect tense shows it is a judgment by the unbeliever about God that he has completed at some point of time in the past, and the force of that judgment continues in his present way of life. It is also "said and done" in the mind of the rejecting unbeliever. And it continues in his mind.

There is no ground of neutrality. John leaves no room for such, as does no other writer of the New Testament, nor does Jesus Himself. The one rejecting Jesus as God's Son in John's day insulted the veracity of Him who cannot lie (Hebrews 6:18; Titus 1:2). The same is true in any age. Infidels, skeptics, agnostics, and atheists (pseudo or true) are doing no less. In rejecting God's witnesses today, they are making God a liar. Jesus said, "he that is not with me is against me" (Matthew 12:30), and ". . .he that is not against you is for you" (Luke 9:50), and "he that is not against us is for you" (Mark 9:40). Cerinthus' denials in John's day were no worse than his latter-day disciples who continue to reject the truth today.

189

Verse 11 And the witness is this, that God gave unto us eternal life, and this life is in his Son.

And the witness is this, that God gave unto us eternal life - Reaching now a climax about the witnesses concerning the Son of God ("witness" in both noun and verb forms appears ten times in vv. 6-11), John claims that the believer has a witness, a testimony within himself: eternal life. He accentuates this eternal life by placing it first in the clause, literally, "that life eternal gave to us the God." Such accentuation is common in Greek grammar but worthy of notice here. This anarthous use of eternal life (no definite article) stresses the quality of the life, rather than making a distinction as to which kind of life it is.

Again John connects eternal life with the Son of God. The results of God's witness in the life of the believer will include eternal life. This is not new to John's writings, even in this epistle (see 3:14; 4:9-10). Add to this the many statements about being "begotten" (2:29; 3:9; 4:7; 5:1,14,18), and one sees that John returns full circle once again in this passage. The believer has eternal life.

Recalling John's progress in argumentation, one notes:

1. God has testified, witnessed to men about His Son.
2. He has used the Spirit, the water, and the blood.
3. He thus brings His Son to mankind for its benefit.
4. Eternal life is in this Son.
5. Those who accept this testimony can have the Son.
6. Those who accept this testimony and have the Son can have eternal life.
7. Those who refuse the testimony cannot have the Son and consequently cannot have eternal life.
8. Additionally, those who refuse must accept the fact they are making out God to be a liar.

Very interesting at this point in John's use of the aorist tense when he claims God "gave" unto us eternal life (EDOKEN, aorist indicative active of DIDOMI). This use of the aorist tense gives the meaning that God completed, at some past time, this action of giving eternal life. Four major possibilities are projected here as to what John is saying: (1) it was completed by the action at the crucifixion of Jesus Christ; (2) it was completed by the entire scope of the incarnation; (3) it was completed only in the sense that eternal life has been promised to Christians, that is, given in promise but not given in fact; (4) it was completed in the life of each individual at the time of their conversion to Jesus Christ.

These possibilities suggest some immediate concerns. Since the action at the cross was universal (1 John 2:2), is eternal life then given to everyone for whom Christ died? The Incarnation was also universal (John 3:16); is eternal life to be given for all those to whom Christ came? If it be only a promise, then is eternal life itself given, or was only the promise given? If so, John would then be using the aorist to refer to the giving of a promise; and if it be only the giving of a promise, why did he not say it that way? If one takes it to be only in promise, the interpretation contradicts what John is saying here: He said God "gave" eternal life; He did not say God gave a promise of eternal life.

There would be no sense in John's pointed argument here if we only have eternal life "in promise." The next verse will claim we have the Son; and if we have the Son, we also have the life. Yet, if we have the eternal life only "in promise," then we would have the Son only "in promise." This is unthinkable, for the vital relationship one has with the Son is absolutely necessary, and without it man is nothing. We do not have just a promise of a relationship with the Son; we now, in the present time, have the relationship! So also, we now, in the present time, have eternal life! One violates the rules of grammar to argue otherwise. It is not necessary to be so afraid of compromising the truth about falling from grace, or eternal security of the believer, that we renounce a clear teaching of the Lord. Proper understanding of eternal life will enhance true arguments about apostasy, not weaken them (see more fully in 2:25).

and this life is in his Son - This shows the single relationship that bears the fruit of eternal life. One must understand this life is in God's Son and can be found there alone. It is from Him, brought by Him to mankind, treasured up in Him, produced by Him, and obtained in Him. Separate from Him, man has no claim on eternal life and no hope of it.

Verse 12 He that hath the Son hath the life; he that hath not the Son of God hath not the life.

The logical conclusion, climax, and crown of John's

progress through the tests about overcoming is now stated. To have eternal life is to have the Son, i.e., accepting God's witnesses in obedient faith, and thus overcoming the world by participating in the life that transcends this world. The one who has this eternal life in the Son has truly been victorious. He has overcome this world. Death now holds no power over him; he will rise again (1 Corinthians 15:50-58). He will have the crown of life (James 1:12), he will dwell forever in the joys of the Lord (Matthew 25:21,23), he will inherit the kingdom where there is eternal life (Matthew 25:34,36).

Since there is a present relationship with the Son, there also should be found some benefits of a present participation in eternal life. Consider that now a Christian can: (1) bear the fruit of the Spirit [Galatians 5:22], (2) present his members to God in service [Romans 6:13], (3) break the habits of sin [Romans 6:1-2, 15-18], (4) crucify the flesh [Galatians 5:24], and (5) walk by the Spirit [Galatians 5:25].

To have the Son of God (TON HUION ECHEI) refers to a vital spiritual connection. It means a relationship. As one can be a citizen of the United States of America, one is thus in a relationship established by one's birth or naturalization. One is similarly a citizen of God's kingdom (Philippians 3:20; Colossians 1:13; Revelation 1:6,9), and this is a relationship also established by birth (John 3:3-5; Titus 3:3-4) or by adoption (Galatians 4:5-7). This birth and adoption can be accomplished only by the power of God. But there is a relationship.

Further, this relationship in God's kingdom also is seen to be tantamount to a relationship with His Son. When one is immersed, one rises to a new life (Romans 6:3-4). Yet when one is immersed, one is immersed into a relationship with Christ (Galatians 3:27; Romans 6:3-4). Since one enters the kingdom by birth, since one is born again to this new life when immersed for the remission of sins, and since immersion is into Christ, it follows that to be in the kingdom is to be in Christ.

Thus, life comes to the sinner when he becomes a believer, obedient to the directions of his Lord and Master. A relationship with Jesus Christ is established and eternal life results.

John has now completed another circle. This continuous weaving and merging may be hard to follow, but the conclusions are seen easily.

1. The sinner can hear God's witnesses.

2. The sinner can accept the witnesses, believe, and obey God.

3. The sinner has accepted the humanity and deity of Jesus Christ (water and blood) as a vicarious offering for sins.

4. The sinner is transformed into a saint, upon his belief.

5. This believer now has a relationship with the Son.

6. The Son has life within Himself and imparts it to the believer.

7. All others are excluded from this eternal life.

Conclusion 5:13-21

A. Boldness in the Assurance of Eternal Life
5:13-15

¹³*These things have I written unto you, that ye may know that ye have eternal life, even unto you that believe on the name of the Son of God. ¹⁴And this is the boldness which we have toward him, that, if we ask anything according to his will, he heareth us: ¹⁵and if we know that he heareth us whatsoever we ask, we know that we have the petitions which we have asked of him.*

Verse 13 These things have I written unto you, that ye may know that ye have eternal life, even unto you that believe on the name of the Son of God.

These things have I written unto you - The antecedent of "these things" (TAUTA) has two possible interpretations: (1) the preceding context, vv. 1-12 only, or (2) the entire epistle. That it refers to the entire epistle seems to be preferred for several reasons. **First,** it seems to parallel the way John treated the concluding portions of his Gospel. There he stressed a purpose for writing, "that ye may believe that Jesus Christ is the Son of God; and that believing ye may have life in his name" (John 20:31). The Gospel was written to produce faith and life in the reader; this epistle is written to produce knowledge and assurance in the life of the Christian. **Second,** all of the tests and grounds of identity are to reassure the saints of their relation to God: walking in the light (1:7), obeying the commandments of God (2:3-5), loving the brethren (2:9-11), believing in the Incarnate Son (2:22-23; 4:1-3; 5:1-5), and practicing righteousness (2:29-3:10a). **Third,** the parallelism and connection between 1:4 and 5:13 so imply: "we are writing" (GRAPHOMEN, present indicative) and "I have written" (EGRAPSA, aorist indicative).¹² The change of tenses seems to imply the finishing of the task, the entire epistle.

The King James Version added an extra clause in v. 13, "These things have I written unto you that believe on the name of the Son of God." This clause is not included in the ASV, RSV, NASB, or the NIV. It is not necessary to the sense of the sentence at all, since it duplicates the last clause of the verse. Due to the grammatical construction of the verse, several textual problems have arisen; but they are not of serious import to the true meaning of the verse and would not change the meaning in substance.[13]

that ye may know - "know" (EIDEITE, perfect subjunctive of OIDA) refers to assured knowledge. It is a clear perception, a proper intellectual understanding that is impressed on the heart. It is nothing startling or new to John, and it should not be to Christians either. We ought to know we have, presently participate in, eternal life. Such statement surely did not bother John, as eternal life seemed to be one of his favorite subjects and expressions. This knowledge accentuated the concept of assurance by the use of OIDA: ". . .freq. used to introduce a well known fact that is generally accepted. . . ,"[14] and ". . .equiv. to it is well known, acknowledged: . . . ."[15] If John had meant that the experience of eternal life was yet only a promise, more likely he would have chosen another verb, GINOSKO, which stresses "come to know." Additionally, soon John will use this same verb OIDA again to stress another assured fact of knowledge, "And we know that the Son of God has come" (v. 20). One of the major reasons for writing the epistle was the assured knowledge of the coming of the Incarnate Son. Yet just as sure is the fact that Christians presently have eternal life, which is another of the major reasons for the book.

that ye have eternal life - In regard to this assurance of present participation in eternal life, one needs to notice several things. **First,** John spoke continually of this eternal life the same as he did present knowledge of the Son of God, as noted above. The same way we can have one, we can have the other. We are not limited in our knowledge to only the promise of knowing something; neither are we limited in our having eternal life to only the promise of receiving this life. **Second,** John and Paul both spoke of eternal life as a present experience. John said the Christian ". . .hath passed

195

out of death into life" (John 5:24), and Paul said that newly baptized persons "might walk in newness of life," and they were "dead unto sin, but alive unto God in Jesus Christ" (Romans 6:4,11). No one can deny that this is a picture of dying to sin, crucifying the old man and having a new life in Christ. **Third,** there are other spiritual concepts that Christians can know, but few arguments are fostered about them. One can know sins have been remitted (Acts 2:38; 22:16), a new birth has been effected (John 3:5; 1 Peter 1:23), help is given in every temptation (1 Corinthians 10:12-13), God will never forsake us in our daily lives (Hebrews 13:5-6), and prayers will be answered (James 1:5; 4:2-3). How does a Christian know all of the above? The Scriptures so teach. If one can know that all these spiritual concepts are presently true, then he can also know that eternal life is presently his in which to participate (see more fully on 2:25).

even unto you that believe on the name of the Son of God - The identification of Jesus Christ as the Son of God occurs seven times in vv. 5-12. "Believe" (PISTEUOUSIN, present indicative) highlights the idea of keeping on believing on the name of the Son of God. One must persevere, else one can be lost by losing faith. Proper faith brings proper obedience, and this equals salvation. Lack of faith does not bring obedience, and this equals damnation (Mark 16:16), a concept and a scripture most denominationalists strive to deny. John wishes to fortify their faith, assure them to knowledge and eternal life, and help their hope.

The "name of the Son of God" sums all that for which the Son of God stands. It certainly stood for that which Cerinthus strove to deny in John's day. This is a very important doctrine; much stress was laid upon it by John, as well as Peter and Paul (see further in 2:12 and 3:23.).

Verse 14 And this is the boldness which we have toward him, that, if we ask anything according to his will, he heareth us:

And this is the boldness that we have - "Confidence" is the translation of the KJV, RSV and NASB, while "assurance" is used by NIV. This is the fourth time in this epistle John speaks of this "boldness" (PARRHESIA) - 2:28;

3:21; 4:17 and 5:14, while he uses it an additional nine times in his Gospel. This "boldness" is a perfect twin to join with the "knowledge" of the last verse. PARRHESIA and OIDA both emphasize personal assurance. (For PARRHESIA see 3:21.) Thus, the Christian may have assured knowledge that he has eternal life and assured boldness that God will answer his petitions! Again, this is not unique or new to scriptures (Ephesians 3:12; Hebrews 4:16).

toward him - is PROS AUTON and is translated "in him" (KJV, RSV), "before him" (NASB), and "in approaching him" (NIV). PROS, when used with the accusative has the basic meaning of "toward,"[16] or "before,"[17]

that, if we ask anything according to his will - Since the Christian continues to believe on the name of the Son of God and has eternal life predicated on such belief, John has added "and" to encourage boldness in our petitions to God. Now he adds these petitions must be consistent with God's will, a fact made very plain by John. Barnes has some wise cautions in this area: (1) prayers must be "in accordance with what he has **declared** that he is willing to grant", (2) answers will be limited by "what **he** sees to be best for us", (3) prayers must be limited "to what it will be **consistent** for God to bestow upon us", (4) promises to hear must be limited "to what will be **for the good of the whole**."[18]

God is no charlatan, and limiting answers to petitions that are according to His will is not unfair at all for mankind. This is so because (1) God is all-wise, (2) God has revealed His will to mankind, (3) God is love and the end result for every man is a product of that love, (4) God wants us to ask, (5) the one who refuses or neglects to ask is the one who is not according to His will anyway, and (6) man also has the right to limit petitions. Even man, when petitioned by other men, has the right to choose his answer. Man is expected to use whatever knowledge and judgment he possesses in dealing with his fellowman. Why should men expect less of God?

"His will" (THELEMA) is used here subjectively, for it truly is God's will, not man's. It is ". . .as a rule the will of God. . .if the will of God should so decree. . .according to his will."[19] Additional thought expresses ". . .if God please or permit."[20]

he heareth us - When God is said to hear the Christian, it means to grant the petition. It is more than mere knowledge of that for which man has spoken; it is the acceptance of those things that are according to God's will and the responding to them. God hears in the sense of answering and granting. It is "the pregnant sense of hearing favorably."[21] God has ever been willing and ready to open His heart in needy mankind (Psalms 34:15; 37:4).

Verse 15 and if we know that he heareth us whatsoever we ask, we know that we have the petitions which we have asked of him.

This type of conditional clause is somewhat unusual in the New Testament, for "if" (EAN) is used with the indicative rather than the more frequent subjunctive. "We know" repeats the verb of assured knowledge (OIDA), and here it is in the perfect tense (OIDAMEN - 2 perf. 1 pers. pl.). However, this construction also is used ". . .with the sense of the present."[22] Though normally the conditional sentence would be supported by the subjunctive tense of the verb, the use of the indicative views the condition as fulfilled.[23] Such can be known for fulfillment of petitions to God and is in line with v. 14. Thus, John repeats the assurance of fulfillment of God's promise. The condition is if we ask "according to His will"; and when we do so, we then know with assurance the prayers will be heard. We know because He has promised.

John reassured the faithful follower of God about a favorable response from God. Has not God promised, "For every one that asketh receiveth" (Matthew 7:8)? God hears us and grants to us is John's point. No doctrine has more assurance than that of granted prayers. We may not understand how or when the answer comes, we may not recognize it when it happens, we may have trouble identifying it, we may lose patience when it is not granted immediately, we may have something else granted than that for which we specifically asked, but **God's answer is on the way!** We are assured of this when meeting the condition. "We know" (OIDAMEN) is the same meaning as in v. 13, where we are told we know that we have eternal life. This verb, within itself, expresses assurance and is a common usage in the New Testament.

B. Boldness in Prayer 5:16-17

¹⁶If any man see his brother sinning a sin not unto death, he shall ask, and God will give him life for them that sin not unto death. There is a sin unto death: not concerning this do I say that he should make request. ¹⁷All unrighteousness is sin; and there is a sin not unto death.

In context, this continues the assurance to the Christian of two things: (1) that he has eternal life [vv. 13-15], and (2) that he can petition God expecting an answer. John circles back to 3:13-24 where he speaks of the same two things: life and prayer. Now he repeats the encouragement to Christians about answers to prayers.

This section has to do with the Christian's duties and relations to erring brethren. This is hard for some commentators to describe, as they do not want to give in to the idea that a child of God can sin in such way as to be lost. One author seems reluctant as the speaks of this section as "post-baptismal sin."²⁴ John has warned the Christian about those who are following the anti-christ, about brethren who are not loving each other, about brethren who love the world, and about brethren who might accept inaccurate doctrines concerning Jesus. Now, he deals with what the Christian should do in his prayer life concerning his brethren. He does have a responsibility to them; what is it?

Verse 16 If any man see his brother sinning a sin not unto death, he shall ask, and God will give him life for them that sin not unto death. There is a sin unto death: not concerning this do I say that he should make request.

If any man see his brother sinning a sin not unto death - "Any man" has to be a brother in this context ("his brother" is TON ADELPHON AUTOU), so this instruction is clearly limited to relations among Christians. This wording does not refer to one's physical family, or any other relationship. "See" indicates that a brother can observe the situation in some way and distinguish between a sin unto death and a sin not unto death.

Here a brother is a sinner, but not that special kind of sinner that is "unto death." Although that kind of brother will be included shortly, John's first instruction has to do with a brother who is not sinning unto death. This sinning, however, is very serious; and we know this because the present tense participle (HAMARTANONTA) is used. This construction demands the sense of continuing sinful practices. The brother is not committing one sin or making one or two mistakes; he is practicing sin. It is his way of life; his habits include this sinfulness. Literally, this is "sinning a sin" (as our ASV text has). Other translations are somewhat misleading, as if the sin were singular: "sin a sin" (KJV), "commit a sin" (NIV), "committing a sin" (NASB). The RSV wanders further afield in using "committing what is not a mortal sin," choosing to adopt Roman Catholic vernacular. This is the only time this expression occurs in the New Testament, but there is no doubt as to its meaning. This erring brother is in a regular practice of sin.

In regard to the idea injected about "mortal sin" (RSV), one can profit from a quotation. "Confusion has resulted from making the distinction between 'mortal' and 'venial' sins and then listing certain gross sins as mortal. Romanists list seven: **superbia, avaritia, luxuria, ira, gula, invidia, acedia (Traegheit,** sloth), and then devise a penitential system that is to be applied by the church, in which the priests measure out the **satisfactio operis** in their sacrament of penance."[25]

"Not unto death" uses PROS for "unto," and it is the same word as v. 14. It refers to "facing" or "toward." Whatever this brother is doing in error will not lead to death (THANATON). Jesus used the same phrase in the same way during the incident with Lazarus, when He said, "This sickness is not unto death" (ME PROS THANATON) [John 11:4]. The deaths in these two cases are different, one physical and one spiritual, but the use of PROS is the same.

he shall ask, and God will give him life for them that sin not unto death - "He shall ask" (AITESEI, future indicative active of AITEO) implies a command to so pray.

201

The future tense presents an incompleted action. This use is thought to be aoristic; and since the origins of the future tense are thought to have come as a variation of the aorist subjunctive, the wording would carry the implied force of the imperative mode. The aorist subjunctive implies doubt, while the future indicative implies a positive action.[26] So here we have a "positive future" carrying the idea that contemplated action in the future should be completed. Pray for this sinner!

"God will give" is actually only "he will give" (DOSEI). Most versions show "God" in italics, and correctly so. There is some controversy about who this "he" might be, but it is not of great importance. Obviously, "he" who gives this life cannot be the petitioner for the sinning brother, else he would not be asking. Obviously, this "he" cannot be the sinning brother, else there would be no need for other brethren to ask on his behalf. So, that leaves the other possibility, God, since He is the only one who can give this life.

"Life" (ZOEIN) given here is the opposite of that which is "unto death." This life is not physical life, but spiritual life that concludes in the state of eternal life, mentioned so prominently throughout the preceding context.

There is a sin unto death - This passage is difficult and one of many interpretations. Note must be taken that this "sin" is anarthous; i.e., it is not "the sin." This demands the interpretation that this "sin unto death" is not a specific sin, nor is it one in some special connotation. Rather, it shows this "sin unto death" is a class of sin, a quality of sin, a state of sin. It is not any specific sin, though many confuse this with the "blasphemy against the Holy Spirit."

"There has been a great diversity of opinion in regard to the meaning of this passage, and the views of expositors of the New Testament are by no means settled as to its true sense. It does not comport with the design of these Notes to examine the opinions which have been held in detail. A bare reference, however, to some of them will show the difficulty of determining with certainty what the passage means, and the impropriety of any very great confidence in one's own judgment in the case. Among these opinions are the following. Some have supposed that the sin against the Holy Ghost is intended; some that the phrase denotes any great and enormous sin, as murder, idolatry, adultery; some that it denotes some sin that was punishable by death by the laws of Moses; some that it denotes a sin that subjected the offender to excommunication from the synagogue or the church; some that it refers to sins which brought fatal disease upon the offender, as in the case of those who abuse the Lord's Supper at Corinth, (see Notes on 1 Corinthians xi 30:) some that it refers to crimes committed against the laws, for which the offender was sentenced to death, ...some that it refers to sins **before** and **after** baptism, the former of which might be pardoned, but the latter of which might not be; and some, and perhaps this is the opinion among the Roman Catholics, that it refers to sins that might or might not be pardoned after death, thus referring to the doctrine of purgatory."[27]

Consideration must be given as to the words used for sin, if proper conclusions can be drawn about this "sin unto death." Previously, John has said, "sin is lawlessness" (3:4). HAMARTANO equals ANOMIA in this statement. In the next verse of the present text, after mentioning "sin unto death," John will say, "all unrighteousness is sin." It will be there that HAMARTANO will equal ADIKIA. So, what we have in John's thinking is that HAMARTANO, ANOMIA, and ADIKIA refer to the same position of man in relationship with God. Distinctions can be seen along finer lines; but for John's purposes in this epistle, a man guilty of any one of these is in the same sad state as if he were guilty of all of them.

The basic meaning of "sin" (HAMARTANO) is "missing the mark."[28] The basic meaning of "lawlessness" (ANOMIA) is "lawlessness, violation of law, iniquity, sin."[29] "Unrighteousness" (ADIKIA) carries the idea of "injustice, wrong; iniquity, falsehood, deceitfulness,"[30] and "wrongdoing. . .unrighteousness, wickedness, injustice. . . said to be sin."[31] One source has a most interesting comment about the relation of these verbs: "ADIKIA is the comprehensive term for wrong, or wrong-doing, as between persons; ANOMIA, lawlessness, is the rejection of Divine law, or wrong committed against it."[32] Thus, this "sin unto death" could be both of these, since John has said sin is both lawlessness and unrighteousness. The "sin unto death" would include actions against other persons and against God's laws also. Note that it would not suffice for one to say if there were sins against other people, those sins would be a violation of God's laws anyway. The use of both words, ANOMIA and ADIKIA, by John to be equal to sin demands that both classes of sins have been direct, not indirect, as would be the above supposed case.

Looking analytically at the "sin unto death," one must remember several things.

1. This sin can be observed by brethren. Being thus seen, such could become the object of prayers, so John mentions the fruitlessness of such prayers. John does not seem to **forbid** praying for the brother sinning a sin unto death; rather, he does **not encourage** such. A Christian has no assurance such prayers will be answered, as he has assurance of other prayers being heard. The injunction to avoid this kind of prayer, which seems to be the implication, emphasizes the idea that, to be avoided, this practice must first have been observed. So a brother can know another brother is acting in this terrible fashion and avoid useless prayers for him to be given life.

2. This sin can be practiced by brethren. It needs to be pointed out that blasphemy against the Holy Spirit was not mentioned as among brethren, but among outsiders (Matthew 12:24; Mark 3:22). They were disobedient believers who refused to come to the Lord and who, knowing the truth, misapplied the power of miracle-working done by the Lord to the devil, not to the Holy Spirit. Since miracles are not being worked today, can anyone blaspheme the Holy Spirit in the way it was done in Jesus' day?

3. This sin was a continual practice. It was a way of life, the usual habit of the brother. If the "sin not unto death" is a continual practice, so also must be the "sin unto death," for both descriptions are similar, one being negative and the other positive.

4. This sin is a general way of life. It is not any specific sin as is shown by the anarthous use of the noun. It cannot be "the sin," and this lends further credence that it cannot be limited to any one sin, such as blasphemy against the Holy Spirit.

5. This "sin unto death" refers to spiritual death. Since

Christ is the source of eternal life in this context and this life is given in answer to the prayers for one sinning a sin not unto death, it follows this death must be eternal death. This "death" is the opposite of whatever the "life" in the passage is. This life cannot be physical life, for the erring brother already has this; and there is no point in giving it to him. Yet some kind of life can be given in answer to the prayers of concerned brethren. It is the eternal life, which his sinning will eventually cause him to miss if he neglects to repent. So, death being the opposite, this death is eternal, spiritual death.

6. This "sin unto death" leads to destruction. Since God has promised to forgive and cleanse erring Christians of those sins of which they will repent and confess to Him (1:9), this must be a case where repentance and confession are not imminent or forthcoming. This is a situation of sin, to keep it in the context of this epistle, when a brother ceases to walk in the light and prefers darkness (1:6). He therefore does not have the continuing cleansing which the Savior offers to those walking with Him in the light (1:8). This is the case of a brother who goes astray and chooses to stay that way in spite of all he has known and experienced.

7. The problem is not an "unforgivable sin," the problem is the impenitent heart of the sinner. This destruction comes similarly as that destruction when one who goes so far in searing his heart and conscience so callously (1 Timothy 4:2) that it is impossible for him to repent (Hebrews 6:4-6). It is not impossible for God to forgive; the problem is all on man's side: he either will not or cannot repent. The sacrifice of Christ can cover sins of only the penitent heart. If someone has no appetite for repentance, there is no sacrifice in earth or heaven that can help him (Hebrews 10:26-31). Truly, this last state is worse than the first (2 Peter 2:20-22).

not concerning this do I say he should make request

This "make request" (EROTESE) is different from the previous "shall ask" (DOSEI) when referring to the brother who is not sinning unto death. There is probably no great significance to this, as John could be using the words interchangeably in this verse. There is a change in tense, however, that is significant. EROTESE is aorist subjunctive, and the use of the subjunctive does imply the doubt of any actual request (see citation by A. T. Robertson above). Therefore, the Christian, having no assurance his prayers for eternal life for this person will be heard, will refrain from such requests. They are not according to the expressed will of God.

The Christian should be bold in requests to God, for there is assurance he will be heard (v. 15). God seeks our petitions and will answer them. He will give life to one erring brother but cannot to the other who continues "sinning a sin unto death." The Christian can pray such a brother would repent, though he should not pray for God to give him life.

Verse 17 All unrighteousness is sin: and there is a sin not unto death.

All unrighteousness is sin - This first clause is similar to 3:4, "sin is lawlessness." There is a change in words (see above), but the force of the thought is the same. All actions that deviate from the Holy nature of Him who is Almighty God are sin. "All thy commandments are righteousness" (Psalms 119:172), so whether they be positive instructions or negative denials, the commandments of the Lord comprise righteousness. To deviate from any one or all is to act in an unrighteous manner.

In context John is perhaps avoiding any chance some may take his statement, "a sin not unto death," to be minimizing some sins. He surely is not. Docetics did minimize sin by claiming their actions done in the physical body were not accountable (see Introduction). Let none say John excuses sin of any sort. Known as the "apostle of love," he is also one of the most outspoken apostles and strongest of teachers against the life of sin. Two facts are crystal clear to John: (1) All types of wrongdoing are sin; i.e., they actually do "miss the mark"; (2) there is a sin (sins) not unto death, and the blood of Jesus is able to cleanse the penitent confessors [see 1:8-9]. John never took sin lightly!

Many sins should have prayers raised for them; and in this context, one type of sin coupled with one type of prayer will be effective. The ineffective prayer is the prayer for eternal life to be given to the man sinning a sin unto death. This constant sinner, settled and comfortable in sin, satisfied with his position and way of life, having no desire for repentance, is not the recipient of eternal life.

and there is a sin not unto death - John encourages prayers for such erring brethren. God can forgive them, as they still are teachable, can be brought to repentance, and have hearts tender enough to respond to Divine appeal. It can be consistent with God's will (v. 14) and eternal life can be given them (v. 16).

After due consideration is given to all these thoughts, does any human being ever know with absolute certainty when an erring brother is beyond the ability of repentance and redemption?

C. Boldness in the Things Christians Know
5:18-21

In this concluding section of the epistle, John begins each of the next three verses with "we know" (OIDAMEN). This is a sense of triumph, victory, assurance from on high, and of conquering with Christ. The use of OIDAMEN is significant to suggest assurance, rather than GINOSKO, which suggests "coming to know" (see v. 13). Three things John says Christians, "my little children" (v. 21), may know: (1) the begotten ones do not practice sin, thus the devil cannot touch them, (2) the begotten ones are the possession of God, (3) the begotten ones have an understanding of Jesus Christ as the Son of God, and of eternal life in this true God.

18We know that whosoever is begotten of God sinneth not; but he that was begotten of God keepeth himself, and the evil one toucheth him not. 19We know that we are of God, and the whole world lieth in the evil one. 20And we know that the Son of God is come, and hath given us an understanding, that we know him that is true, and we are in him that is true, even in his Son Jesus Christ. This is the true God, and eternal life. 21My little children, guard yourselves from idols.

Verse 18 We know that whosoever is begotten of God sinneth not; but he that was begotten of God keepeth himself, and the evil one toucheth him not.

We know that whosoever is begotten of God sinneth not - The first fact that "we know" is that the Christian does not continue to practice sin. "Sinneth not" (OUK HAMARTANEI present indicative) has the force of continuing in the action contemplated. (For fuller discussion, see 3:9.)

On the use of the word "begotten" (GEGENNAMENOS perfect passive participle of GENNAO), one must understand the perfect tense describes an action taken in the past with results still present in the present. (Fuller discussion may be found in 3:9.)

but he that was begotten of God keepeth himself - "He that was begotten of God" presents quite a study and puzzle to many. There is much disputation about this second use of "begotten," as it is an unusual change in tense. The first use of GENNAO in this verse above is a perfect passive participle. This second use is an aorist passive participle (GENNETHEIS). Thus, many take this second use of "begotten" to refer to Jesus Christ and not the Christian. If this be true, it would read, "the one begotten of God (Christian) does not continue to sin because the begotten one (Jesus Christ) keeps him." This is a very comforting thought, and incidentally, a teaching that has plenty of foundation in other scriptures (Matthew 11:28-30; Romans 8:28-32; 1 Peter 1:3-5; 2 Peter 1:8-11; Jude 1). Yet, that is not the thought of this scripture.

The texts as well as the translations of this verse vary, and there is a textual problem. Without straying too far into the disputations, it will suffice to offer three points: (1) John never uses GENNAO in reference to Jesus Christ anywhere else in his writings; and if used here, the usage would be a complete turnabout in his vocabulary, something that is considered very unlikely by most language scholars; (2) the change to the aorist could be read "keepeth himself";[33] and (3) John is in a hortatory section here and will shortly close this section with an exhortation "guard yourselves" in v. 21. So the reading of our text (ASV) is preferred. Purveyors of the false doctrine of "eternal security" cannot gain a foothold here.

"evil one toucheth him not" - Lenski has an interesting translation, "does not fasten himself upon him."[34] The use of the definite article before this evil one can only strengthen the idea this one is the devil. "Toucheth" (HAPTETAI, present indicative middle of HAPTO) has the sense of "touch for the purpose of harming, injure,"[35] and ". . .by impl. to harm."[36] The wicked one will try to fasten himself, thus the middle voice, on the Christian. He cannot do so as long as the begotten one clings to family values and teachings. As long as the begotten one lives up to family traits, the evil one cannot touch him. The Christian cannot do this by his own strength alone. Many helps and assurances are there for him, like those with which John has filled this epistle.

Verse 19 We know that we are of God, and the whole world lieth in the evil one.

We know that we are of God - The second fact of assurance that "we know" is that we belong to God. We are possessed and controlled by Him, not Satan. John draws from previous truths already expressed fully in this epistle to come to this concluding statement: "in him" (2:5-6), "of us and not of us" (2:19), "begotten of him" (2:29), "children of God" (3:10), "abideth in him" (3:24), "of God" (4:4). The true status of the disciple is now brought to its conclusion in John's writing: The Christian is in God's family and kingdom. "Of God" (EK TOU THEOU) is literally "out of God." He is our source of life and being. We belong to Him in every way.

and the whole world lieth in the evil one - "World" (KOSMOS) has prior use in this epistle and is similar, though somewhat different from its use here (2:15; 4:4-5). Previously, it referred to all that is under the control and influence of the devil, animate or inanimate. Yet, here it refers more to the persons under Satan's control. This is true due to the contrast John describes. There is one group of persons who belong to God while the other group of persons belongs to the evil one. "We" is set in apposition in this sentence to the "whole world," thus the necessity for this use of the "world" to refer to persons.

"Lieth" (DEITAI) means "to lie under an influence, to be involved in."[37] The RSV and NASB translate this "in the power of," while the NIV uses "under the control of." As the saved have a special relationship to God, the lost have their relationship to the "evil one."

Verse 20 And we know that the Son of God is come, and hath given us an understanding, that we know him that is true, and we are in him that is true, even in his Son Jesus Christ. This is the true God, and eternal life.

And we know that the Son of God is come - Here is the third and final fact of assurance John presents in this concluding context: We know that the Son of God is come. Such declaration of the Incarnation is to be expected to be

210

included as one of the major facts, if one is familiar with the purpose of the epistle, and with John's argumentation thus far. John began his epistle with the emphatic declaration of this truth (1:1-3), circled in, through, around, over and under this truth all throughout the letter, wove this truth into nearly every piece of his beautiful fabric, and now concludes with this last stirring shout of triumph: **Jesus Christ is the Son of God!**

and hath given us an understanding, that we know him that is true - John sums up what all Christians know and what he has been declaring. Christians have plenty of evidence given by John, and all the other inspired prophets who wrote New Testament books, as to the life and work of this Jesus. God made it possible that Christians are not left bereft of any needful truth. "Understanding" (DIANOIAN) is not a new faculty of intellect, nor is this any new truth given only to believers and not to unbelievers, and neither is it any special inner illumination given as a second work of grace by the Holy Spirit. It may include a capacity of spiritual understanding, due the acceptance of spiritual beliefs about the Son of God. Those who accept Jesus as the Son of God are ready in their hearts to accept all else that is said and proven by credible evidence. Those who deny Him as the Son of God will refuse any further facts about redemption as they are not the "good soil" that will receive the seed (Luke 8:8,15). Their hearts are not ready for any further understanding and cannot receive it due to the fact they deny the teachings of God's word.

Further, two different verbs for "know" are used in this one verse: OIDA and GINOSKO. "We know that the Son of God is come" uses OIDA, the kind of knowledge that gives full assurance. "We know him that is true" uses GINOSKO, the knowledge that is acquired; i.e., we "come to know." So this understanding Christians are given is the fact that they "come to know" the true one, Jesus Christ the Son of God. Reception of this knowledge, upon credible testimony, is progressive, ongoing, and continuing acquisition of knowledge about Him (compare v. 13). This knowledge of God and the Son of God is a major thrust throughout the New Testament. Paul often emphasized it: "For I know him whom I have believed," (2 Timothy 1:12) "till we all attain

211

unto the unity of the faith, and of the knowledge of the Son of God," (Ephesians 4:13) and "that I might know him" (Philippians 3:10). John, in the Gospel, presented this also: "And we have believed and know that thou art the Son of God" (John 6:69). Again, "And this is life eternal, that they should know thee the only true God, and him whom thou didst send, even Jesus Christ" (John 17:3).

"Him that is true" begins the last thrust in John's argument. "True" (ALETHINON) carries not only the idea of "true, dependable, . . .in accordance with the truth," but it also carries the idea of "genuine, real. . .of God in contrast to other gods, who are not real."[38] So John is setting the stage of emphasis for the last exhortation in v. 21. Jesus Christ is the "real one," the genuine one. The veracity of John's statement is borne out by others: "in him should all the fulness dwell," (Colossians 1:19) "For in him dwelleth all the fulness of the Godhead bodily," (Colossians 2:9) and "that God was in Christ reconciling the world to himself" (2 Corinthians 5:19).

and we are in him that is true, even in his Son Jesus Christ - To be in Him is to be in union with Him, united in a spiritual relationship, a fellowship. The relationship is sustaining, special, unique. It is a relationship in which men are connected to Jesus Christ. This connection to genuine Deity (the "Real One") is only through Jesus the Son. John claims we can **know** Him as the Son of God, plus we can be **in Him** that is true, who is the Son of God. Therefore, this knowing Him is to be in Him. And this is the connection of the Christian to the Godhead or Trinity. Care should be exercised here lest errors in making unscriptural separations between Persons in the Godhead are made (see below).

This is the true God, and eternal life - Perhaps the division here between v. 20 and v. 21 is unfortunate, as it seems they fit together best. Emphasis is upon true worship and knowledge versus idolatry. And John closes with the warning about idolatry.

There is much controversy here whether this "true God and eternal life" is Jesus or the Father. Some say all references to "Him" and "God," from v. 13 through v. 21, are all references to the Father. Others claim the expres-

212

sions refer to Jesus, the Son. This latter idea is preferable for several reasons. **First,** the most natural grammatical construction would allow taking the antecedent of "this" to be "his Son Jesus Christ," as it is the nearest noun to which it could refer. **Second,** John's use of eternal life previously has been to stress the reality of the Incarnate Son of God as the source of eternal life (1:2-3; 2:24-25; 3:14; 5:11,13). **Third,** John's overriding theme of the epistle is to show the reality of deity in this Jesus, that He is no less the nature of deity than the Father or Holy Spirit; and this is the clearest, most concise, direct, and pointed statement that could be made. The entire epistle has been pointing to this, and John does not disappoint his readers. **Fourth,** if this statement were to refer to the Father, it would be tautology and misuse of a truism. This would have John saying, "We know the true God, we are in the true God and this is the true God."[39] **Fifth,** to switch from the Son to Father at this point might foster the very error John was combatting, the erroneous teaching that claimed Jesus was less than the Father. If John had been proceeding in his argument about this man Jesus, giving Him all types of honor and glory, but then, in order to speak of the true God and eternal life, he switched to speaking about the Father, it sadly would have cemented in their minds this error of supposed difference in quality of the deity of Jesus.[40] **Sixth,** the best understanding of the nature of God precludes such separations anyway. To know Jesus is to know the Father, and to know the Father is to know Jesus (John 8:19; 17:3; 14:7). To hate Jesus is to hate the Father also (John 15:23). To deny or confess the Son is the denial or confession of the Father (1 John 2:23). To honor the Son is to honor the Father (John 5:23). So many such things are given within scriptures about God, the Deity, (whether referring to one person in the Godhead or to all) that there are times distinctions should not be made. **Separations** among them ought never be made, for such is the nature of God that there is no such thing as one separate from the other. "Jehovah our God is one Jehovah" (Deuteronomy 6:4). **Distinctions** can be seen within the godhead as to personality and work, but **separations** must be avoided. They are not separate from one another. Any relationship a person has with one cannot be thought of as separate from the other persons of the Godhead. Any concept of separation simply does not conform to the biblical teachings about the nature of God.

Verse 21 My little children, guard yourselves from idols.

My little children - John closes with so much love for his readers, as if it were just bursting from him. The expression "my little children" was also used early in the epistle (2:1). Thus John opens and closes this letter in tender love of the Lord's disciples, his brethren in Christ, and sets the tone and example for his readers to love the brethren likewise.

guard yourselves from idols - "Guard" (PHULAXATE, aorist imperative of PHULASSO) calls for heeding a warning, or, as a unique definition suggests, "to keep in abstinence, debar."[41] Any imperative verb has the idea of future reference within it, and the use of the aorist calls for immediate action.[42]

"Idols" (EIDOLON) refers to anything of an appearance or likeness, since it comes from EIDOS, which meant "image, shadow or phantom in secular Greek."[43] It is also the common word for such worship of likenesses in the New Testament, as the word appears in various forms and usages over thirty times. In all the major cities throughout the Roman world, idolatry was rampant in these times. John's readers were assailed on every hand by influences to follow idols. One can read of temples in Ephesus to worship Artemas (Diana of Acts 19), Serapis, and Domitian. Additionally, there were known to be statues of Zeus, Dionysus, Nike, and Bes.[44] If idolatry were not a very serious problem in the days of John's writing, why had there been warnings about idolatry in other inspired books: Romans, Corinthians, Galatians, Colossians, and Thessalonians.

There is a thought the Gnosticism and Docetism, and the followers of Cerinthus, espoused such beliefs as would lead to idolatry. Perhaps John is speaking about literal idols, as well as idolatry in a mental or figurative sense. Those who deny the true God have mental images, or idols, which they serve and serve falsely. One can worship a philosophy

214

(Colossians 2:8) or the "wisdom of this world" (1 Corinthians 1:20-25). And this might be included in John's gentle warning.

Most of "my little children" no doubt were converted from idolatry. So, this closing thought is called for and one that is vital. False doctrine about Jesus the Son of God can eat away at one's faith and a falling away could result.

"The dearest idol I have known,
    Whate'er that idol be,
Help me tear it from Thy Throne,
    And worship only Thee."[45]

[1]R. C. H. Lenski, *The Interpretation of the Epistles of St. Peter, St. John and St. Jude*, (Augsburg Publishing House, Minneapolis, Minnesota, 1963), p. 519.

[2]Lenski, *Interpretation*, p. 520.

[3]Samuel Bagster, *Analytical Greek Lexicon*, (Samuel Bagster & Sons, London, 1852, Revised Edition by Harold K. Moulton, Zondervan Publishing Co., Grand Rapids, Michigan, 1978), p. 66.

[4]William F. Ardnt and F. Wilbur Gingrich, *A Greek-English Lexicon of the New Testament*, (University of Chicago Press, Chicago, Illinois, 1957), pp. 133-134.

[5]W. E. Vine, *An Expository Dictionary of New Testament Words*, (Riverside Book and Bible House, Iowa Falls, Iowa, 1952), p. 509.

[6]Donald W. Burdick, *The Letters of John the Apostle*, (Moody Press, Chicago, Illinois, 1985), p. 366.

[7]J. W. Roberts, *The Living Word Commentary, The Letters of John*, (R. B. Sweet Co., Inc., Austin, Texas, 1968), pp. 131-132.

[8]A. T. Robertson, *Word Pictures in the New Testament*, (Broadman Press, Nashville, Tennessee, 1933), Vol. VI, *The General Epistles and the Revelation of John*, pp. 240-241.

[9]Thomas Hartwell Horne, *An Introduction to the Critical Study and Knowledge of the Holy Scriptures*, (W. Blackwood and Sons, Edinburgh: and R. Milliken and Son, and John Cumming, Dublin, 1839), pp. 448-471, note especially p. 469.

[10]Albert Barnes, *Notes on the New Testament, James, Peter, John, and Jude*, Baker Book House, Grand Rapids, Michigan, 1949 reprint), pp. 342-343.

[11]A. T. Robertson, *A Short Grammar of the Greek New Testament*, (Hodder & Stoughton, New York, New York, 1908, Third Edition), p. 161.

[12]Burdick, *Letters*, pp. 384-385.

[13]Burdick, *Letters*, p. 386.

[14]Arndt and Gingrich, *Lexicon*, p. 558.

[15]Joseph Henry Thayer, *A Greek-English Lexicon of the New Testament*, (American Book Co., New York, N.Y. 1889; being Grimm's Wilke's *Clavis Novi Testamenti, Translated Revised and Enlarged*, 1879, Harper & Brothers), p. 174.

[16]Arndt and Gingrich, *Lexicon*, p. 716.

[17]A. T. Robertson, *Grammar*, p. 123.

[18]Albert Barnes, *Notes*, p. 347.

[19]Arndt and Gringrich, *Lexicon*, p. 355.

[20]Bagster, *Lexicon*, p. 192.

[21]Burdick, *Letters*, p. 388.

[22]Bagster, *Lexicon*, p. 283.

[23]Burdick, *Letters*, p. 388.

[24]C. H. Dodd, as quoted in Alexander Ross, *The New International Commentary on the New Testament, the Epistles of James and John*, (Wm. B. Eerdmans Publishing Company, Grand Rapids, Michigan, 1954), p. 221-221, in footnote Number 1.

[25]Lenski, *Interpretation*, pp. 536-537.

[26]A. T. Robertson, *Grammar*, pp. 141-142.

[27]Albert Barnes, *Notes*, pp. 343-344.

[28]Bagster, *Lexicon*, p. 17.

[29]Bagster, *Lexicon*, p. 31.

[30]Bagster, *Lexicon*, p. 7.

[31]Arndt and Gingrich, *Lexicon*, p. 17.

[32]Vine, *Dictionary*, p. 186.

[33]J. W. Roberts, *Letters*, p. 143.

[34]R. C. H. Lenski, *Interpretation*, p. 538.

[35]Arndt and Gingrich, *Lexicon*, p. 71.

[36]Bagster, *Lexicon*, p. 49.

[37]Bagster, *Lexicon*, p. 227.

[38]Arndt and Gingrich, *Lexicon*, p. 36.

[39]Lenski, *Interpretation*, p. 543, and Barnes, *Notes*, p. 354.

[40]Albert Barnes, *Notes*, p. 354.

[41]Bagster, *Lexicon*, p. 431.

[42]Burdick, *Letters*, p. 397.

[43]Arndt and Gingrich, *Lexicon*, p. 220.

[44]E. M. B. Green, and C. J. Hemer, *The Illustrated Bible Dictionary*, (Inter-Varsity Press, Leicester, England, 1980), Vol. 1, pp. 461-462, and also Burdick, *Letters*, p. 407.

[45]Ross, *NIC*, p. 275.

EPISTLES
OF
JOHN

NOTES
ON
2 and 3 JOHN

Introduction

The brevity of these letters leads many to feel they were not well-quoted among early writers and that they were not recognized as canonical. However, credence for these letters is much the same as that for the first epistle.

It is thought by some that John wrote both of the last two letters on the same day![1] By others, these two letters have been called "twin sisters."[2] In both letters the same general thrust and outline seems to have been followed, i.e., commendation and encouragement about personal faith, dealing with the trials and discouragements, warnings about false teachers, and dealing with false teachers within the congregations.

Author

The author of both books is without a doubt the apostle John. **First,** the similiarity of vocabulary with First John, as well as the Gospel of John, is so striking that it cannot be avoided. It is hardly accepted that someone would go to all this trouble to be an imitator of John. Terms, expressions, and words are so noticeable that it is easy to have John come to mind when reading the book. Six words and eleven expressions in Second John are the same as First John, and the remarkably heavy use of them multiple times within this short letter of only thirteen verses is hardly a coincidence. In Third John there are five words and six expressions very similar to those in Second John, and again the coincidence argument is without much validity.[3] **Second,** the weight of evidence from the writings of the early fathers points conclusively to John the apostle. Iranaeus, Clement of Alexandria, Dionysius, Eusebius, Cyprian, and the Muratorian Fragment all refer to these books and to a plurality of such letters.[4] **Third,** The sentiment, tone, and manner are consistent with the aged apostle. In his work at Ephesus in the twilight of his life, it fits that he would style himself the "the elder," as he does in the salutation to both these letters. Exactly what this appellation means is another point of controversy, but it fits into the style of the aged apostle. Rather than style himself "the apostle," he chooses a lesser designation to the elect lady and Gaius. **Fourth,** the very use of this appellation may be most fitting to be applied only to John. It would hardly fit any other New Testament writer as well, as it does not refer to a work in the local congregations of overseer. Rather, it seems best to refer to age, experience, and situation of venerable life. **Fifth,** the fact that John was not accustomed to affixing his name to his writings is also a point that fits with his authorship.

To Whom Addressed

The second letter is written to "the elect lady and her children," and the conjecture about his use of "elect lady" (EKLEKTE KURIA) has led to much study and disputation. Two major thoughts are advanced: (1) This is addressed to an "elected lady" named "Eclecte" or "Cyria" and her children, or (2) this is addressed to a local church and John is using the term "elect lady" figuratively in personification. Scholars are pretty well divided on this subject and strong arguments can be given for either position.

The case for a personification of a local church is stated by several arguments. (1) The plural personal pronoun for "you" (HUMAS, HUMIN) in verse 6 and 8 indicate this EKLEKTE KURIA is not a single person. (2) The use of the plural verbs in the same verses strengthens this claim. (3) This type of personification of a local congregation or the universal church is common throughout the New Testament. (4) Early church literature, e.g., the **Shepherd of Hermas,** used this personification.[5] (5) A local church would be more apt to need warnings against false teachers. (6) The command to love one another would fit a congregation better than an individual.[6]

The case for reference to an individual woman should be looked into closely. (1) If the salutation had been to a congregation, it would have been specified, as that practice seems to be the uniform mode of the New Testament. (2) It is highly unlikely John would depart from the literal mode of writing First John and Third John to enter into a long figure of speech for an entire letter. (3) It is highly improbable John would have personified a local congregation as a woman, since this type of mystical figure of speech was used only in poetry, prophecy, or some composition where figurative language abounds. (4) The mentions made of "children," (vv. 1,4 and 13) [her sister's children also] are not those that would be used in addressing a local church. (5) It accords best with apostolic usage that the person's name to whom the letter is designated would be addressed directly.[7] (6) The simplicity and tenderness of the epistle stamp it as personal. (7) The use of the plural pronouns (HUMIN and HUMAS) seems to fit a woman and her children better than a church and its members.[8] (8) The word KURIA occurs nowhere else in the New Testament except Second John; and in First Peter 5:13, there is a similar reference to "She (suneklekte) that is in Babylon, elect together with you. . . ," where an elect sister is obviously designated but not named either.[9] (9) The sustaining of an allegory of this kind, as supposed if it refers to a church, would be highly unlikely in so slight a letter. (10) If it were an allegory, it would destroy any distinction between the lady and her children, as the church (or "lady") is composed of believers ("children"), and the two are identical. Such redundancy would make little sense. (11) There is really no need to prefer a mystical meaning to this epistle.[10]

The arguments are long and detailed, but the heavier weight is clearly on the side of the literal understanding. There really is no compelling reason to take "lady" figuratively, and there is certainly no harm in doing so. It seems to be the easier of the ways to look at it, so it is treated that way in this study. Thus, we have the only inspired book in the Bible to be addressed to a woman.

The third letter is addressed to Gaius, an individual also, but not easy to identify either. There were three men named Gaius mentioned in the New Testament: (1) Gaius of Macedonia, a companion of Paul in travel [Acts 19:29]; (2) Gaius of Derbe, one of the seven baggage carriers (monies collected for the poor in Judea) accompanying Paul on the return from the third missionary journey [Acts 20:4]; (3) Gaius of Corinth, Paul's host and one whom he baptized personally [Romans 16:23; 1 Corinthians 1:14]. Whether it be one of these three is not known with certainty, and many scholars feel a fourth man, otherwise unknown in New Testament writings, may well be the recipient. Gaius was a common name in these times;[11] and as it had been over thirty years since the events had transpired with the other three men, it might well be another Gaius altogether. That he was an exceptional man is seen easily as he is addressed as "the beloved, whom I love in truth." He was prospering spiritually and lived consistent with the truth (vv. 1-4), and was unusual in his hospitality and care for traveling teachers (vv. 6-8).

Date of the Books

Due to the similarity of First John, most understand these books to be written about the same time, between A.D. 90 and 95. It matters little whether Second John or Third John was written first, especially if one accepts the notion they were written on the same day. The mention of the antichrist in v. 7 of Second John, however, has led some to argue this book was written soon after First John, with an interval passing before the completion of Third John.

The use of "the elder" in both books to refer to the author lends credence to the idea this was toward the close of the life and work of John, thus the late date suggested.

Purpose of the Epistles

Energetic evangelism and excitement of studying with traveling missionaries were the overtones of the day. It seems that the more persecutions there were, the more urgent spreading the good news of salvation in Jesus Christ became. Men were traveling throughout the Empire and great works were being accomplished. Yet, there were somber clouds within the Empire, as false teachers were also energetic in their work.

The rise of the Roman highway system, plus the continuing stimulus of world commerce, made traveling over land and sea much easier, less expensive, and thus more feasible for both true and false teachers. The deployment of Roman troops throughout the Empire also contributed to the safety of travel, and many more were willing to risk the dangers.

Hospitality must have been at an all-time high within the culture and especially among Christians. Such had been urged in other letters predating John's letters (Romans 12:13; Hebrews 13:2; Titus 3:13-14; 1 Peter 4:9). Thus John, in the second epistle, felt the need to caution one dear lady and her friends about accepting ("receiving them. . .giving them greeting") any and all teachers into their homes. Discernment must be maintained lest one be guilty inadvertently of participating in their false teachings by such support.

In avoiding the error of false teachers, however, John prefaced his warnings to Cyria with beautiful and encouraging words that (1) John loved the family, (2) that together they shared in the knowledge of the truth and its work in the world, (3) their walking in the truth was a cause of great rejoicing, and (4) that they evidently were practicing well the admonition to love one another and that this should continue. At the close John added yet another encouragement, that he hoped soon to see them, at which time their joy could be made full.

In the third letter John felt the need to commend Gaius for his unusual hospitality, and then he proceeded to deal with a man in that congregation who refused proper hospitality to traveling preachers. In fact, this man not only refused to give his own hospitality, but he also incited faction and disruption in regard to those who did show care and love. John also informed Gaius of his own impending visit.

Thus we, the readers of all centuries, share for a lifetime a few moments in the history of the first century congregations. We get a small glimpse into some of the joys, encouragements, activities and dangers of the daily lives of these saints. Short though these epistles may be, they are treasures of inspiration for eternity.

---

[1]R. C. H. Lenski, *The Interpretation of the Epistles of St. Peter, St. John and St. Jude*, (Augsburg Publishing House, Minneapolis, Minnesota, 1963), p. 549.

2Guy N. Woods, *A Commentary on the New Testament Epistles of Peter, John and Jude*, (Gospel Advocate Company, Nashville, Tennessee, 1954), p. 331.

3Donald W. Burdick, *The Letters of John the Apostle*, (Moody Press, Chicago, Illinois, 1985), pp. 414-415, 442-443.

4Albert Barnes, *Notes on the New Testament, James, Peter, John and Jude*, (Baker Book House, Grand Rapids, Michigan, 1949), pp. 356-359; Alexander Ross, *The New International Commentary on the New Testament, The Epistles of James and John*, (Wm. B. Eerdmans Publishing Co., Grand Rapids, Michigan,1954), pp. 124-125; Burdick, *Letters*, pp. 413-414.

5J. W. Roberts, *The Living Word Commentary, the Letters of John*, (R. B. Sweet Company Inc., Austin, Texas, 1968), p. 150.

6Burdick, *Letters*, p. 416.

7Barnes, *Notes*, pp. 359-360.

8Burdick, *Letters*, p. 416.

9Woods, *Commentary*, p, 338.

10Ross, *NIC*, pp. 129-130.

11Ross, *NIC*, p. 131.

OUTLINE OF 2 JOHN

I.   Salutation 1-3
II. Commendation 4
III. Exhortation 5-6
IV. Caution 7-11
V.   Conclusion 12-13

OUTLINE OF 3 JOHN

I.   Salutation 1-2
II. Commendation 3-8
III. Denunciation 9-10
IV. Exhortation 11
V.   Recommendation 12
VI. Conclusion 13-14

Notes on Second John

I. Salutation 1-3

¹The elder unto the elect lady and her children, whom I love in truth; and not I only, but also all they that know the truth; ²for the truth's sake which abideth in us, and it shall be with us for ever: ³Grace, mercy, peace shall be with us, from God the Father, and from Jesus Christ, the Son of the Father, in truth and love.

In this Second Epistle of John, readers will encounter again several of John's favorite words and phrases in his vocabulary. Notice the following will be seen in this short letter: truth, to love, to know, to abide, Jesus Christ the Son, to walk, commandment, from the beginning, to love one another, confess not that Jesus cometh in the flesh, antichrist, world, hath or hath not God. These expressions are common to John and not new to the student of John's epistles.

As was customary with John, he does not mention himself by name, but he does send a greeting from "the elder" in such way that there is little doubt that the recipient knew the sender. Whether he specified the recipient is a matter of dispute, but it is thought to be to a special woman and her family in one of the congregations in Asia. Since most of these letters in the first century were hand delivered, it was not necessary to provide further identification.

John follows the normal pattern of such letters to churches or individuals. He gives a greeting followed by commendations and then proceeds to the business and purpose of the letter. This letter concerns hospitality to traveling teachers and the accuracy of doctrine they hold.

Verse 1 The elder unto the elect lady and her children, whom I love in truth; and not I only, but also all they that know the truth;

The elder unto the elect lady and her children - John refers to himself here as "the elder" (HO PRESBUTEROS), a term in the New Testament which has several meanings and uses. (1) It was used to refer to men on the special council of the Jewish people, the Sanhedrin [Acts 23:14-15]. (2) It was used to refer to members of local councils in individual cities [Luke 7:3]. (3) It described men and women of age [1 Timothy 5:1-2]. (4) The term pictured the twenty-four beings around the throne of God [Revelations 4:10]. (5) The term came to be used in a special sense among Christians and congregations, depicting men who were overseers and shepherds of the local congregations [Acts 14:23; 1 Timothy 5:17-19; Titus 1:5]. (6) There is the possibility of another use in this context by John as a title of dignity, respect, and honor along with the idea of experience and aged.[1] Whether John refers to himself in some special way, or merely as an aged teacher and Christian, is not of great import. It is of note that he does not designate himself as "the apostle," though within this short book he will indeed have to use strong language to deal with a dangerous and unscriptural doctrine. Some feel he could have expressed more authority if he had done so, but to come in this letter simply as the aged and beloved teacher was plenty for inspiration.

"The elect lady" was a woman of John's acquaintance within one of the churches in Asia. That this refers to an individual woman has more the weight of argument (see Introduction). Her name could have been either of the two words used by John: EKLEKTE or KURIA. The first means "elect" and the second means "lady." It was normal for names in that day to mean something, so either name could have been hers. If it were the first word, the address would perhaps have been "to the lady Eklekte" or "to the Lady Electa." If it were the second word, it would have been "to the elect Kuria." For KURIA, one scholar uses an English spelling of "Cyria"; thus, it is found in many present-day writings.[2] It does seem, however, most natural to take this salutation as being one to a lady and her family who had been showing hospitality to teachers visiting in the local congregation and accepting her hospitality.

whom I love in truth; and not I only, but also all they

that know the truth - Common bonds with the truth and with those who know the truth are the bonds of love John has with this family. "Whom I love" has the plural pronoun (HOUS) indicating John's love for the entire family, not just the woman. All others who know the truth have the same bond of love with this family. It is possible John is saying "whom I love truly," for the first use of "truth" does not have the definite article. However, since the second reference to "truth" is literally "who know **the** truth," it is more likely both uses of the word refer to the same thing — the truth of the gospel.

This is John's first of five uses of "truth" (ALETHEIA) in this book alone. John actually refers to truth twice more with the pronouns "which" and "it" in v. 2. He used the word nine times in the First Epistle and will use it four more times in Third John, making eighteen times in these three books. In the Gospel he used the word twenty-two times. Truth is extremely important, important in John's writings, important in the teachings of the Lord, important in Paul's letters, and must continue to occupy a place of importance in the hearts and minds of servants of the Lord in all centuries. This context, speaking about "the truth," the entire gospel of the Lord Jesus Christ, needs to be understood clearly when one studies the problem later in vv. 9-11 as to what is meant by "doctrine of Christ." John sets the context of the book with six references made to the entire body of truth which the New Testament congregations had received from the Lord, His apostles, and His prophets.

Standing in opposition to this truth are the deceivers, the non-confessors, the anti-christ, those who lose rewards, those who go onward and abide not in the doctrine of Christ, and those who, in reality, have no fellowship with God. Those who know truth and those who walk in truth are standing on the one hand, while opposers are on the other hand. There is no compromise between truth and error, truth and lies, truth and deception, truth and darkness, abiding in truth and abiding not in accurate doctrine. There are no common grounds, no grey areas of doubt, no possibilities of tolerant excuses. One is either an upholder of truth or one is an enemy of truth.

The woman and her family to whom John addressed the

book were evidently known by others within the fellowship of the truth. These others loved the family in the same way John did. They were said to "know the truth" (HOI EGNOKOTES TAN ALETHEIAN), and since the perfect tense is used, John claims they knew the truth in the past, and the results of such knowledge continue in the present. Coupling this understanding of the verb tense with the basic meaning of GINOSKO, that is, coming to know, one realizes these to whom John referred came to know the truth in the past, and still cling to it in the present (see 1 John 2:3).

Verse 2 for the truth's sake which abideth in us, and it shall be with us for ever;

for the truth's sake which abideth in us - This third mention of truth (a definite article "the" stresses a specific body of truth, TAN ALETHEIAN) shows the reason why John and the others love this family and are in felllowship with them. This family knows the principles of truth, they abide in the commandments of the truth, they love each other due to the fellowship found in this truth, and this interacting is all based upon whether the truth abides in them. This truth is "the doctrine" (vv. 9-10), so important in these times, and includes all the words of inspiration by which God's will is conveyed adequately to man.

This body of truth abides in both John and this family. "Abideth" (MENOUSAN, present participle) is one of John's favorite words. It includes the idea of "stay, continue, . . . dwell, lodge, . . . sojourn, remain, . . .endure, persevere, be constant, . . . to abide, be in close and settled union."[3] Since this is present tense, it amplifies the idea of constancy. The body of truth settles down and continues to dwell within the hearts and lives of this lady and her children, as well as the apostle John. To emphasize this even further, John adds the fact that "it" (the body of truth) shall be with them forever (EIS TON AIONA). AIONA carries two major ideas in its meaning: (1) illimitable duration or eternity, and (2) an era, age, or segment of time.[4] John no doubt has the first idea in mind, that of eternity. The truth is eternal (Matthew 24:35), and John affirms that this body of truth will be with believers not only in this age, but endlessly, eternally. The life of the church in the first century was being threatened by those who opposed the truth; thus, John encourages this lady about her relationship to truth.

Verse 3 Grace, mercy, peace shall be with us, from God the Father, and from Jesus Christ, the Son of the Father, in truth and love.

Grace, mercy, peace shall be with us, from God the Father - This was a common form of greeting in most of the New Testament letters with some variations. "Grace," prominent of Paul's salutations also, generally referred to God's state of mind toward the sins of mankind. "The apostles and N.T. writers at the beginning and end of the Epp. crave for their readers the favor ('grace') of God or of Christ, to which all blessing, esp. spiritual, are due:. . . .Moreover, the word CHARIS contains the idea of kindness which bestows upon one what he had not deserved; . . . ."[5] "Mercy" is the extension of God's grace, it is grace in action toward the miseries of sinful mankind. ELEOS is "mercy; kindness or good will towards the miserable and afflicted, joined with a desire to relieve them; . . . ."[6] "Peace" (EIRENE) carries out the progressive idea of grace in action by showing the state which results from such grace and mercy. This EIRENE refers to ". . .a conception distinctly peculiar to Christianity, the tranquil state of a soul assured of its salvation through Christ, and so fearing nothing from God and content with its earthly lot, of whatsoever sort that is: . . . ."[7] Since God the Father is gracious toward sinful man, mercy flows freely from His throne resulting in peace of mind to the forgiven sinner, the Christian. This triple formula is John's way of giving yet another assurance to the believer.

and from Jesus Christ, the Son of the Father, in truth and love - Some manuscripts add "Lord" to "Jesus Christ," as in the KJV; but if "Lord" is used this way by John, it would be the only time in his writings. Common to Paul, such use of the triple designation is not common with John. John is meeting the Gnostic problem directly with the claim that such grace, mercy, and peace are equally from Jesus Christ. He shares deity with the Father and is the divine cause for such grace, mercy, and peace. The repetition of the preposition "from" (PARA), used now to refer to Jesus

Christ, further emphasizes that such grace, mercy, and peace have been received from the Son as well as the Father. John counters the heresy of the anti-christ in vv. 7-11; but prior to doing so, John states assurance in the true nature of Jesus Christ. Within Himself Jesus Christ is able to be the author of grace, mercy, and peace. He can do so since He is deity, equal with the Father in nature and attributes. He came to declare the Father (John 1:18), and those who recognize Him as deity can recognize the Father properly as well (John 14:9).

"In truth and love" makes known the vital link between "grace, mercy, and peace" with the grand principles of God's word and God's love. John uses "truth" for the fourth time and for the second time connects it with "love." These two grand principles walk arm in arm with grace, mercy and peace and cannot be disconnected from them. Being faithful to the truth and walking in the commandments of that truth, one of which is love, are the necessary ingredients to having grace, mercy and peace. It is unthinkable that one could walk in error and practice hatred and still have the grace, mercy and peace from God!

II. Commendation 4

⁴I rejoice greatly that I have found certain of thy children walking in truth, even as we received commandment from the Father.

I rejoice greatly that I have found certain of thy children walking in truth - John had come into contact with several of the children in this family, and he was happy to give their mother a commendation for finding them walking in the truth. This had happened previously, as John uses the aorist passive (ECHARAN, from CHAIRO). Some call this an "epistolary aorist,"[8] since it is being stated from the viewpoint of the reader. The KJV and RSV translate it as regular aorist, "I rejoiced," the NIV says "It has given me great joy," and the NASB translates it, "I was very glad."

John does not mean to imply that certain of the children in the family are the only ones walking in truth, as the word "certain" ("some" in the RSV) is in italics and not found in the original text. Literally, the text translated, "I have found of the children of thee." This could mean one of two things. First, as suggested, it could mean John had become acquainted with only some of her children, and he was rejoicing to find them faithful to the truth in their manner of life. Second, it could mean some of the children were faithful and others were not. This second idea would necessitate a rather large assumption; and without any evidence to the contrary, it is better to understand John had been in contact with only some of the children.

Truth, though used anarthously here, refers to the prior uses of the same word. Thus it is body of revealed truth through Jesus Christ the Son of the Father. "Walking" in this truth (PERIPATOUNTAS, present participle) stresses a manner of life, a continuous activity. John used this same stress of activity in 1 John 1:6-7 in reference to walking in light or walking in darkness. This expression is common to both John and Paul in their epistles.

even as we received commandment from the Father

- The word "commandment" occurs four times in this short letter — (1) "received commandment from the Father' [v. 4], (2) "not as though I wrote to thee a new commandment" [v. 6], (3) "that we should walk after his commandments" [v. 6], and (4) "This is the commandment, even as ye heard from the beginning" [v. 6]. Since two of the last three (used in the singular) refer to the command to love one another, it is thought by many this first use also refers to the command to love one another. However, since the entire body of truth has been under consideration by John in the first four verses of the salutation, it is also possible this commandment could be commandments in general from the Father. In the First Epistle, John spoke of obedience to all the commandments of God (1 John 3:22) and of doing the truth and walking in the light (1 John 1:6-7). And here in v. 6, when the word is plural, commandments, it cannot be confined to the single command to love another. So it is possible John is concluding his salutation with the stress of obeying all the commandments of the Lord. The commandment to love one another would be included, but it is doubtful John saw Cyria's children walking only in brotherly love. It is much more likely John saw them walking after the commandments of God in many ways, including brotherly love.

III. Exhortation 5-6

⁵And now I beseech thee, lady, not as though I wrote to thee a new commandment, but that which we had from the beginning, that we love one another. ⁶And this is love, that we should walk after his commandments. This is the commandment, even as ye heard from the beginning, that ye should walk in it.

John has now completed the salutatory part of his letter and is ready to turn to the major concerns, the relationship of truth and love. In a special way, this truth and love will be discussed in view of hospitality to visiting preachers and teachers. Love must be discriminating if it is the love that pleases God. Love must discriminate between truth and error and those who teach either. So, ready to engage the task, John reminds this family of the commandment of God to love one another.

Verse 5 And now I beseech thee, lady, not as though I wrote to thee a new commandment, but that which we had from the beginning, that we love one another.

And now I beseech thee, lady - John makes the transition by using "now" the same as he did in the First Epistle (2:28). He is ready to make a request of the woman to whom the letter is addressed. "Beseech" (EROTAO) seems to be less urgent than "ask" (AITEO), a word most often used for a supplicant to a person of higher education. Rather, it is used when the asking person is familiar with and on equal ground with the person who is asked.[9] And EROTAO is also a word that carries more authority and dignity.[10] The repetition of the word "lady" (KURIA) adds emphasis and suggests the expression, "I beseech thee, Cyria." It is perfectly proper for him to use this familiar address, as he doubtless is well known and loved by this family as the aged and venerable apostle.

not as though I wrote to thee a new commandment - The similiarity between this wording and 1 John 2:7 is inescapable. Both of them must refer back to John 13:34-35 and can be considered one of the most forceful arguments that John is the author of all three books. It is interesting to note that John used the plural pronoun "you" (HUMIN) in 1 John 2:7, but he used the singular "you" (SOI) in the present verse. This suggests even more that this letter was being written to an individual woman. Other than one or two minor variations like this, the passage states the same truths as 1 John 2:7 (where see for fuller discussion).

but that which we had from the beginning - Similar phrases are used in 1 John 2:24 and 3:11. The use in those passages seems to refer to the time of the beginning of the preaching of the gospel, and there is no reason to claim John means anything different here. It has always been the case in following Jesus Christ, from the very beginning of his work among men, that men would know the commandment to love one another.

that we love one another - The object of John's dignified request now is stated — that we love one another. This is the badge of identification among Christians (John 13:34-35) and that to which John calls the attention of Cyria. All other statements in this epistle will center on and be thrust out from this cardinal principle which John proclaims so continuously. He will ask her to recognize deceivers and the anti-christ because of this love. He will ask her to refuse the hospitality of her home to such travelers because of this love. This love is something that must permeate every facet of one's life and existence.

Verse 6 And this is love, that we should walk after his commandments. This is the commandment, even as ye heard from the beginning, that ye should walk in it.

And this is love, that we should walk after his commandments - Walking after His commandments and keeping His commandments are virtually the same. John has already stressed the idea of keeping the commandments (1 John 5:3), as in John's mind there was no true love without duty. "Love divorced from duty will run riot, and duty divorced from love will starve."[11] One cannot separate love and obedience and have the kind of love and obedience that will please the Lord. "Walk" (PERIPATOMEN, present subjunctive) refers to linear action, a continuing walk. It is

234

the process of living. The life of a Christian consists in obedience and the one who does not do so cannot claim to be a lover in the sense of this godly love. Thus, Cyria must make distinctions as travelers come into her sphere of life and be careful to exclude those who do not love God correctly. If they do not teach the proper doctrines, they are not walking after His commandments. If they walk after the commandments of God, they would be teaching the truth and the truth only.

This is the commandment, even as ye heard from the beginning, that ye should walk in it - Lessons that one first hears in the school of discipleship will include love. This particular commandment, the one to practice brotherly love, is known by one and all among individuals in the churches of the first century. The translators of the RSV felt this to be so plain they substituted "love" for the pronoun "it." Thus the RSV reads "that you follow love." This does not change to any great extent the meaning of the passage, but taking such liberties with the text becomes more commentation than translation.

IV. Caution 7-11

⁷For many deceivers are gone forth into the world, even they that confess not that Jesus Christ cometh in the flesh. This is the deceiver and the anti-christ. ⁸Look to yourselves, that ye lose not the things which we have wrought, but that ye receive a full reward. ⁹Whosoever goeth onward and abideth not in the teaching of Christ, hath not God: he that abideth in the teaching, the same hath both the Father and the Son. ¹⁰If any one cometh unto you, and bringeth not this teaching, receive him not into your house, and give him no greeting: ¹¹for he that giveth him greeting partaketh in his evil works.

John enters now into the major topic of the letter, addressing the serious caution that he wanted to send to Cyria. She evidently was a woman of warm and loving hospitality and was known for generosity with traveling teachers. He had saluted her, commended her for having children who walked in truth, exhorted her concerning obedience and love, and is now ready to urge an important caution. This caution is of particular importance for the most hospitable Cyria; and since this was a circular letter, it would be of equal importance to all Christians who might read it. Well-intentioned and loving people throughout the entire church needed to know and respect this important distinction. There was too much danger that churches would be decimated by influential teachers who were following Cerinthus and the Gnostic heresy.

Verse 7 For many deceivers are gone forth into the world, even they that confess not that Jesus Christ cometh in the flesh. This is the deceiver and the anti-christ.

For many deceivers are gone forth into the world - The use of the subordinate conjunction "for" (HOTI) looks forward in the subject matter John stresses in v. 8, "Look to yourselves." John is not saying brotherly love ought to be practiced because many deceivers have gone out into the world; rather, he is saying **even though** brotherly love is to be practiced, it must be practiced with some discrimination **because** there are many deceivers gone forth into the world. Therefore, one must be on the lookout for these false teachers. As it is our duty to show the world what true Christianity is by the love we practice among ourselves, it is also a duty to keep ourselves away from false teachers and from unwitting support of their cause.

John used some strong wording in the First Epistle to describe these false teachers, including "liars" (2:22), "lead you astray" (2:26), "false prophets" (4:1), "spirit of the anti-christ" (4:3). Now in this Second Epistle he adds "deceivers." A "deceiver" (PLANOI) is "deceiving, seducing; a deceiver, impostor,"[12] and "a vagabond, tramp, impostor. . .hence univ. a corrupter, deceiver. . . ."[13] In noun form this word occurs only three other times in the New Testament (Matthew 27:63; 2 Corinthians 6:8; 1 Timothy 4:1), but John used the verb form in 1:8; 2:26; 3:7 where it is translated "lead you astray."

Some of these teachers may well have gone out from among the congregations (2:19) and were known to be ". . .not of us; for if they had been of us, they would have continued with us: but they went out, that that might be made manifest that they all are not of us." It certainly would have been a test of Cyria's faith if some of these teachers, personal friends of long standing, returned to her city and expected the hospitality of her home.

even they that confess not that Jesus Christ cometh in the flesh. This is the deceiver and the anti-christ - In John's mind there was no difference in the one who did not confess the coming of Christ in the flesh and in the one who was the deceiver. This was not a claim that there was no one who lived in Nazareth named Jesus; rather, it was a claim that the one named Jesus from Nazareth was not God Incarnate. John therefore is not speaking of a general class of unbelievers who were ignorant of all these teachings. He is referring to the Gnostics who were perverting the teachings about Jesus being the Christ. They believed in Jesus, but only in a heretical sense that he was the physical son of Joseph and Mary. They taught that God came upon Jesus at His baptism and left Him prior to the crucifixion. This meant they denied the virgin birth, the incarnation, and most of all, the propitiatory death and giving of His blood upon the cross (see Introduction).

Some argue this "cometh in the flesh" refers to the second coming of the Lord and not His birth to Mary. It is possible according to the grammatical construction of it to mean a future coming since "cometh" (ERCHOMENON) is a present participle. Lenski argues this is a timeless present."[14] Burdick offers four arguments to support this view: (1) No one in the first century was denying His second coming in the flesh; (2) the Gnostics denied the coming of God in the flesh when Jesus first appeared; (3) the same phrase is used previously by John in 1 John 4:2, there the perfect tense is clearly used to refer to Christ's first coming; and (4) the immortal resurrection body is normally thought of when referring to the second coming; not flesh."[15] (For a fuller discussion of Christ coming in the flesh, see 1 John 4:2.)

This false teaching is clearly the product of deception and it stems from the spirit of the anti-christ. John does not have in mind just one person who may be styled "the anti-christ"; he is referring to all those under the influence of this pernicious heresy. It is doubtful John is warning this lady about giving hospitality to only one man, "the anti-christ"; rather, he warns her of all those who might be conspirators with him or under his influence (See 1 John 2:22).

Verse 8 Look to yourselves, that ye lose not the things which we have wrought, but that ye receive a full reward.

Look to yourselves, that ye lose not the things which we have wrought - The use of the present imperative (BLEPETE, present imperative of BLEPO) puts readers on their immediate and constant guard. The same phrase is used in Mark 13:9 and is translated, "But take ye heed to yourselves." BLEPO is used for the "faculty of sight," but also "to have an eye to, to see to."[16] Some of the gains already made could be lost. Apostasy is possible.

"We have wrought" is questioned by many textual students, who say the translation should be "ye have wrought." Evidence is fairly well divided between the two translations.[17] If our text is correct in using, "we," then it is saying some of the accomplishments made among them by John's teachings could be lost. If the proper translation is "ye," then it refers to accomplishments they had made under the teaching and leadership of all their teachers. Either way makes little difference as to its ultimate meaning. Christians can grow in the grace and knowledge of the Lord (2 Peter 3:18) whether the impetus be from any one teacher or from various teachers.

John is emphatic about several dangers. They are in danger of not being vigilant about themselves, and John encourages them to look introspectively. They are in danger of serious mistakes which could cost them what has already been wrought. They are in danger of marauding false teachers. They are in danger of apostasy. It would make little sense for John to write to them using this language if it were impossible for a child of God to lose his soul after once being saved. Such language just could not be used if it were impossible to fall from grace.

but that ye receive a full reward - "Full reward" (MISTHON PLERE) implies an interesting concept little known or taught. MISTHOS generally refers to "dues paid for work, wages, hire:" but also "of divine recompense. . .of the rewards which God bestows, or will bestow, upon good deeds and endeavors. . . ."[18] If there are full rewards, there are also lesser rewards. And the New Testament so teaches that rewards are not the same as eternal life. Eternal life is given to all of those who will be with the Saviour in heaven; rewards are given additionally according to each man's works. John spoke often of this eternal life (John 3:36; 5:24; 6:47; 1 John 5:13). Jesus also promised life (Matthew 25:46; Mark 9:43-45; Luke 18:30). Paul wrote of this eternal life (Galatians 6:8; 1 Timothy 4:8; 6:12). James mentioned this crown consisting of life (James 1:12).

Different from this eternal life, in addition to it, are the promised rewards. Jesus said those persecuted would have "great" reward (Matthew 5:12; Luke 6:23) as well as those who loved their enemies and did good to them (Luke 6:35). Not all men are persecuted this way, so not all Christians in heaven will obtain this "great reward." Jesus said He would render to every man according to his deeds (Matthew

16:27) and He spoke of the master who rewarded the ten talent man with the unused one talent (Matthew 25:28). His giving the talent to the man who already had ten other talents, rather than to the man with four talents, has puzzled many. An accurate concept of rewards will help allay such puzzlement. Jesus also spoke of one given "authority over ten cities," while another was given only five cities (Luke 19:17,19). Why the difference in the rewards? If this Parable of the Pounds refers to the second coming of the Lord, then the Master's coming and distributing different rewards suggests there are different rewards to be given at the judgment.

Notice also that Paul spoke of rewards that reflect individual labors (1 Corinthians 3:8) and that some could even suffer loss of rewards but still be saved themselves (1 Corinthians 3:12-15). He also taught each man will be judged by the deeds done in his own body, whether good or bad (2 Corinthians 5:10). Coupling this with John's later description of Jesus rewarding each man according to his work (Revelations 22:12), it is inescapable that these "rewards" are individual and differ with each person. Yet each saved person will have eternal life; how could there be any difference among individuals if all of them have the same eternal life? The proper answer comes when one understands eternal life is the same for all saved persons, but rewards differ according to the individual. Thus the proper concept of rewards as taught in the New Testament shows that rewards are different from eternal life. It is well to remember, too, that what is true in rewards will also be true in punishment, as some will receive "many stripes" and others "few stripes." According to Luke, ". . .to whomsoever much is given, of him shall much be required: and to whom they commit much, of him will they ask the more" (Luke 12:47-48).

John is pleading with his readers to guard themselves lest they lose their full reward, that is, the complete and perfect measure of rewards their abilities and opportunities could bring to them. It is possible to see that all Christians saved by grace will inherit eternal life and that each Christian thus saved eternally will also be rewarded by the Lord according to individual abilities, opportunities, and fulfillment thereof.

Verse 7 Whosoever goeth onward and abideth not in the teaching of Christ, hath not God: he that abideth in the teaching, the same hath both the Father and the Son.

Whosoever goeth onward - With the warning of the previous verse in mind, John writes of those who make the fatal error of leaving the truth. Upon leaving the truth, they must realize they have also left the fellowship of both the Father and the Son. They may feel they have made progress; John describes it as going too far and leaving the bounds of truth. There is some disagreement in text here, as the KJV has "Whosoever transgresseth," which is a translation of PROBAINON. The weight of evidence seems to be that the earlier and more reliable manuscripts used PROAGON, thus our text has "goeth onward," NASB has "goes too far," NIV uses "runs ahead," RSV has "goes ahead," NEB uses "runs too far ahead," and TEV says "goes beyond." John is describing someone who professes progress, but who actually left the proper doctrine. He has strayed from the path. Gnostics felt they had obtained a loftier plane of understanding and a superior knowledge. John simply tells them that they have gone so far they are out of fellowship with God. PROAGON oftens means "lead forward, lead or bring out someone. . .go before, lead the way, precede. . . ," but within this context it means, "anyone who goes too far and does not remain within the teaching."[19] Another adds, "The meaning is, **whosoever advances beyond the limits of Christian doctrine.**"[20]

Wedges are often driven between groups when one group claims to be progressive and the other is accused of being stodgy or even regressive. Men will often boast of being "progressive" and churches often style themselves so. John is saying progress is good only when it stays within the bounds of what is actually true, not what men might want to style as the truth. "There is an advance which involves desertion of first principles; and such advance is not progress but apostasy."[21]

and abideth not in the teaching of Christ - The persons under consideration were going outside the truth in their advances, for they were leaving the truth as taught by

241

Christ. They were not abiding (ME MENON, present participle) in this truth, simply meaning they did not "stay . . .continue. . .dwell. . .lodge. . .remain. . .abide, [remain] in close and settled union. . . ."[22] Their professed progress was no progress in spirituality at all; rather, it was the loss of everything.

"The teaching of Christ" (TA DIDACHE TOU CHRISTOU) can be understood within proper Greek grammar either of two ways: (1) **subjective genitive,** "the teaching which Christ did"; or (2) **objective genitive,** "the teaching about Christ himself." If it be the former, then this teaching refers to the entire body of truth brought by Christ, normally called the "gospel." If it be the latter, then this teaching would be limited to the truth about Christ being the Son of God, the very thing the Gnostics challenged. It would be proper to understand it either way insofar as the grammatical construction is concerned. Other considerations have to be studied to see the correct application.

Within the immediate context preceding this verse, the deceiver and the ant-christ are mentioned. John's great emphasis on these opposers of the Son of God throughout 1 John, as well as in the present letter, has led many to conclude all that John has in mind is the truth about the Incarnation. This was what Cerinthus, the Gnostics, and the Docetics had denied. Therefore their claim is that this is all that John has in mind. Scholarship of the world, grammarians, lexicographers, historians, and commentators through the last two centuries have been about evenly divided on this passage. Scholars on both sides of the argument have provided copious quotations. Some declare it refers only to the **teaching about Christ,** while others insist it includes **all that was taught by Christ and His apostles.**

A search of the context will help considerably. It is true that two verses previously John mentions the deceiver and anti-christ. Yet, it is also true that one more verse previous, v. 6, mentions walking in Jesus' "commandments." Then going back another verse, v. 5, one finds that within those "commandments" there is a special "commandment" to be followed — "that we love one another." Thus, John's prior context includes plural commandments from the Lord, one of which is to love each other. This commandment to love one another does not bear directly on whether Jesus is God in the flesh, but John is surely concerned about love in this context. And this command to love one another is only one of the commandments (plural) that John mentions.

Then going back yet another verse, v. 4, John speaks of walking in the "truth." It is to be remembered John speaks of "truth" six times in this short letter and the word refers to the entire body of truth as revealed by Jesus (see comments on verse 1). Since plural commandments are referred to and one of them concerns brotherly love, it is difficult to say John is concerned in the present verse with only one basic teaching about Christ, whether or not He is the Son of God. John is concerned about all the truth, everything which the Son of God revealed. The context demands one to realize John's "teaching of Christ" includes all truth. One of the basic truths would be, of course, the Sonship of Jesus, but "teaching of Christ" is not limited to that narrow a scope.

Similar uses are found many times within scripture. The "doctrine of the Pharisees and Sadducees" (Matthew 16:12) refers to what they taught, not what is taught about them. The "teaching of Balaam" (Revelation 2:14) cannot refer to any teaching about Balaam, but it must refer to the teaching that Balaam did, as the verse goes on to say, "who taught Balak to cast a stumblingblock before the children of Israel. . . ." The "doctrine of the Nicolaitans" (Revelation 2:15) likewise is not what is taught about them, but what they were teaching. This is such a normal understanding that the same grammatical construction (Acts 2:42 — TA DIDACHE TON APOSTOLON) is translated "apostles' teaching" rather than "the teaching of the apostles." Since it obviously could not refer to any teaching about the apostles themselves, the translators took the liberty of using the possessive with the noun form, "apostles'," rather than a prepositional phrase "of the apostles."

If that approach had been used in 2 John 9, the verse would have read "Whosoever goeth onward and abideth not in Christ's teaching." And that is exactly what the writer has in mind. Thus, the evidence clearly points to the use of "doctrine of Christ" as being **subjective genitive,** all the

243

teaching done by Christ and His apostles. This would include the all-important doctrine of His deity and His humanity, but would not be limited to just the question of His person.

The difference this treatment makes in present-day application is important. In the study and practice of fellowship among believers, if one loses fellowship with God only when one denies Jesus's Sonship, then there is hardly any other basis on which to base fellowship. One could believe and teach all kinds of false doctrines and still be in fellowship with the Lord's people, if only he continued to declare Jesus is the Son of God! This would mean all denominations that hold to the deity of Jesus would be in true and scriptural fellowship. They could build man-made churches; teach copious falsities about the second coming of Christ; worship actions, work of the church, moral standards within personal lives of the saints, etc., but still be in fellowship. All this would be true if this "doctrine of Christ" is objective genitive, referring only to the teaching about Him as the Son of God. This leaves open all the speculation and conjecture men might devise, though Jesus warned of the "tradition of men" (Mark 7:7-9). Paul limited what a man could teach to the doctrines that were taught by the inspired apostles that were first century doctrines (Galatians 1:8-9). Not only should the doctrines have originated with the apostles, the doctrines must have been taught originally in the first century. Doctrines originating later than the first century could not qualify as "certified" gospel (see Galatians 1:11 KJV). Anything else, anything less, or anything in addition to this body of truth is not part of the "faith which was one for all delivered unto the saints" (Jude 3).

hath not God - The professed progress made by these false teachers did not lift them to the loftier plane, rather, it stripped them naked of any fellowship and communion with God. They have not the true knowledge of God; therefore, they have no fellowship with God either. One may cry "I know Him" but be terribly deceived (1 John 2:4).

he that abideth in the teaching, the same hath both the Father and the Son - To have the Father and the Son is simply to be in fellowship and communion with them. To have One is to have the Other. The state of Godhood is so structured that any separation to the extent of dividing fellowship would be to deny the One Jehovah. It is interesting that John often repeats truths in opposite terms. His statement about this same fellowship is found in 1 John 2:23-24. "Whosoever denieth the Son, the same hath not the Father: he that confesseth the Son hath the Father also. As for you, let that abide in you which ye heard from the beginning." In that passage he speaks of truth abiding in the believer. In our current passage John speaks of the believer abiding in the truth. It means the same stated either way. To be out of fellowship with the Son is to be out of fellowship with the Father. It is preposterous to reject the truths taught by Jesus and claim to be faithful to the Father. The Modernists, Muslims, Hindus, Buddhists, and devil-worshippers ought to beware. All their pretensions about spirituality and fellowship with the Creator of this universe go by the wayside when they reject Jesus Christ the Son of God.

Verse 10 If any one cometh unto you, and bringeth not this teaching, receive him not into your house, and give him no greeting:

If any one cometh unto you, and bringeth not this teaching - Because the case under consideration with this hospitable woman concerns traveling teachers, John warns her about whom she ought to give her help. If a teacher is to receive her help and hospitality, he is to be faithful to the gospel. When EI ("If") is used with the indicative ERCHETAI ("cometh", present indicative from ERCHOMAI), it is considered a conditional clause, "the condition determined as fulfilled."[23] This implies that the woman had already been visited by traveling teachers who should not have received her hospitality. These were not chance meetings, casual visits, or harmless socializings. This was a serious reality which would harm the woman if she continued to help them. These teachers were not bringing "this teaching," literally "this **the** teaching" (TAUTAN TAN DIDACHAN), the teaching referred to in the previous verse, as it is the article of previous reference. Any person who came was to be loyal to all the body of truth and certainly loyal to accurate teaching about Jesus.

receive him not into your house, and give him no greeting - These false teachers were not to enjoy the normal hospitality afforded to traveling teachers of the day. Since inn and guest house accommodations were so limited in that day, most travelers stayed in private homes, particularly among believers in the first century. It would not mean that acts of kindness and love would never be shown. John is not leaving open any chance for someone to be rude and boorish. It would not mean that help in circumstances of survival of life could not be offered. According to Barnes, it does include, however, a number of things Christians must avoid: (1) countenancing them as religious leaders and teachers; (2) attending their instruction; (3) receiving them into one's house and entertaining them as one would a true teacher; (4) commending these teachers to others; and (5) lending their names or influence in any way to propagate their error.[24] To this could be added the caution of avoiding opportunities to allow false teachers to "shipwreck" one's faith (1 Timothy 1:19-20) or to "overthrow the faith of some" by letting their "false word eat as doth a gangrene" (2 Timothy 2:17-18). Real dangers were in the mind of John, not some trivial social problems in the area of hospitality.

The word used here for "greeting" (CHAIREIN, present infinitive) comes from CHAIRO which means "to rejoice, be glad, be joyful, be full of joy, . . .a term of salutation, hail! . . .to greet."[25] It was a common form of salutation in the Grecian world of the day (Acts 15:23; 23:26; James 1:1), used similarly to the way "Shalom" was, and still is, used among the Hebrews. It included the idea of wishing them well-being, peace, or Godspeed, and was used both as a greeting and a farewell. The KJV uses the Elizabethan expression "neither bid him God speed." Since such false teachers are doing the work of the deceiver, the anti-christ, the Devil, one who is faithful to the convictions of truth cannot wish them well in their work. There must be no wish for success or God's help in the enterprise of these false teachers doing the Devil's work. If it would have puzzled the faithful Christians of that day to see their brethren offering such greetings and help to false teachers, is it any wonder that many are puzzled in modern days by even elders and preachers who "give greetings" to denominational preachers and churches with no qualms of conscience? To be faithful to the Lord, one must be careful of what he countenances and what he encourages.

Verse 11 for he that giveth him greeting partaketh in his evil works - John states the danger he wanted Cyria to avoid. Knowing her love for the truth, her walk in truth, and the rejoicing of even knowing her children walked in the truth (vv. 1-4), John understood she would not want to do anything to harm the truth. "For" (GAR) introduces the reason for John's sharp cautions to her. She is in real danger, the danger of working against the Lord rather than for Him. Her hospitality, no matter how well intentioned or honestly given from a heart overflowing with love for the Lord and His teachers, was in reality taking part in false teaching. She was encouraging evil works, even helping them to continue. "Partaketh" (KOINONEI, present indicative of KOINONEO) means to "have in common, share. . .to become implicated in, to be a party to. . . ."[26] Another lexicographer adds, "to enter into fellowship, join one's self as an associate, make one's self a sharer or partner. . . ."[27] So John gives one of his sharpest statements and strongest of warnings. She must not continue in her fellowship with false teachers. She must not invest her time, talents and money in destructive heresies. Love for God and His truths take precedence over any of her good desires to entertain and encourage traveling evangelists. She must first of all ascertain if these travelers are faithful to accurate doctrine. Warnings of such sharp nature were not unknown among other New Testament writers either (Romans 16:17-18; 2 Corinthians 6:14ff; Galatians 1:6-9; Philippians 3:18-19; 1 Timothy 4:1-4; 2 Timothy 4:1-5; 2 Peter 2:1-22

V. Conclusion 12-13

¹²Having many things to write unto you, I would not write them with paper and ink: but I hope to come unto you, and to speak face to face, that our joy may be made full. ¹³The children of thine elect sister salute thee.

The letter now draws to a close. After a rather sharp caution, John closes in a most tender and solicitous manner. He saluted her, commended her, exhorted her, cautioned her, now he closes with an earnest expression of a desire for a personal visit.

Verse 12 Having many things to write unto you, I would not write them with paper and ink: but I hope to come unto you, and to speak face to face, that your joy may be made full - What these things were that John wanted to communicate to her is not known. Some conjecture that he wanted to bring out many of the things he had written in the First Epistle in order to reinforce the caution about false teachers. That might well be, but there is no way to know what has not been revealed. That he carried these things on his heart continually is expressed by "having" (ECHON, present participle). This additionally supplies the thought of a cause and might be expressed "Because I still have many things to write unto you. . . ."

"I would not write them" (OUK BOULETHE, aorist indicative form BOULOMAI) is somewhat unusual, since literally it is "I purposed not." Since he already used the infinitive "to write," it can be understood his purpose was connected to the previous infinitive, "to write." The use of the aorist indicating past tense is understood again as an epistolary aorist; that is, when those who received the letter read it, John's purpose could be said to have occurred in the past.

"With paper and ink" is interesting, as John refers to papyrus. This is the only time this word "paper" appears in the New Testament, though it is found in the LXX in Jeremiah 36:23. The "paper" (CHARTA) of that day differed from animal skins (MEMBRANA) as used by Paul when requesting the "parchments" (2 Timothy 4:13). "The papyrus reed grew in ancient times in great profusion in the Nile and was used as a material for writing. From Egypt its use spread to other countries and it was the universal material for writing in general in Greece and Italy during the most flourishing periods of their literature. The pith of the stem of the plant was cut into thin strips, placed side by side to form a sheath. Another layer was laid upon this at right angles to it. The two layers were united by moisture and pressure and frequently with the addition of glue. The sheets, after being dried and polished, were ready for use. Normally, the writing is on that side of the papyrus on which the fibres lie horizontally, parallel to the length of the roll, but where the material was scarce the writer used the other side also (cp. Revelation 5:1). Papyrus continued to be used until the seventh cent., A.D., when the conquest of Egypt by the Arabs led to the disuse of the material for literary purposes and the use of vellum till the 12th. century."[28]

The ink (MELANOS) means "black" or as one said "black stuff."[29] It was usually soot, lampblack, or carbon of some sort mixed with water and gum, allowed to harden into sticks for later use. Though the writing instrument is not mentioned here (see 3 John 13), it was made from a reed that was usually split and sharpened to a proper point.

but I hope to come unto you, and to speak to you face to face, that your joy may be made full - John would rather discuss many of these things personally with this woman than to use only the short, written messages. Although the blessing of joy being made full can come from such personal interviews, it is rarely attained from letters. Some read into this that there were hurt feelings and deep wounds which John wanted to heal in a personal visit. This again is speculation, and not every likely, as John seems to expect joy to come out of their meeting. "Face to face" is literally "mouth to mouth" (STOMA PROS STOMA), a common expression denoting conversation between persons. It usually carried with it the idea of personal and confidential conversation and may be reminiscent of God speaking with Moses "mouth to mouth" (Numbers 12:8).[30]

The argument over whether this is John's joy or the woman's joy that is to be made full is of little consequence. The personal visit would turn out to be joyful from both viewpoints; her joy would be made full from the viewpoint of having a personal visit from this aged apostle and John's joy could be made full in being able to communicate all the things stored up in his heart that he wanted to tell her.

Verse 13 The children of thine elect sister salute thee.

The children of thine elect sister salute thee - Those who interpret this letter as addressed to a church metaphorically spoken of as "the elect lady" will say this "elect sister" is the congregation where John resides. The weight of evidence does not bear out this acceptance of such a metaphor (see Introduction). It would be most difficult to place both the women and the children in such a metaphor. If the women represented two congregations, those congregations were made up of individual members. That would not leave anything for the children to represent. If you wanted to claim that the children represented the individual members of each congregation, then there would be two congregations composed of something other than individual members. The metaphor just will not work.

It seems John is sending greetings from the children of the addressee's sister. We know that this sister was a Christian for she also was called "elect." Whether she was alive or dead is not known; it could have been that she was not present where John and the children were when the epistle was sent, thereby not sending her greetings along with theirs. It could be that these children were the bearers of the news that improper hospitality was being shown by Cyria. All such things as these can be looked at briefly, but too much time spent can lead to dangerous speculations.

Thus, we obtain a glimpse into the times of the first century. We see some of the joys which enriched the lives of the early Christians, feeling a little bit of the quiet peace that comes when there is love and fellowship among believers. There is also a dignified sense of success and accomplishment when teachers and students continue to grow in the grace and knowledge of the Lord Jesus Christ. We see some of the problems the early congregations faced, even while one of the apostles was still alive. We are emboldened when we see the courage and fortitude it took to deal with these early problems. These problems are not exclusive to the first century, and we are the better by being able to study the inspired solutions with the apostle John.

What a jewel of a little book written to a jewel of a lady!

[1]See William F. Arndt and F. Wilbur Gingrich, *A Greek-English Lexicon of the New Testament*, (University of Chicago Press, Chicago, Illinois, 1957), pp. 706-707;

Also Joseph Henry Thayer, *A Greek-English Lexicon of the New Testament*, (American Book Co., New York, N.Y., 1889; being Grimm's Wilke's *Clavis Novi Testamenti, Translated Revised and Enlarged*, 1879, Harper & Brothers), pp. 535-536.

[2]Thayer, *Lexicon*, p. 365.

[3]Samuel Bagster, *Analytical Greek Lexicon*, (Samuel Bagster & Sons, London, England, 1852, Revised edition by Harold K. Moulton, Zondervan Publishing Co., Grand Rapids, Michigan, 1978), p. 263.

[4]Ardnt and Gingrich, *Lexicon*, pp. 26-27.

[5]Thayer, *Lexicon*, p. 666.

[6]Thayer, *Lexicon*, p. 202.

[7]Thayer, *Lexicon*, p. 182.

[8]Guy N. Woods, *A Commentary on the New Testament Epistles of Peter, John and Jude*, (Gospel Advocate Co., Nashville, Tennessee, 1954), p. 341.

[9]W. E. Vine, *An Expository Dictionary of New Testament Words*, (Riverside Book and Bible House, Iowa Falls, Iowa, 1952), p. 71.

[10]Richard C. Trench, *Synonyms of the New Testament*, p. 140, as quoted by Donald W. Burdick, *The Letters of John the Apostle*, (Moody Press, Chicago, Illinois, 1985), p. 423.

[11]A. Plummer, in a quote by Alexander Ross, *The New International Commentary on the New Testament, The Epistles of James and John*, (Wm. B. Eerdmans Publishing Co., Grand Rapids, Michigan, 1954), p. 229.

[12]Bagster, *Lexicon*, p. 386.

[13]Joseph Henry Thayer, *A Greek-English Lexicon of the New Testament*, (American Book Co., New York, New York, 1889; being Grimm's Wilke's *Clavis Novi Testamenti, Translated Revised and Enlarged*, 1879 Harper & Brothers), p. 515.

[14]Lenski, *Interpretation*, p. 566.

[15]Burdick, *Letters*, pp. 425-426.

[16]Bagster, *Lexicon*, p. 71.

[17]J. W. Roberts, *The Living Word Commentary, The Letters of John*, (R. B. Sweet Co., Inc., Austin, Texas, 1968), p. 162.

[18]Thayer, *Lexicon*, p. 415.

[19]Arndt & Gingrich, *Lexicon*, pp. 708-709.

[20]Marvin R. Vincent, *Word Studies in the New Testament,* (Charles Scribner's Sons, New York, 1911), Vol. II, *The Writings of John,* p. 395.

[21]Plummer, quoted by Burdick, *Letters,* p. 427.

[22]Bagster, *Lexicon,* p. 263.

[23]A. T. Robertson, *A Short Grammar of the Greek New Testament,* (Hodder & Stoughton, New York, New York, 1908), Third Edition, pp. 161-162.

[24]Albert Barnes, *Notes on the New Testament, James, Peter, John and Jude,* (Baker Book House, Grand Rapids, Michigan, 1949), p. 365.

[25]Bagster, *Lexicon,* p. 433.

[26]Bagster, *Lexicon,* p. 235.

[27]Thayer, *Lexicon,* pp. 451-452.

[28]Vine, *Dictionary,* p. 829.

[29]Ross, *NIC,* p. 232, footnote 3.

[30]Barnes, *Notes,* p. 366.

Notes on Third John

I. Salutation 1-2

¹*The elder unto Gaius the beloved, whom I love in truth. ²Beloved, I pray that in all things thou mayest prosper and be in health, even as thy soul prospereth.*

Though the apostle John is not mentioned here in the salutation by name, there is universal acceptance that he is the author. This letter is going to a man of his acquaintance, Gaius, most likely one of his own converts (v. 4). This letter revolves around three men: Gaius, Diotrephes, and Demetrius. Gaius and Diotrephes are members of the same congregation and there is a possibility Demetrius is also. He could have been the messenger who took John's letter and thus might be included as one of the travelers that the church was hindered in receiving. He could have been a member of the local church that received this letter and was returning home. It is more likely, from the language of verse 12 that he was a stranger to Gaius and needed recommendation.

The letter is brief, almost a twin to the Second Epistle in length and language. It is thought by some that these two letters were written on the same day and went to individuals within the same congregation (see Introduction for fuller discussion).

Within this letter is one of the sharper writings of John, the apostle usually styled the "apostle of love." He calls upon his authority as an apostle (v. 10) since Dioptrephes refuses to accept John, i.e., "receiveth us not" (v. 9). Both the Second Epistle and the Third offer a look into the relatively unknown side of this aged apostle when he is called upon to deal with those who are rebels and reject the truth. By inspiration John refuses to tolerate such rebellion.

Verse 1 The elder unto Gaius the beloved, whom I love in truth - "The elder" (HO PRESBUTEROS) had reference

253

perhaps to six things in the New Testament (see 2 John 1). Whether John is coming simply as an older man or whether he is coming in a sense of a man of dignity, rank, age, honor, and experience is not known. He is surely addressing Gaius from a position of age and experience in the truth; and with his dealing with Diotrephes, it is probable that he is coming with a special rank of honor and dignity also. The idea that he was an overseer in a local church, as was Peter, is not substantiated.

The New Testament mentions three men named Gaius, one of Macedonia, one of Derbe, and one of Corinth (see Introduction). It is most likely that a fourth man, entirely different from any one of these, is the recipient of this letter. As it has been over thirty years since any of these three men have been mentioned, it is most likely there was an additional man to whom John was writing. Gaius was a common name used in the Roman Empire, some say as common as "John Smith."

This man Gaius, whichever one he was, was "beloved," (AGAPATO, from AGAPATOS). This adjective, used four times by John in this short letter for Gaius (vv. 1,2,5,11), is a common form of address throughout the New Testament (used sixty-two times). It means "dear, beloved . . .Oft, in direct address."[1] It also includes "worthy of love."[2] This may refer not only to John's heartfelt esteem of Gaius, but also to what the brethren in the general area thought of him. Gaius was obviously a man held in high regard in the area and in the congregation.

whom I love in truth - Not only was Gaius the "beloved" one, esteemed highly by all who knew him, he was also a man whom John loved personally. Grammatically this could be translated "whom I truly love," since "in truth" (EN ALETHEIA) is anarthous here. However, from the use of the word "truth" three more times in verses 3 and 4, twice with the definite article (TAN ALETHEIA), it is likely John's usage is interchangeable. He makes no difference in meaning whether or not "truth" has the definite article.[3] So John is speaking clearly of those who walk within the bounds of truth and have fellowship together in Jesus Christ.

Verse 2 Beloved, I pray that in all things thou mayest

prosper and be in health, even as thy soul prospereth.

Beloved, I pray that in all things thou mayest prosper and be in health, - By using the vocative "Beloved" (AGAPATE), John continues to stress his regard for Gaius. He used this term of address a total of nine times in First and Third John, three of which are in Third John. These triple references to love in regard to Gaius in these two introductory verses is not surprising when one considers the animosity Gaius must have endured from Diotrephes. Since John considered the hospitality and support offered to these teachers by Gaius to be "faithful work" (v. 5), a work of love (v. 6), a work well done (v. 6), and a work of fellowship in the truth (v. 8), he would encourage Gaius at every opportunity. Yet this was the very thing Diotrephes abhorred and fought. Thus John repeats with emphasis that Gaius is operating in the right circle, the circle of love and truth.

The verb translated "I pray," (EUCHOMAI) means "to pray, offer prayer, . . .to wish, desire";[4] and additionally, "2. to wish: TI, 2 Corinthians xiii.9; foll. by acc. with inf. 3 John 2, adhere to the religious sense, to pray, pray for, in both the preceding pass.]; . . . ."[5] The KJV uses "I wish," though it is far more common to see it translated as in our text, "I pray" (RSV, NASB, NIV). "This kind of prayer occurs in papyrus letters of the second century with noticeable frequency, although the form varies from letter to letter."[6]

"That in all things" (PERI PANTON) is placed in an impressive word order, since it is placed first in the sentence, immediately after "Beloved" and prior to "I pray." Since one also notices "thy soul" (SOU HE PSUCHE) is placed last in the sentence, it is surmised that John intends to emphasize these two things by this construction.[7]

John mentions three things about which he is concerned with Gaius — financial prosperity, physical health, and prosperity of soul. The verb translated "thou mayest prosper," literally "thee to prosper" (SE EUODOUSTHAI, present passive infinitive of EUODOO), is used by Paul to refer to a proposed prosperous journey to Rome (Romans 1:10) and to refer to the way each individual determines his weekly financial offering (1 Corinthians 16:2). Since Gaius had obviously been helping the evangelists of the day, John is wishing him well in regard to finances so that he might be able to continue such hospitality in setting them forward on their journeys (v. 6).

To wish one to "be in health" (HUGIAINEIN) was "very common in private letters."[8] It simply means "bodily health"[9] and is the very word used by Dr. Luke to describe physical health (Luke 5:31; 7:10; 15:27). Interestingly, all of the other eight uses of this word in the New Testament are metaphorical in reference to sound doctrine, sound words, and sound faith (1 Timothy 1:10; 6:3; 2 Timothy 1:13; 4:3; Titus 1:9,13; 2:1,2). As the body can have strength and vitality in the physical sense, the teachings of evangelists can have strength and vitality in a spiritual sense. Thus, Paul spoke of "sound" doctrine as "healthful" doctrine (see footnote in ASV, 1 Timothy 1:10). In the present passage the word has to refer to physical health since Paul goes on to add the mention of prosperity of soul.

even as thy soul prospereth - Gaius was a man who was growing stronger in the faith as a Christian should. In fact, his spiritual growth was seen as the measure by which he might in the future grow financially and in physical health. He was an outstanding man as his spiritual prosperity was outdistancing his material prosperity. How often just the opposite case is seen. Many caring souls lament the fact that Christians are not prospering spiritually and wish they would prosper as much as they do in material things! "Here, incidentally, is the standard by which to determine how rich one may safely become: **just so long as the soul prospers!** So long as one enjoys soul prosperity, his riches bless and benefit not only himself, but others; when they impair spiritual health, the interests of the soul demand, as in the case of the rich young ruler (Mark 10:17-31) that a surgical operation be performed and they be severed from us!"[10] John thus wishes Gaius might prosper as well financially and physically as he had in spiritual attainments. Of how many could such a prayer be well offered today?

This produces several points of variance between Gaius and Diotrephes. Gaius was rich in spiritual values, activities, knowledge, manner of life, and the respect of those among whom he lived. Diotrephes exhibited much of the opposite, being mean, self-willed, spiteful, proud, arrogant, and rebellious to truth. What more could John say to point out these two men were of opposite spiritual stances?

II. Commendation 3-8

³For I rejoiced greatly, when brethren came and bare witness unto thy truth, even as thou walkest in truth. ⁴Greater joy have I none than this, to hear of my children walking in the truth. ⁵Beloved, thou doest a faithful work in whatsoever thou doest toward them that are brethren and strangers withal; ⁶who bare witness to thy love before the church: whom thou wilt do well to set forward on their journey worthily of God: ⁷because that for the sake of the Name they went forth, taking nothing of the Gentiles. ⁸We therefore ought to welcome such, that we may be fellow-workers for the truth.

John enters into a commendation of Gaius as he has been showing hospitality and help to preachers. Word has reached John about these things and he is commending Gaius for walking as a Christian should, "in the truth." Even before the whole church was this known, and John adds a strong implication that Gaius ought to continue such practices.

Verse 3 For I rejoiced greatly, when brethren came and bare witness unto thy truth, even as thou walkest in truth.

For I rejoiced greatly - Or it could be said, "I was very glad," as this is another case of the epistolary aorist (ECHAREIN). This was a common form in letters of the day,[11] and John is joyful at the news from Gaius.

when brethren came and bare witness unto thy truth, These brethren may have been sent by John to the church where Gaius and Diotrephes lived. If so, they had been received by Gaius and rebuffed by Diotrephes. And this rebuff may have included most of the entire congregation, as is implied in verse 10, "casteth them out of the church." There are two present tense participles, "came" (ERCHOMENON) and "bare witness" (MARTUROUNTON), which stress the idea that brethren came back to John repeatedly and bore witness repeatedly to the condition of Gaius. Their testimony was not just a one-time event; rather, it was the fact that all the brethren who traveled into the city where Gaius lived and who were blessed by his generosity came to John on various occasions and told of Gaius' support.

"Unto thy truth" does not refer to Gaius being truthful, but to the fact he was devoted to the truth of the Lord. In this and the following verses the word "truth" is used three times. Each time it "refers to the same thing, the objective divine truth or reality which forms the Word and gospel. This always remains objective whether we have it as ours or not, whether we walk in it or in its opposite, the lie. Having it in our hearts does not change it and make it subjective; the subjectivity — if we **must** use the word — is only our possession. All comments which make either SOU TA ALETHEIA or EN ALETHEIA or both subjective are unwarranted. These brethren reported that Gaius acted in harmony with the gospel truth and doctrine (2 John 9,10), that thus this truth was his (SOU), in his heart. The conduct of Gaius was the open evidence for what was in his heart. This rejoiced John greatly. The conduct of Gaius was his expression of love."[12]

even as thou walkest in truth - The use of the present indicative (PERIPATEIS) shows Gaius was continuing to walk in the truth. Though it does not have the article, "truth" (ALETHEIA) must refer back to the previous uses of truth in these verses. It does not mean Gaius truly walks but it means Gaius walks in the truth, the entire scope of the doctrine revealed through Christ.

Verse 4 Greater joy have I none than this, to hear of my children walking in the truth.

Greater joy have I none than this, - " 'Greater' is made doubly emphatic, first by position at the beginning of the sentence, and secondly by the double comparative (MEIZOTERAN.)"[13] "Joy" (CHARAN) simply means "joy, gladness and rejoicing."[14] John is giving much emphasis to the feelings brought to his heart by the report of these brethren.

"This" is actually a plural pronoun and would usually have been translated "these things." Most likely it refers to

259

the activities of Gaius and the brethren there which brought joy to John. It is not unusual, however, for the plural to be used for the singular.[15]

to hear of my children walking in the truth - John seems to indicate that Gaius and others in that congregation were John's converts, as this is his usual reference. It could merely mean those over whom John had been exercising great spiritual care and concern and those with whom he had been closely associated. The fact that his joy was coupled with their walking testifies once again that John's idea of love and faithfulness was activity in the Lord. "Walking" is a present participle (PERIPATOUNTA) and in this verse means "to maintain a certain walk of life and conduct."[16] The present tense doubles the idea of such maintaining, as it requires the iterative sense of the verb. They continually walked in the truth as a habit of life.

Such word of faithful children gladdens the heart of any gospel preacher or teacher. The fact men and women would persevere is one of the greater satisfactions the teacher has. And such is true as well among parents. "There is nothing that would give more peace to the dying pillow of the Christian parents, than to be able to leave the world with with assurance that his children would always walk in truth."[17]

Verse 5 Beloved, thou doest a faithful work in whatsoevever thou doest toward them that are brethren and strangers withal;

Beloved, thou doest a faithful work - For "beloved" see verse 2. The faithful work is literally a "faithful thing" that Gaius has been doing. The RSV uses "a loyal thing," but that translation seems to be a bit more commentative. The KJV has "thou doest faithfully" as if the word were an adverb. The NIV has "you are faithful" which is much closer to the proper use of this adjective.

in whatsoever thou doest toward them that are brethren and strangers withal; - John uses the aorist subjunctive (ERGASA), translatedd "doest," to imply future actions, as well as Gaius' present actions. Lenski translates the expression "whatever thou mayest (actually) perform."[18] The word translated brethren (ADELPHOUS) simply means fellow Christians, a term used by John twenty times in these three epistles. More than likely, it refers to those who lived in nearby cities and visited frequently and were thus well known, as opposed to the other class of persons who received Gaius' help. "Strangers" (XENOS) usually refers to foreigners, but here it means those travelers with whom Gaius is not acquainted. If John did indeed send some missionaries who were received by Gaius, they were among this class of strangers. One student takes this to mean not two classes of men received by Gaius, but "to them that are brethren and **that** strangers."[19]

Verse 6 who bare witness of thy love before the church: whom thou wilt do well to set forward on their journey worthily of God:

who bare witness of thy love before the church - In verse 3, John had used the present participle (MARTUROUNTON) for bearing witness, but here he uses the aorist (EMARTURASAN) "bare witness." The RSV used "testified" in verse 3 and in the present verse uses "have testified." In verse 3 it was present tense and in the present tense it is aorist, not perfect tense as the RSV seems to say. The KJV uses "have borne witness," again tending toward the perfect tense. What John is simply saying is that he views the repeated testimonies of these men, as to the love of Gaius before the church, as one single incident which happened in the past. This is a common use of the aorist even though it may refer to repeated action over a long time. It often views the whole period as one point of time. "The thing to bear in mind is that the aorist represents the actions as a point. In itself it may have continued a long time. It is precisely the idea of the aorist (undefined action) that it does not distinguish between complete or incomplete action. It may be used of either."[20] Thus, John uses the aorist to indicate that these actions of men who told about Gaius' love before the church might not yet have been completed. All this witnessing is viewed as a single incident.

"Before the church" is taken by most to mean Ephesus, since secular history has John living there at this time.[21] John uses the word "church" (EKKLESIA) only three times in all of his writings, and all three occur in this letter. Whether John meant "church" to refer to the congregation or to the assembly of the congregation is not known. It could refer to either, but in verse 9 it will obviously refer to the church as a called-out body of people, a congregation, who belong to the Lord.

whom thou wilt do well to set forward on their journey worthily of God: - John does not issue a direct command to continue supporting these teachers, neither does he issue a direct request. He simply commends Gaius, because the hospitality he had already been giving would be continuing to do well. Stated this way, John's words would not fail to imply to Gaius that he had the stamp of approval from the Apostle John. Gaius might be suffering embarrassment and persecution from Diotrephes, but he knew that his present course of action pleased the Lord. John was using a common form of saying "please set them forward." The phrase "you will do well" is "very common introducing a command or request, almost = our 'please' or 'kindly.' It is generally followed by an aor. part., as in 3 John 6, ..."[22] Thus, John uses the aorist participle (PROPEMPSAS) which means "to furnish with things necessary for a journey."[23] When Gaius is thus encouraged to continue these actions of love toward the travelers, it means to furnish them with whatever they will need to do their traveling. When the needs are local in the city where Gaius resides, such would include a place to stay and meals. When the missionaries leave and head toward other cities, the injunction means to give them food, clothing, money, or anything else necessary to help them accomplish their mission (see Romans 15:24; 1 Corinthians 16:6,11; 2 Corinthians 1:16; Titus 3:13). "Worthily of God" could refer to the manner in which one would treat God, or the manner in which God has treated us, or a manner that would bring praise to God, or even in a manner that "befits God's service" (RSV).

Verse 7 because that for the sake of the Name they went forth, taking nothing of the Gentiles.

because that for the sake of the Name they went forth - This is the first of two reasons that John gives for helping these itinerant preachers; they went out for the sake of the Name. The second reason will follow, as they took nothing of the Gentiles. The article TOU before ONOMATOS (**the** Name) makes this name a very particular name, not just any name. To do something that way in a name means to do it for all that the name represents — the nature, character, and purposes of the one who wears the name. "Name" appears 209 times in the New Testament and over 150 times it refers to the Lord Jesus Christ. When these travelers worked, taught, suffered, and walked those many miles, they did it all for the sake of Jesus Christ, who He is, what He did for us, and what He teaches us to do to follow Him to glory.

The apostles, after being beaten in the presence of the council, rejoiced they were counted "worthy to suffer dishonor for the Name" (Acts 5:41). Ananias was told, "Go thy way: for he is a chosen vessel unto me, to bear my name before the Gentiles and kings, and the children of Israel: for I will show him how many things he must suffer for my name's sake" (Acts 9:15-16). In the problem of circumcision, the apostles, elders, and the whole church at Jerusalem wrote to the brethren who were Gentiles in Antioch, Syria, and Cilicia about "men who hazarded their lives for the name of our Lord Jesus Christ" (Acts 15:26).

Ignatius is said to have written to Ephesus with the common expression of Christians describing his prison term as "in bonds for the Name's sake."[24] "When the agents of persecution came to ferret out the martyr, and when civil and papal edicts shut the door of sympathy, occasionally help could be obtained by knocking at the door of others, and whispering, 'In the Name!' "[28]

taking nothing of the Gentiles - This is the second reason why these preachers ought to be supported by those in Gaius' congregation. They took nothing of the "pagans" as Lenski translates ETHNIKON.[26] The word is defined as "3. in the N.T. savoring the nature of pagans, alien to the worship of the true God, heathenish; . . . the pagan, the Gentile."[27] The RSV and NIV use "heathen." This was somewhat the rule, or custom, of the earlier evangelists, especially Paul. He did not wish any kind of misunderstanding about his motives and did not claim his right to support in some congregations, even from the brethren (Acts 18:3; 20:34; 1 Corinthians 9:6-18; 2 Corinthians 11:7-11; 1 Thessalonians 2:9). Nothing will undermine the respect of a teacher more quickly and thoroughly than a perception that he is doing his work for financial advantage. And nothing will help melt the hearts of the stubborn more quickly than a sacrificial life of a gospel preacher!

These two reasons for supporting these teachers, treated so inhospitably by Diotrephes, and so well by Gaius, are now seen. They are going forth for the sake of the Name, plus they are being careful about misunderstandings in financial affairs, taking nothing of the Gentiles. John is ready to express a conclusion to such a situation.

Verse 8 We therefore ought to welcome such, that we may be fellow-workers for the truth.

We therefore ought to welcome such, - It seems John is giving particular emphasis to "we" (HUMEIS) as opposed to the "Gentiles," i.e., the unbelieving pagans. Since these travelers did not take support from unbelievers, it was all the more urgent that "we" believers give them proper hospitality and "setting forward" on their journeys. Two reasons for their lack of support mentioned previously — they would not accept support from unbelievers and they often chose to support themselves for reasons of expediency — did not obviate the responsibility of Christians whom they taught to support them. "To welcome" leaves out some of the ideas contained in the original word (HUPOLAMBANEIN). Its literal connotation includes "to take up and carry away,"[28] and "to receive as a guest, support."[29] Various translations all help in understanding this — KJV has "to receive such," NIV has "to show hospitality," RSV and NASB have "to support," and Marshall's Interlinear uses "to entertain." John speaks not only of warm and loving greetings, but he also means for Gaius to continue to support these men financially in their travels. Since this word is a present active infinitive, it directs Gaius to continue such welcoming as a habit. One missionary worker was quoted as saying his work was similar to exploring a deep mineshaft and added, "I will go down, if you hold the ropes."[30]

Lenski points out this is a paronomasia. Since these traveling teachers "take nothing" from the Gentiles (v. 7), we ought to "take them up under" and support them.[31]

that we may be fellow-workers for the truth - "Fellow-workers" (SUNERGOI) was a favorite word with Paul, being used fourteen times as he emphasized sharing the work of the gospel (Romans 16:3,9,21, etc.). This is the only time John uses it, though he had expressed the same idea with other words in warning the "elect lady" about fellowshipping false teachers (2 John 10-11). John's warning to the lady was given in the negative lest she share in a bad work, while to Gaius John urges continued cooperation in order to be a sharer.

"For the truth" can be taken literally, that supporters of teachers are sharing in the work of the gospel itself. This phrase might also be taken metonymically; that is, we may be fellow-workers with those teachers who evangelize the truth. Either way, it shows the privilege and honor afforded to those who choose to be supporters.

It is interesting to notice that here John writes that men are fellow-workers with God in spreading the gospel, but the reverse is also true — God cooperates with men and shares in the work of men too! "And they went forth, and preached everywhere, the Lord working with them, and confirming the word by the signs that followed" (Mark 16:20). The same word is used to speak of God's work among men (SUNEREGO).

III. Denunciation 9-10

⁹I wrote somewhat unto the church: but Diotrephes, who loveth to have the preeminence among them, receiveth us not. ¹⁰Therefore, if I come, I will bring to remembrance his works which he doeth, prating against us with wicked words: and not content therewith, neither doth he himself receive the brethren, and them that would be forbiddeth, and casteth them out of the church.

John thus far has saluted Gaius and his brethren (vv. 1-2), then commended them for their love and hospitality, as they were doing a faithful work to brethren and strangers (vv. 3-8). All this has built a most forceful case for the genuine godly character and commitment to Christ for the man Gaius. Now John begins to show the man who stands so much in the opposite vein of character, Diotrephes. For the "Apostle of love," as he is so often called, to be so forceful in denunciation is surprising to some. It ought not to surprise believers when negative things must be said and done in the name of the Lord. Few farmers would be successful if they did not clear away the brush, rocks, and weeds prior to planting the new seed. The major object is not such clearing, but clearing away the land is necessary for a good crop and harvest.

Verse 9 I wrote somewhat unto the church: but Diotrephes who loveth to have the preeminence among them, receiveth us not.

I wrote somewhat unto the church - This is a simple aorist (EGRAPSA) expressing a past action. John had previously written a letter of commendation for some travelers to the church. The letter and the men had been rejected by Diotrephes. "Somewhat" (TI) merely means "something," including that it was a certain letter. John is referring to a certain letter that he had sent to the church. Possibly it accompanied the men as they traveled.

This letter is not known now. Lenski argues this refers to

2 John but lacks enough evidence to argue conclusively.[32] Paul spoke of other letters (Colossians 4:16) and surely it could be argued that the content of the New Testament does not cover all possibilities of the correspondence throughout the lifetime of all the apostles. They may have sent many letters, both inspired and uninspired. They may have been urged by the Spirit to write letters which are not now contained in the New Testament, but we have full assurance that what is within the New Testament is full and complete (Jude 3; Galatians 1:8-9; 2 Timothy 3:16-17). We have everything God intended to preserve for all generations. It is possible, even likely, that many letters were sent by John and the other apostles that were not necessarily inspired. What would keep any of these great teachers from writing many letters of exhortation and teaching the same as would we today? Mentioning other letters not contained in our Bibles, therefore, ought not to be shattering to one's faith in God and His Word.

This letter was written to the church (EKKLESIA), and John did not mean the universal body of God's people. Such a letter would have been most difficult to distribute to the entire brotherhood. This letter written by John contained specific instructions for that specific congregation about receiving and helping these teachers. It surely could have applied to other churches they might have visited, but John does not mention such.

but Diotrephes, who loveth to have the preeminence among them, receiveth us not - John uses a strong adversative conjunction "but" (ALLA) to show the seriousness of this rejection. A lesser conjunction often used is DE, but John chose the stronger. This is the only mention of this man Diotrephes in the New Testament, but his name has become a synonym for something ugly and hurtful to the Lord's people. "Diotrephes" means "nourished by Zeus, or foster-child of Zeus,"[33] giving some the idea that this man had come out of a pagan culture.

The phrase "loveth to have the preeminence" ("loves to be first" — NIV, NASB) comes from PHILOPROTEUON. "It is a compound verb, made up of a verb meaning 'to love' and a verb meaning 'to have first place.' It is rather interesting to observe that the second verb occurs just once in the N.T., in Colossians 1:18, where it is used of Christ, 'that in all things He might have the preeminence, might have first place.' Christ is the only Head of the Church; there is no room in it for 'little Popes,' like Diotrephes."[34] What a contrast this is! On the one hand there is Jesus Christ, who **deserved** to have all preeminence but "humbled himself, becoming obedient even unto death, yea, the death of the cross" (Philippians 2:8). On the other hand, there is Diotrephes **desiring** the preeminence and deserving none of it. He only did those things which showed his arrogance and self-will.

There are many conjectures that Diotrephes was the preacher, an overseer, or a deacon in charge of the money, etc., but no conclusive evidence has emerged. What we do know is that he was a domineering man in the local congregation with Gaius and that he evinced many qualities of leadership, though he misused them. As he asserted his own will and ambition, he denied even the authority of an apostle as he strove to assume control over the fellowship procedures of the local church.

The verb "loveth to have the preeminence" is a present tense participle, indicating this was a persistent pattern of life for Diotrephes. Had this been only one case of refusal to visiting teachers, it would not have required the attention John gave it.

"Received us not" did not refer to a refusal to accept John in person. When Diotrephes refused to "receive" John, it was a refusal to accept the word of the letter John sent along with these teachers. The NASB makes a comment here, rather than a translation, as it uses, "does not accept what we say," This explains the single word "us" (HAMAS), as it truly does include what John said in the letter. This is not just a simple rejection of John personally or just a rejection of men as credible whom John had sent; it is also a rejection that John had any right to speak to the affairs of the local church.

Such rejection is tantamount to rejecting John's authority as an apostle, for surely the apostles had not only such rights, but duties to perform as instruments of the Holy Spirit. They were still giving out the Truth as it was being revealed through them. Therefore, when John's word was rejected, John's apostleship was rejected also, and ultimately the authority of God was rejected. Peter used this same line of reasoning with Ananias, "thou has not lied unto men, but unto God" (Acts 5:4). The same was true in the days of Moses when Korah, Dathan and Abiram rebelled. Moses said, "But if Jehovah make a new thing, and the ground open its mouth, and swallow them up, with all that appertain unto them, and they go down alive into Sheol; then ye shall understand that these men have despised Jehovah" (Numbers 16:30). It was also true in the case of the prophet Samuel, "And Jehovah said unto Samuel, Hearken unto the voice of the people in all that they say unto thee; for they have not rejected thee, but they have rejected me, that I should not be a king over them" (1 Samuel 8:7). It is still true today and in every age that a rejection of God's teachers and leaders is a rejection of God Himself. When men preach the truth today, accurately from the Word of God, and it is rejected out of hand, the rejection is not so much of the preacher as it is a rejection of the Word of God. When men refuse to follow the lead of God's duly appointed overseers in local churches, they are not just refusing men personally; they are, in actuality, refusing God. This is true because they refuse God's appointed and constituted leadership. Let congregations beware lest they make the same mistake as other rebels to God's authority.

Verse 10 Therefore, if I come, I will bring to remembrance his works which he doeth, prating against us with wicked words: and not content therewith, neither doth he himself receive the brethren, and them that would he forbiddeth and casteth them out of the church.

Therefore, if I come, I will bring to remembrance his works which he doeth, prating against us with wicked words - John intends to come to visit this congregation (v. 14); and when he does visit personally, he intends to bring before the church these evil works of Diotrephes. John, with all his loving and gentle spirit, is not intimidated by Diotrephes. He refuses to let him continue in his desire to be the "church boss." It is of note this is a matter for the entire church, not just a select few men or leaders within the group. It is obvious John refers to a public meeting, open to all members of the congregation.

"If I come" (EAN ELTHO) does not leave any doubt as to John's coming, for this same conditional conjunction was used by John to refer to the second coming of the Lord also (see 1 John 2:28 and 3:2). "Bring to remembrance" (HUPOMNASO, future indicative of HUPOMIMNASKO) "signifies to cause one to remember, put one in mind of. . . "[35] NASB and NIV use "call attention," RSV simply has "bring up."

This may be an example of doing what the Lord said to do when wrongs were done between brethren (Matthew 18:15-18). John is having to deal with these things from a long distance away. He had first sent a letter which Diotrephes refused. Other brethren were involved in this and were witnesses to it. Next, John intends to bring this matter before the whole assembly. He has not had the chance to speak with Diotrephes personally about these matters, but the error has gone far beyond anything personal and John is anxious about saving the church.

The first evil that Diotrephes has done is said by John to be "prating (PHLUAREO) against us with wicked words," indicating "talk nonsense (about), bring unjustified charges against. . . ."[36] Paul used the adjective form of this to speak about "tattlers" or "gossips" (1 Timothy 5:13). The words that Diotrephes used were not just idle words, they were also "wicked words" (LOGOIS PONAROIS). Such words were malicious and vicious.

and not content therewith, neither doth he himself receive the brethren, and them that would he forbiddeth and casteth them out of the church - Three more charges against Diotrephes are now added. In addition to (1) prating with wicked words, Diotrephes also (2) refuses to receive the teachers sent by John, (3) he forbids all others within the church to receive them, and (4) if anyone did receive them, Diotrephes would exert every effort to exclude them from the fellowship of the church. He was not satisfied with venting his own private feelings against these visiting teachers sent from John; he also demanded that others fall in line with his thinking. If the members did not fall into line, they would suffer the same ostracism as these visiting teachers. Many within this congregation evidently wanted to show hospitality, but Diotrephes would brook no challenge to his way, his authority. He would have any dissenters ostracized too, whether or not they believed and taught the same as these visitors. The dissenters would be ostracized only on the grounds they disagreed with Diotrephes.

All four verbs used by John to describe the actions of Diotrephes are in the present indicative tense ("prating" - PHLUARON, "receive" - EPIDECHETAI, "forbiddeth" - KOLUEI, and "casteth out" - EKBALLEI). These are things Diotrephes continually does, and John can reasonably expect them to continue if someone does not stand in his way. This is a way of life for Diotrephes. He wants to gain control of the local congregation, and these are the normal and continuing actions one can expect from him. It is probable that the last two verbs ("forbiddeth" and "casteth out") are conative. Diotrephes surely had been speaking evil about John and had been refusing to accept in respect and honor those teachers John had sent. Whether Diotrephes had succeeded in forbidding the church to accept them is doubtful. And whether he had succeeded in casting believers out of the fellowship of the local church is also doubtful. Consider that Gaius was still there, also Demetrius; and it seems both of them are still able to worship and function within the local group. If so, then Diotrephes was merely striving to forbid and cast out but had perhaps not been able to accomplish it completely. This does not lessen the force of John's sharp criticism of Diotrephes. The evil the man did plus the evil he was continually attempting to do were actions worthy of rebuke and censure by John.

Whether Diotrephes was successful would make no difference in one's fellowship with God. By using the term "casteth them out of the church," John did not intend to leave the impression that God would honor in that local group what this domineering leader might accomplish. Diotrephes might mark them, avoid them, cause others to do likewise, and additionally block any support from the local members. They might be led by this evil man to refuse any fellowship with the teachers. Yet this gives no indication as to what God might do. It is God who adds saved persons together in fellowship (Acts 2:27), and boisterous actions to the contrary will not please God. There are occasions when God demands that believers be cut off from fellowship (1 Corinthians 5; Romans 16:17; Ephesians 5:11; etc.), but these are delineated clearly within scripture. Capricious, selfish, arrogant, self-serving actions do not obligate other Christians to follow suit.

The tragedy of one evil and ambitious man within a congregation must not go unnoticed. Who can count the local churches that have suffered greatly from such preachers, elders, deacons, teachers or outspoken men within the group? How many horrendous divisions have been caused by such men and women? Hearts, lives, soul-winning efforts, families, tender souls of new converts, and countless opportunities of missions and evangelism have been shattered due to one or two persons who act as did Diotrephes. Here is the true "dog in the manger" principle, or as one preacher puts it, "I don't like to do visitation, and I don't even like them that do!" As the dog in the fable prevented the ox from eating the hay, even though the dog himself did not want the hay, so Diotrephes demanded others to refuse the teachers from God.

It is so easy to be narrow, unbending, and self-righteous in our commitment to truth. Once convinced of the argument for an interpretation, it is difficult to tolerate any other view. Men can self-destruct spiritually when they choose a certain interpretation or teaching, then refuse to tolerate anyone who believes differently. Yet, they, like Diotrephes, often take it one step further, for **they refuse to tolerate anyone who will tolerate the one differing from the preacher's view!** They "don't like that view, and don't even like them that do like those of that view!" The temptation to control and exercise power causes many a man and woman to be a "modern-day-Diotrephes." Jesus said, "Whosoever shall exalt himself shall be humbled; and whosoever shall humble himself shall be exalted" (Matthew 23:12). James quoted the wise man (Proverbs 3:34), "God resisteth the proud but giveth grace to the humble" (James 4:6). In the context spoken for the benefit of shepherds of local congregations, Peter said, "Likewise, ye younger, be subject unto the elder, Yea, all of you gird yourselves with humility, to serve one another: for God resisteth the proud, but giveth grace to the humble" (1 Peter 5:5).

IV. Exhortation 11

¹¹Beloved, imitate not that which is evil, but that which is good. He that doeth good is of God: he that doeth evil hath not seen God.

After this sharp denunciation of Diotrephes, John is now ready to exhort Gaius to do differently. If he is worthy of the commendations John had given him (vv. 3-8); then he will be willing to apply this exhortation to his own life.

Verse 11 Beloved, imitate not that which is evil, but that which is good - This is the fourth time John uses "beloved" in this book and the ninth time in the three epistles (see v. 2). The Greek grammatical construction in this part of the verse suggests asyndeton, as the change of topic is rather abrupt. John uses the vocative (AGAPETE) to address Gaius and then uses a construction that is somewhat puzzling. He literally tells Gaius not to keep on imitating the evil, but to keep on imitating the good. "Imitate not" is a strong negative (ME) used with the imperative (MIMOU, present imperative from MIMEOMAI), and usually means to quit doing something that is already a practice. In view of the commendations already mentioned in this letter (vv. 4-5), surely John does not mean that Gaius had been practicing the same thing as Diotrephes. John had to use the present imperative to express the latter part of the clause, "but (imitate) that which is good," and thus the present imperative was used for both clauses. It probably means Gaius may have had a tendency to listen and follow Diotrephes, and he was surely to put a stop to that.

The verb translated "imitate" (MIMEOMAI) is used only three other times in the New Testament (1 Thessalonians 3:7,9; Hebrews 13:7). A noun form of the word is used seven times and is usually translated "followers." Vine says it is "always used in exhortations, and always in the continuous tense, suggesting a constant habit or practice."[37] This word seems to be similar to the English word "mimic."

He that doeth good is of God: he that doeth evil hath

not seen God - Two present tense participles are used here to emphasize continuing practice, "doeth good" (AGATHOPOION) and "doeth evil" (KAKOPOION). This general principle is characteristic of John's letters (see 1 John 2:29; 3:6-10). "Of God" is another of John's favorite expressions to describe the family characteristics (see 1 John 3:10; 4:4-6; 5:19). To "see God" (EORAKEN, perfect tense from ORAO) is reminiscent of "whosoever sinneth hath not seen him, neither knoweth him" (1 John 3:6; see also John 14:9; Hebrews 11:27). "These expressions are simply variations of John's rich vocabulary for describing fellowship with God and Christ. Action contrary to the spirit and manner of God endangers fellowship with God by destroying its basis. A Christian who belongs to God's family must not act as though he belonged to the other group."[38]

V. Recommendation 12

¹²*Demetrius hath the witness of all men, and of the truth itself: yea, we also bear witness; and thou knowest that our witness is true.*

Demetrius hath witness of all men, and of the truth itself - Twice in the New Testament the name Demetrius appears, here and in Acts 19:24. There was a silversmith in Ephesus who was involved in the riot when Paul was there, but there is no reason to assume this man is the same as the one in Ephesus. Some argue that Demas (Colossians 4:14; 2 Timothy 4:10; Philemon 24) is a shortened form of Demetrius, but again, there is no evidence for such conjecture. We know three things about this man from the text: (1) he was generally held in high esteem by the brethren, (2) he had good witness of the truth itself, and (3) John also gave him good witness. It is probable that he was the bearer of this letter from John and that he was unknown to Gaius. This is why John is careful to show his qualifications in the letter, as he does not want Demetrius treated as other visiting evangelists have been treated by Diotrephes.

"Hath the witness" (MEMARTUPETAI, perfect tense) shows an action that has been completed in the past with the effect still showing in the present. It was an assured fact that Demetrius had a good report from the brethren. "All men" is a hyperbole simply referring to the general acceptance of this good man by the brethren.

"Of the truth itself" is somewhat vague and may be taken either as the body of truth as an objective witness or as the Holy Spirit Himself. It is unlikely to be the Holy Spirit giving personal witness to this man, as such is not known throughout the New Testament as the normal work of the Spirit. More likely is the case that Demetrius' life is in harmony with the truth; i.e., he walks in harmony with the truth and thus the truth witnesses to his way of life. The good report of all the brethren is linked with this and is the reason why they can give their good report. They have seen his life to be in harmony with the truth.

yea, we also bear witness; and thou knowest that our witness is true - John adds his personal testimony to that of the brethren and the truth, making the third witness. "Bear witness" (MARTUROUMEN) is present tense, showing John continues to affirm the faithfulness of Demetrius. With all these recommendations, Gaius ought to be able to see that Diotrephes would not refuse to accept Demetrius.

VI. Conclusion 13-14

¹³I had many things to write unto thee, but I am unwilling to write them to thee with ink and pen: ¹⁴but I hope shortly to see thee, and we shall speak face to face. Peace be unto thee. The friends salute thee. Salute the friends by name.

John concludes this short book with very personal statements. The tenderness and personal concern shown here is typical of John. He would like to discuss many other things, but these will have to wait until a personal meeting can take place. This close is similar to the one in 2 John and, of course, argues that both books were written by the same author.

Verse 13 I had many things to write unto thee, but I am unwilling to write them to thee with ink and pen: - Putting things down in writing does not give the expression, eye contact, and body language so readily apparent in personal conversation. Perhaps the things which John wished to discuss were so delicate that he would prefer to discuss them personally. Perhaps there were some things that needed more time, a fuller discussion, so that writing was not the better way. Then, it could have been that John did not have the time to write fully enough and he would just wait until he visited with Gaius.

To write with "ink and pen" suggests 2 John 12, except there he mentions "paper and ink." Ink (MELANOS) was a form of soot, carbon, or lampblack mixed with oil and gum. It was allowed to harden and was stored in stick form for future use. The pen (KALAMOU) was a sharpened reed, often split to produce sharper points.

Verse 14 but I hope shortly to see thee, and we shall speak face to face. Peace be unto thee. The friends salute thee. Salute the friends by name.

but I hope shortly to see thee, and we shall speak face to face - No doubt about John's intentions, as he certainly intends a personal visit. At that time he would not only deal with the rebel Diotrephes (v. 10), he would also be able to finish his exhortations to Gaius and the brethren. In John's mind, this visit is somewhat urgent as he intends to come "shortly" (EUTHEOS), though this word is not used in the similar conclusion of 2 John. Interestingly, this same word is used when Jesus rescued Peter from sinking in the sea (Matthew 14:30-31) and might lend emphasis to the idea of urgency. "Face to face" (STOMA PROS STOMA) is literally "mouth to mouth" and simply refers to the time when they can have personal conversation. The same expression is used in the close of 2 John, v. 12.

Peace be unto thee. The friends salute thee. Salute the friends by name - The RSV lists this as verse 15 as does also the Greek text, but none of the other major translations do so. John uses the same expression (EIRENE SOI) in his farewell as the Lord used when He greeted the apostles after His resurrection (John 20:19,21; Luke 24:36). It was a common greeting and farewell statement (Luke 10:5; 1 Peter 5:14).

"The friends" (PHILOI) is an unusual way of referring to Christians, as this is the only place it is used. This idiom was common, however, in the papyri letters.[39] Jesus did call Lazarus "our friend" (John 11:11), He did speak of a man laying "down his life for his friends" (John 15:13), and He did say "Ye are my friends, if ye do the things that I command you" (John 15:14). These references are all very personal, and there is no reason for one to conclude Jesus wanted the group to be called by such a name. John wants Gaius to receive greetings from all those with him as he writes the letter and wants Gaius to greet all the Christians in his congregation also. This is a personal greeting between friends. With all the hostility, anger, and confrontation that is going on in the situation with Diotrephes, it is not unusual for John to use this term for those who are faithful to the Lord. That it is intensely personal is shown also by the fact it is to be "by name." John urges Gaius to greet each of his Christian friends name by name. Reminiscent of Jesus' words is the practice here by John, "To him the porter openeth; and the sheep hear his voice: and he calleth his own sheep by name, and leadeth them out" (John 10:3). John, as the aged and loving apostle, desires that personal greetings be tenderly involved as he bids them farewell.

What a wonderful glimpse into the life and times of the first century! The personal rapport these men had with their students, the tender concern, name by name, soul by soul, person by person, is a far cry from the formal "big business" approach of many churches today. True it was they had many deep theological problems with which to be concerned in their letters, but oh, how wonderful it is that they also were concerned with individual souls. John, in this short little letter, is concerned gravely with Gaius, Diotrephes, Demetrius, all the friends who are with John as he writes the letter, and the friends who are with Gaius. The sweetness of such a scene is a wonderful study in the value of each single soul and the continuing concern that the Lord wishes all His followers to have for one another.

"We seldom hear this epistle quoted but in the reproof of lordly tyrants, or prating, troublesome fellows in the Church. And yet the epistle contains many excellent sentiments, which, if judiciously handled, might be very useful to the Church of God. But it has been the lot both of the **minor prophets** and the **minor epistles** to be generally neglected; for with many readers **bulk** is every thing; and **no magnitude** no goodness."[40]

[1]William F. Arndt and F. Wilbur Gingrich, *A Greek-English Lexicon of the New Testament*, (University of Chicago Press, Chicago, Illinois, 1957), p. 6.

[2]Samuel Bagster, *Analytical Greek Lexicon*, (Samuel Bagster & Sons, London, England, 1852, Revised Edition by Harold K. Moulton, Zondervan Publishing Co., Grand Rapids, Michigan, 1978), p. 2.

[3]Donald W. Burdick, *The Letters of John the Apostle*, (Moody Press, Chicago, Illinois, 1985), p. 447.

[4]Bagster, *Lexicon*, p. 177.

[5]Joseph Henry Thayer, *A Greek-English Lexicon of the New Testament*, (American Book Co., New York, N.Y., 1889; being Grimm's Wilke's *Clavis Novi Testamenti, Translated Revised and Enlarged*, 1879, Harper & Brothers), p. 264.

[6]Burdick, *Letters*, p. 447.

[7]Alexander Ross, *The New International Commentary on the New Testament, The Epistles of James and John*, (Wm. B. Eerdmans Publishing Co., Grand Rapids, Michigan, 1954), pp. 234-235.

[8]James Hope Moulton and George Milligan, *The Vocabulary of the Greek New Testament,* (Wm. B. Eerdmans Publishing Co., Grand Rapids, Michigan, 1960), p. 647.

[9]A. T. Robertson, *Word Pictures in the New Testament,* (Broadman Press, Nashville, Tennessee, 1933), Vol. VI, *The General Epistles and the Revelation of John,* p. 260.

[10]Guy N. Woods, *A Commentary on the New Testament Epistles of Peter, John and Jude,* (Gospel Advocate Co., Nashville, Tennessee, 1954), p. 357.

[11]Burdick, *Letters,* p. 448.

[12]R. C. H. Lenski, *The Interpretation of the Epistles of St. Peter, St. John, and St. Jude,* (Augsburg Publishing House, Minneapolis, Minnesota, 1963), p. 580.

[13]A. Plummer, *The Pulpit Commentary,* (Wm. B. Eerdmans Publishing Company, Grand Rapids, Michigan, 1950), Vol. 22, *Epistles of Peter, John & Jude, the Revelation,* p. 2.

[14]Bagster, *Lexicon,* p. 433.

[15]Burdick, *Letters,* p. 449.

[16]Bagster, *Lexicon,* p. 320.

[17]Albert Barnes, *Notes on the New Testament, James, Peter, John and Jude,* (Baker Book House, Grand Rapids, Michigan, 1949), p. 372.

[18]Lenski, *Interpretation,* p. 581.

[19]Ross, *NIC,* p. 235, footnote Number 1.

[20]A. T. Robertson, *A Short Grammar of the Greek New Testament,* (Hodder & Stoughton, New York, New York, 1908), Third Edition, p. 138.

[21]Adam Clarke, *A Commentary and Critical Notes,* (Abingdon-Cokesbury Press, New York and Nashville), Vol. II, *Romans to Revelation,* pp. 941 and 934.

[22]Moulton and Milligan, *Vocabulary,* p. 522.

[23]Bagster, *Lexicon,* p. 346.

[24]Plummer, *Pulpit Commentary,* p. 2.

[25]Woods, *Commentary,* p. 361.

[26]Lenski, *Interpretation,* p. 581.

[27]Thayer, *Lexicon,* p. 168.

[28]Moulton and Milligan, *Vocabulary,* p. 658.

[29]Arndt and Gingrich, *Lexicon,* p. 853.

[30]Ross, *NIC,* p. 236.

[31]Lenski, *Interpretation,* p. 584.

[32]Lenski, *Interpretation,* pp. 584-585.

[33]Thayer, *Lexicon,* p. 152.

[34]Ross, *NIC,* p. 237, footnote 3.

[35]W. E. Vine, *An Expository Dictionary of New Testament Words,* (Riverside Book and Bible House, Iowa Falls, Iowa, 1952), p. 946.

[36]Arndt and Gingrich, *Lexicon,* p. 870.

[37]Vine, *Dictionary,* p. 578.

[38]J. W. Roberts, *The Living Word Commentary, The Letters of John,* (R. B. Sweet Co., Inc., Austin, Texas, 1968), p. 179.

[39]Robertson, *Word Pictures,* p. 266.

[40]Clarke, *Commentary,* p. 943.

Bibliography

Arndt, William F. and Wilbur F. Gingrich, *A Greek-English Lexicon of the New Testament*, (University of Chicago Press, Chicago, Illinois, 1957).

Bagster, Samuel, *Analytical Greek Lexicon*, (Samuel Bagster & Sons, London, England, 1852, Revised edition by Harold K. Moulton, Zondervan Publishing Co., Grand Rapids, Michigan, 1978).

Barnes, Albert, *Notes on the New Testament, James, Peter, John and Jude*, (Baker Book House, Grand Rapids, Michigan, 1949).

Baxter, J. Sidlow, *Explore the Book*, (Zondervan Publishing House, Grand Rapids, Michigan, 1960), Vol. Six.

Blaiklock, E. M., *The Illustrated Bible Dictionary*, (Inter-Varsity Press, Leicester, England, 1980), Vol. 2.

Burdick, Donald W., *The Letters of John the Apostle*, (Moody Press, Chicago, Illinois, 1985).

Clarke, Adam, *A Commentary and Critical Notes*, (Abingdon-Cokesbury Press, New York and Nashville), Vol. VI, *Romans to Revelation*.

Dana, H. E. & Julius R. Mantey, *A Manual Grammar of the Greek New Testament*, (The Macmillan Company, New York, New York, 1948).

Douglas, J. D., *The Illustrated Bible Dictionary*, (Inter-Varsity Press, Leicester, England, 1980), Vol. 2.

Green, E. M. B. and C. J. Hermer, *The Illustrated Bible Dictionary*, (Inter-Varsity Press, Leicester, England, 1980), Vol. 2.

Halley, Henry H., *Halley's Bible Handbook*, (Zondervan Publishing House, Grand Rapids, Michigan, 1971), Twenty-Fourth, Revised.

Hastings, James, *A Dictionary of the Bible*, (T. & T. Clark, Edinburgh, Scotland, 1910), Vol. II.

Henry, Matthew, *An Exposition of the New Testament*, (William Mackenzie, London, England), Vol. X.

Horne, Thomas Hartwell, *An Introduction to the Critical Study and Knowledge of the Holy Scriptures*, (W. Blackwood and Sons, Edinburgh: and R. Milliken and Son and John Cumming, Dublin, 1839).

Huther, Joh. Ed., *Meyer's Commentary on the New Testament, Critical and Exegetical Handbook to the General Epistles of James, Peter, John and Jude*, (Funk & Wagnalls Publishers, New York, 1887).

Lenski, R. C. H., *The Interpretation of the Epistles of St. Peter, St. John, and St. Jude*, (Augsburg Publishing House, Minneapolis, Minnesota, 1963).

Macknight, James, *Apostolical Epistles*, (Thomas Nelson, Edinburgh, Scotland, 1829), Vol. IV.

Marshall, Alfred, *The Interlinear Greek-English New Testament*, (Zondervan Publishing House, Grand Rapids, Michigan, 1968, published by special arrangement with Samuel Bagster & Sons, Ltd., London).

Marshall, I. H., *The Illustrated Bible Dictionary*, (Inter-Varsity Press, Leicester, England, 1980), Vol. 2.

McGarvey, J. W. & Philip Y. Pendleton, *Thessalonians, Corinthians, Galatians and Romans*, (The Standard Publishing Company, Cincinnati, Ohio, 1916).

M'Clintock, John & James Strong, *Cyclopedia of Biblical, Theological, and Ecclesiastical Literature*, (Harper & Brothers Publishers, New York, 1894), Vol. IV.

Moulton, James Hope and George Milligan, *The Vocabulary of the Greek New Testament*, (Wm. B. Eerdmans Publishing Co., Grand Rapids, Michigan, 1960).

Plummer, A., *The Pulpit Commentary*, (Wm. B. Eerdmans Publishing Company, Grand Rapids, Michigan, 1950), Vol. 22, *Epistles of Peter, John & Jude, The Revelation*.

Roberts, J. W., *The Living Word Commentary, The Letters of John*, (R. B. Sweet Co., Inc., Austin, Texas, 1968).

Robertson, A. T., *A Short Grammar of the Greek New Testament*, (Hodder & Stoughton, New York, New York, 1908), Third Edition.

Robertson, A. T., *Word Pictures in the New Testament*, (Broadman Press, Nashville, Tennessee, 1933), Vol. VI, *The General Epistles and the Revelation of John*.

Ross, Alexander, *The New International Commentary on the New Testament, The Epistles of James and John*, (Wm. B. Eerdmans Publishing Co., Grand Rapids, Michigan, 1954).

Smith, William, *A Dictionary of the Bible*, (John Murray, London, England, 1893), Second Edition, Vol. I., Part II.

Thayer, Joseph Henry, *A Greek-English Lexicon of the New Testament*, (American Book Co., New York, N.Y., 1889; being Grimm's Wilke's *Clavis Novi Testamenti, Translated Revised and Enlarged*, 1879, Harper & Brothers).

Unger, Merrill F., *Unger's Bible Handbook*, (Moody Press, Chicago, Illinois, 1967).

Vincent, Marvin R., *Word Studies in the New Testament*, Charles Scribner's Sons, New York, 1911), Vol. II, *The Writings of John*.

Vine, W. E., *An Expository Dictionary of New Testament Words*, (Riverside Book and Bible House, Iowa Falls, Iowa, 1952).

Webster, Noah, *Webster's New Twentieth Century Dictionary Unabridged*, (World Publishing Co., Cleveland and New York, 1940), revised by Jean L. McKechnie, 1968.

Woods, Guy N., *A Commentary on the New Testament Epistles of Peter, John and Jude*, (Gospel Advocate Co., Nashville, Tennessee, 1954).